FORENSICS SERIES VOLUME 2

Duo Practice and Performance

• • •

Thirty-five 8–10 Minute
Original Dramatic Scenes

FORENSICS SERIES VOLUME 2

Duo Practice and Performance

• • •

Thirty-five 8–10 Minute Original Dramatic Scenes

By Barbara Lhota and Janet B. Milstein

YOUNG ACTORS SERIES

A Smith and Kraus Book

Published by Smith and Kraus, Inc.
177 Lyme Road, Hanover, NH 03755
www.SmithKraus.com

The scene "Romance" is excerpted from the play of the same title, which first appeared in Smith and Kraus's *Women Playwrights: The Best Plays of 2001*.

First Edition: February 2003
10 9 8 7 6 5 4 3 2 1
Manufactured in the United States of America

Cover design by Lisa Goldfinger
Text design by Julia Hill Gignoux, Freedom Hill Design

Contents

ACKNOWLEDGMENTS

Lisa Herceg, for her understanding throughout
and her editing of the scene intros

Merel Marine

Dr. James M. Brandon

Dan Foss

Jaye Morrison

David Scheidecker

Michael Graupmann

Darlene F. Olson

Ricky Staub

Emily Casey

Joanna Ericson

Karen Milstein

Elizabeth Monteleone

Julia Hill Gignoux

Lisa Goldfinger

and

Eric Kraus and Marisa Smith for their belief,
support, and incredible patience

Introduction

When I was fifteen years old, I joined the Forensics club. I certainly couldn't afford the golf, ski, or equestrian clubs and stooping to the bowling club with those goofy shoes was just too much for me to bear. Besides, I wasn't all that good at sports, but boy, could I talk when encouraged. Truth be told, I had no idea what the word *forensics* meant in this context, but it had a nice ring. It sounded scientific—even intellectual and academic—in a cut-people-up-for-evidence-kinda-way. I vaguely understood that it had to do with speech and competition and interpretation, but that's all I knew.

I first heard about forensics through a couple of cool sophomores who were chatting it up. Their dangling carrot was that each week in late fall, and all through the winter into early spring, we would visit high schools across the state for speech competitions on Saturdays. This meant that each week we would have the glorious opportunity to mingle with tons of other teenagers, including boys. Wow! As a teenager, the idea of meeting fresh blood on a regular basis is always incredible, but for those stuck in an all-girl's Catholic school, this was a ray of light, a glimmer of sunshine in a dark, dusty corridor of despair.

At the first meeting, Mr. Sill, the director of the theater and speech department and saintly builder of all sets for all plays performed at my high school, introduced us to the basics. He even explained the origin of the word *forensics* in terms of speech. Apparently, the ancient Greeks created the word. It was applied to speeches that were given to persuade groups of people toward a certain way of thinking. The forensic speeches used evidence, examples, and arguments that would win over the group, not unlike the evidence from expert medical forensic witnesses. This was precisely why I joined this sort of club—

to win people over. I was, in fact, shy and wanted desperately to fit in and make friends.

After hearing about all of the various events, I felt most captivated by the interpretive categories. It wasn't that extemporaneous and impromptu didn't interest me, but the idea of creating anything written while being timed scared me half to death. Persuasive and informative speeches sounded fun, though not necessarily a natural fit. But interpretation of a short story or a scene, now that was my forte—something I could do in my sleep. For years I had been interpreting music, drama, and old TV shows for my brothers and sisters in our living room—finally, an audience that would appreciate my talent instead of telling me to buzz off.

By the end of my introduction to forensics, I knew this was the club for me: cool, arty, verbal kids who got to express themselves and inspire each other. Mr. Sill told us that this club would enhance our speaking abilities and build our confidence. I needed that. But I still had a lot of fear swirling around me. Would I be good? Would I ever win a competition or even get past the first rehearsal? Who would be my partner for the duo competition? Would I lose my lunch like I heard this one girl did before her first competition? Of course, all fears dissolved as I started to work on the material with my coach.

Four years later, I was the president of the club. While competing, I learned a lot about storytelling, the human condition, interpretation, acting, and it did enhance my speaking abilities and self-confidence.

After high school, I went on to compete in college events. This was equally, if not more, satisfying. At those events, you could see the development of eloquent after-dinner speakers, talented actors, and convincing young lawyers.

Looking for fresh material was always a challenge. I spent hours pouring over tons of plays, short stories, and poetry collections in the library. I would never discourage students from doing this. It's a wonderful opportunity to discover new playwrights and authors you can really appreciate. However, finding scenes that met all of the rules of the competition was challenging, if not downright impossible. Apparently, things have not changed.

As an acting teacher, Janet had many young students involved in forensics who would repeatedly ask her if she knew of any great eight-minute scenes. They were having trouble finding suitable material that was not overdone. Janet spoke to me about this problem and together we set out to offer a solution. Janet's idea was to create a sourcebook full of balanced eight-to ten-minute scenes specifically geared toward high school and college forensics duo students. Our goal was to write active and accessible scenes, with rich, balanced characters and unique, topical situations. I think we've accomplished that. In this book, you will find thirty-five scenes that are as original as we suspect you are. A brief synopsis, including the ages of both characters, precedes each scene.

Barbara Lhota

Tips from the Pros: What Coaches, Directors, and Judges Think

In order to make this book more useful, we talked to high school and college coaches, directors, and judges to get their opinions on the duo forensics event. We asked a series of questions—a survey of sorts. We found the tips enlightening and the comments offer some insight as to what to expect in terms of rehearsal, performance, and competition.

• • •

WHAT DO YOU LIKE ABOUT THE DRAMATIC DUO EVENT?

"It provides a 'slice of life' opportunity to explore experiences and viewpoints student may otherwise never encounter, and helps them to understand the problems of others."
— Merel K. Marine

"I like that it is the only 'individual' event that requires a partner. This one peculiar factor makes the event so important as the speaker develops the skills of timing, teamwork, and when someone misses a cue, improvisation."
— Dr. James M. Brandon

"It gives young actors a chance to develop characters with a variety of emotional levels; it also allows them some freedom to analyze the motivations of the characters in-depth and with less restriction."
— Jaye Morrison

"I think that learning how to perform with a partner is a really important acting skill and communication tool. This was always my favorite event because it allowed me as a performer to share my time on stage with someone else and also allowed me to play off of someone else. Learning how to build a scene and how to react to another performer's energy is an important skill that cannot be learned in solo interpretion events."

— Michael Graupmann

"The oral interpretation of dramatic literature without 'acting it out' is an opportunity and an artistic challenge that is exciting as well as fun!"

— Darlene F. Olson

WHAT ARE THE RULES?

Time limits? Eight minutes for most high school competitions and ten minutes for most college competitions.

Movement? The answers here varied from none at all to unlimited. If you are not permitted to move, you have the opportunity to show off your vocal skills and imagination. The key is to follow your league's rules for each individual competition to the letter. Some coaches and judges complained that rules were frequently and unfortunately ignored. Because of that, some scenes that were better than others in terms of presentation received lower scores than their competitors. If you do not follow the rules of a sport, you most likely will be penalized or disqualified no matter how much talent you possess.

Are set pieces allowed? Again, answers varied here from none at all, to a table and chair, to just chairs. Follow your individual league's rules. Some judges commented that if you are allowed to use furniture—use it creatively. Let the blocking enhance and clarify the story.

Should the script be held or memorized? It tends to vary from league to league.

"Script in hand, and the script should be used during the performance (i.e., it CAN be used as a prop, but it MUST be looked at from time to time. This is another rule too often ignored."

— Dr. James M. Brandon

"Memorized!"

— Merel K. Marine

"Scripts need to be memorized but also black binders held to give recognition to the authors."

— Michael Graupmann

HOW DO YOU CREATE AN INTRO FOR DUO COMPETITION?

"The student should be speaking in his or her own voices; the intro should include both speakers, and it should reflect the tone and intent of the piece. Introductions should be accessible, but not overly explanatory."

— Dr. James M. Brandon

"I usually like to use part of the scene or the result of an improv as an attention catcher or "teaser" and then follow with a brief "out of character" shared narrative intro. I also like to incorporate singing when the talent and theme make it appropriate."

— Merel K. Marine

"I try to give the audience a sense of who the characters are and draw them into the scene immediately. Often the scene begins and then a *short* intro, which includes the title and author, is given."

— Jaye Morrison

"I always make sure to give a helpful bit of outside knowledge first. This can be historical, literary, or scientific information that applies. Then I relate this nugget of insight to the relationship in the piece, perhaps giving plot or character background that needs to be known beforehand . . . Extra points for creativity, humor, and elegant phrasing."

—Michael Graupmann

"I prefer a very brief introduction to the scene. If we don't need background information to understand the scene, don't give it to us. Also, don't smack us in the face with the 'theme.' Show us, don't tell us. Remember: The shorter the intro, the more time you have to perform."

— Dan Foss

WHAT DO THE JUDGES LOOK FOR IN THIS EVENT?

"I feel some judges too often concern themselves with the rule book. However, communication of text and hopefully subtext are important. Quality of the literature should be important, and acting skill is important. I personally rate the extent to which I am emotionally moved as most important, followed by creative and appropriate composition, blocking, and naturalness of performance."

— Merel K. Marine

"Who knows? Depth of character? Acting ability? But unfortunately, often good, original scripts and acting itself become secondary to the emotional 'umph' of the script."

— David Scheidecker

"Commitment to the playwright's literature—to interpret the playwright's intention or purpose first and foremost. Authentic, practiced interpretation beginning and ending with vocal and physical suggestions of the two characters."

— Darlene F. Olson

"Confidence. Poise. A student who uses the full range of his or her voice. A student who is believable. A student who can give the appearance of spontaneity. A student who has selected and performed material that is within his or her range. A student who clearly enjoys what he or she is doing. ENERGY!"

— Dr. James M. Brandon

"I want to see two characters complete a journey in eight minutes. Have the actors worked together to create a believable relationship? Have they demonstrated a clear understanding of their characters' goals?"

— Dan Foss

WHAT SORT OF REHEARSAL SCHEDULE WOULD YOU RECOMMEND FOR THIS TYPE OF COMPETITION?

"It depends on the student, but before the first read-through of the piece before an audience, the student MUST complete, at minimum, an hour of rehearsal for every minute of stage time. So a ten-minute duo should be rehearsed at least ten hours before ever approaching an audience. This ten-hours does NOT include mere read-throughs and line memorization time."

— Dr. James M. Brandon

"Depending on the amount of scenes with which one has to rehearse, I recommend one rehearsal per week at the following schedule:

1st Rehearsal: Half hour read-through and discussion/improvisation

2nd Rehearsal: One hour blocking session

3rd Rehearsal: One hour off-script review of blocking and polish/ business

4th Rehearsal and all subsequent rehearsals: Alternate half hour and one hour sessions, depending on problems. Include special rehearsal sessions to keep things fresh."

— Merel K. Marine

"I believe that a great deal of work needs to go into the initial staging and blocking of a duo, for the purpose of getting both partners comfortable and able to manipulate the text to suit their own needs. When the words and actions feel natural and spontaneous, they are at the desired level of performance . . . Nothing seems less inspired than over-practiced duo. For this reason, I think students have to know their own work habits."
—Michael Graupmann

"I want to see my duet scene partners three to four times a week for an hour at a time. This gives us the time to review the judges' critiques from the previous weekend and give attention to that feedback in our rehearsals."
— Dan Foss

DO YOU HAVE ANY TIPS ON HOW TO KEEP THE PIECE FRESH SINCE IT IS PRESENTED SO FREQUENTLY?

"A) Switch roles. B) 'Mute' acting (communicate the script via facial expressions and movement only). C) Rehearse as a humorous scene to find the humor that should exist in all scenes. Don't be afraid to be outrageous. D) Improv problems that may have existed between characters prior to the opening of the scene. E) Give each character a secret subtext to carry throughout the scene. This is never to be shared with the partner. This should provide interpretation variety from rehearsal to rehearsal or performance to performance."
— Merel K. Marine

"Remember that judges want you to succeed and provide you with feedback that will improve your performance. Don't discount comments with which you may not necessarily agree. Try everything your judges recommend in rehearsal. Even if it doesn't work for you, you may still learn something new about your character from attempting a different approach."
— Dan Foss

"Pick it up before each tournament and try to read it again 'for the first time.' You'll be surprised at what you find."

— Dr. James M. Brandon

"We sometimes switch roles. We often alter blocking. Sometimes we add vocal music in the intro. We do many dramatic exercises to help discover the characters and make them fuller during the season."

— David Scheidecker

"Experiment casting each scene as a different movie genre: mystery, sci-fi, farce, musical, and so forth. Finding new hidden meaning will reveal a wealth of new life to a piece."

— Michael Graupmann

"We try to expand their thinking—think outside the box; try new things with delivery and blocking."

—Jaye Morrison

"Never settle into your performance so much that it doesn't change—even if you're winning! Often judges will see you more than once in a season. We love to find that even the best scenes have progressed and improved. Look for new moments each time you rehearse or perform. Watch for what your scene partner is giving you and ensure that you are returning the favor!"

— Dan Foss

• • •

We would like to thank those who kindly offered their helpful advice. In the pages that follow, we hope you find a scene that sets your soul ablaze—that you simply MUST do. Be sure to check out the other books in our Forensics Series. Good luck in all competitions and remember—have FUN!

Barbara Lhota and Janet B. Milstein

ACCEPTANCE LETTER

Tina, 38 years old, arrives home from a long evening at the bowling alley. She is eager to plan Charlie's big birthday/graduation party. Charlie, 18 years old, is not at all enthused. He sits in a chair with his head buried in a book when Tina enters.

TINA: *(Sing-songy.)* Heeelllooo! I'm home. *(Seeing him.)* Hey, kid. Get your filthy sneakers off the chair. How ya doin'?

CHARLIE: *(Shrugs.)* I don't know.

TINA: Well, how was your day?

CHARLIE: I don't know.

TINA: Twelve years. Twelve years of teachers goin' on about my son's academic aptitude. He's bright, he's gifted, he's absolutely brilliant and yet, every time *I* ask him a question, it's "I don't know."

CHARLIE: *(Getting up.)* Anyway . . .

TINA: I'm kidding. Now, don't walk away from me. Guess what I did tonight? Guess.

CHARLIE: Why don't *you* guess what *I* did?

TINA: Okay, but you go first. I'll give you a hint. It has to do with your birthday.

CHARLIE: Oh great.

TINA: Don't "oh great" me. It's good news. I got party favors. It's a whole Hawaiian theme.

CHARLIE: I'm going to be eighteen years old, Mom, not eight!

TINA: Oh boy, eighteen, Charlie! That's ancient.

CHARLIE: I'm just saying I don't want a theme party.

TINA: Oh come on, we're not talkin' Mickey Mouse. It's Hawaiian. It's fun. It's festive. We'll even do *(Sing-songy.)* *liquor* provided we have some designated drivers.

CHARLIE: I really don't want a party anymore.

TINA: What? Don't be ridiculous. I stopped at the bakery. The cake's amazing. It's a hoola girl doll-thingy. The grass skirt's a vanilla cake with loads of frosting. The doll's wearing a coconut bra. Very sexy. Your friends will love it.

CHARLIE: I don't have any friends to invite.

TINA: Come on now, you're just being silly. Everyone from the bowling alley's planning on coming. They're your friends.

CHARLIE: No, they're *your* friends, Mom. And I don't want anything to do with them. I have nothing in common with them.

TINA: Oh, well, below your standards, huh? I suppose the gang will get over it. But Mel and Lorraine will be hurt. I guess you have lots of kids from school you'd rather have come.

CHARLIE: No. I wouldn't know who to invite. I don't have any friends at school.

TINA: Jerry and *(Sing-songy.) Lisa* to start.

CHARLIE: I don't have a thing for her. How many times do I have to tell you that?

TINA: Okay, okay. I just think she's adorable. Anyway, small groups are fun. Four's definitely a party. And you can definitely do four, Charlie.

CHARLIE: May I be excused now?

TINA: Wait. I thought you were going to help me unload the car. I got all kinds of crap in there. My feet are killin' me! It's warm for March, huh?

CHARLIE: Do you want me to unload or not?

TINA: Not. I want you to sit. Come here.

(Charlie moves closer to her.)

TINA: Sit. *(He does.)* Whatcha been doin'?

CHARLIE: *(Gesturing to his book.)* Oh, parachute jumping, skydiving, what's it look like?

TINA: Like you're rereading your trigonometry book for the fiftieth time, practically in the dark.

CHARLIE: *Was* reading. *Was* is operative.

TINA: You're going to ruin your eyes.

CHARLIE: And why do you say *the fiftieth time* as if that were a bad thing to do?

TINA: I didn't say it was bad. I just don't understand, Charlie, why you don't loosen up.

CHARLIE: Most parents would be thrilled. They'd love it if their kid were reading about math or physics. You act like it's some sort of downfall.

TINA: I just want you to enjoy life. I don't understand why you aren't out with a girlfriend or hanging with some friends.

CHARLIE: Why aren't you?

TINA: Because I worked for nine hours at the bowling alley and then I went shopping for a party I thought you were excited about.

CHARLIE: Emphasis on *thought.*

TINA: Yes. Fine. I don't know what's the matter with you, but apparently you're angry with me for some unknown reason. And I seem to be put in the position of guessing why.

CHARLIE: I never said I was angry with you.

TINA: You don't have to say it. You exude it from every pore.

CHARLIE: So did I get any *mail* in the last few days?

TINA: Oh my God! Is that what this is all about? I should have known.

(Charlie looks down.)

TINA: Charlie, I know you're nervous about these school applications, but you did apply to the two most difficult universities in the United States.

CHARLIE: So . . . so?

TINA: So . . . there's, uh, well, a lot of bureaucracy. They're big. It's easy to get lost in the shuffle.

CHARLIE: Oh. So you're saying my application got lost in the shuffle?

TINA: It could happen. I don't know. I'm simply saying that I honestly think you ought to reconsider staying home the first year. Maybe going to the community college in Alpena.

CHARLIE: Oh my God, why? Why would I do that, Mom?! We've been over this. All my teachers understand. Why don't you? You do realize I'm in the top 1 percent in the state? I'm not trying to brag, I'm not! But I just don't belong in Black River and you know it.

TINA: I know you'll go to a much better school eventually. I just think you could use another year under your belt. I mean, you're young for your age. That's good. I think you'll mature in a year. You'll know what you really want.

CHARLIE: I know what I want now! The only problem is that it's not what *you* want.

TINA: What I want has nothing to do with it. MIT and Harvard are too expensive.

CHARLIE: So it's the money? That's why you got rid of it?

TINA: Got rid of what? *(Pause.)* Charlie?

CHARLIE: *(Beat.)* My acceptance letter. My acceptance to MIT.

TINA: What are you talking about?

CHARLIE: See you never guessed what I did today. So I'll tell you. I got a phone call. Guess who? *(Beat.)* Don't you want to guess, Mom?

TINA: No. Tell me.

CHARLIE: Oh, you can do better than that. You already had a hint. It was the head of the math department at MIT. He asked why I hadn't responded to a letter sent out almost two weeks ago. I guess I played it off . . . said we had rotten luck with our mail lately. The only reason he even called me, since he never does that, is that Mr. Franklin, my math teacher, is a personal friend of his. Mr. Franklin wondered why I wasn't notified either way. *(Beat.)* The thing is I think I *was* notified . . . only I never saw it.

TINA: I was going to give it to you, Charlie.

CHARLIE: When? After it was too late to accept? After you convince me that I would just be a number there, lost in the shuffle?

TINA: I never intended on holding onto it. I just couldn't let go of it. I was going to give it to you soon. And nothing—I swear *nothing* has come from Harvard yet.

CHARLIE: Yeah, well, forgive me if I call tomorrow because I don't trust you anymore.

TINA: I was proud of you when I read it.

CHARLIE: Could have fooled me! It was mine!

TINA: I know. I'm sorry. I just . . . I didn't think I could afford it by myself. I was trying to figure. I thought Grandpa would have had more money to leave behind. I thought—

CHARLIE: Who cares. I'll get financial aid. I'll get scholarships. Maybe not a full one, but I can take out loans.

TINA: Oh, Charlie, I don't want you to start your life in debt. Grandpa always used to say it was a terrible way to—

CHARLIE: Grandpa was wrong! He was wrong to make you quit school because he didn't want to take out loans. You were really smart. It was so dumb!

TINA: No, don't blame Grandpa for my quitting. Getting pregnant didn't help. Not that I have ever regretted that.

CHARLIE: Anyway, the point is you could have done so much more. We could have lived better.

TINA: It's not so bad . . . what I've done. Who I am. How we've lived, is it?

CHARLIE: Mom, be honest, you work in a run-down bowling alley in a nothing town.

TINA: It's not a nothing town. It may not be as intellectual or cultured as you'd like, but there are nice people here. They're good people, and they have been very, very good to us. I had nothing but a bunch of bruises and a shattered ego when I arrived here. I got a job, and I made good friends and I built a bowling league at the bowling alley that's alive, and active. It's a good . . . it's a nice life.

CHARLIE: And you'd like me to stay here? Go to school at Alpena Community College?

TINA: Just a year. It's not that bad. I'll work part-time at Walgreen's to make extra cash. Then you'll go away next year, and you won't have to take out as much in student loans.

CHARLIE: One year? Maybe, maybe I could do it. Work at the paper mill. They need engineers. That's a challenging job. And engineers make a pretty good salary.

TINA: Yeah. Yes, exactly! Meanwhile you enjoy the lake and waterskiing. You work at the forest preserves for extra cash. We'll throw three major kickbutt cookouts a summer.

CHARLIE: And I give up hope of ever being on the Genome project, or designing rockets that orbit Saturn, or creating technologies that defy the very laws of gravity! I know I'm weird. But I love trig! I love physics, and chemistry, and Latin! And Mom, I will invent something. I don't know what yet, but it'll be big, or part of something big. I have big expectations—huge, and yet, your expectations for me are so small. That's what I don't get. You say you love me, but you act as if you hardly know me. Because if you did, you would know I could survive a four-year university. It's all I ever prepared for and dreamed of.

TINA: I don't have small expectations for you, Charlie. I know you're special. I've always known. Don't you get it? I don't want you to leave.

CHARLIE: But you can leave with me! We could get a place together.

TINA: No. No. Where would I work?

CHARLIE: There are jobs in bowling alleys in Cambridge. There're probably tons.

TINA: But I don't know anyone there in Cambridge.

CHARLIE: You'll know me.

TINA: Your head will be swirling about with vectors and, god willing someday, women. There won't be time for me. And that's as it should be.

CHARLIE: All these years you've had me fooled. You always pretended to be such a wild free-spirit. Margarita parties at Christmas.

TINA: That was a hit last year, huh?

CHARLIE: Yeah. The party girl who would do anything, go anywhere if only she had more money and less kid. The truth is that you're afraid of anything outside of here, aren't you?

TINA: I wouldn't say afraid exactly. But I suppose I wouldn't be considered all that wild. Too much competition.

CHARLIE: I remember when that guy, that cousin guy from New York . . . Mel's cousin . . .

TINA: Dan.

CHARLIE: Yeah. Dan Walters. Exactly. When he visited last year.

TINA: What about him?

CHARLIE: He liked you. He tried to kiss you in the kitchen last Christmas.

TINA: No he didn't. Not exactly.

CHARLIE: Yes he did. I saw it. And you wouldn't let him do it.

TINA: Maybe I didn't like him, smartie pants.

CHARLIE: Oh you *liked* him all right. You did that giggle thing all night. You were just afraid you'd like him too much and have to go off to New York, which would be scary.

TINA: I don't know. Maybe. I do like this little town, Charlie. I like our little house and the lake. It's nice, almost perfect. I wish we could play crazy eights and hang out forever.

CHARLIE: I wish we could too. But I need so badly to meet people more like me. I can't stay here with you just because you want me to. Can't you see that? It'll destroy me.

TINA: And leaving here would destroy me. So what's a desperate mother to do? Let him go, though you know his leaving will hurt more than anything else you've ever experienced? Or resort to stealing letters out of the mail? I chose stealing a letter. Foolish. Selfish.

(Charlie nods gently.)

TINA: I know you think my life was wasted, Charlie, but I am so proud of what I've done.

CHARLIE: I know. "The bowling alley has more than a hundred active league members."

TINA: Darn tootin'! And it was dead before I started managing it, but that's not what I meant.

CHARLIE: I know we have a great house.

TINA: No, that's not what I was going to say either.

CHARLIE: Oh God, not the Haunted Hussie parade?

TINA: No! You. You, Charlie. It's *you* I'm proud of. I always have been. Always. *(Pause.)* Oh shoot, we're not gonna get all mushy. It's not our style. So would you like to see your acceptance letter, young man?

CHARLIE: Yes. Maybe we could bring it to the bowling alley. I'd like to show it off.

TINA: Yeah? Then we could invite the whole obnoxious lot to a certain b-day party?

CHARLIE: Okay. But no Hawaiian theme!

TINA: What?! Who put you in charge? It will be Hawaiian all right! I got a dozen lays, and a couple of hoola-hoola skirts to prove it. I know it's *your* party, but *I'm* throwing it. Now, shut up and get the car. I'll grab the letter.
(She starts to move.)

CHARLIE: *(Calling.)* Mom? *(She stops, but doesn't turn.)* I'll miss you too. Tons.

TINA: I know, Charlie. I know.

MAINTAINING SANITY

Clover, 22, has been taking care of her little brother, River, 19, since she was a little kid. Their mother Mimi, an artist, was an unpredictable lady who had periodic psychotic episodes. As a result, the kids have fallen into definite roles. Clover plays the mother and River, the troubled child. Two years ago, their mother died after a quick bout with cancer. As she was dying, Clover vowed she would take care of River and the house. River, now in his first year of college, is starting to resent his sister's constant need to keep things under her control. He uses the basement of their house to get a little privacy. His sister wants to know exactly what he does down there. She fears that he may have a breakdown someday like their mother. River is also concerned. He fears that his sister has no life of her own and that she will never let go of his. In this scene, they confront each other.

CLOVER: Where have you been for the last two days?

RIVER: *(Shrugs.)* Hanging out at the library.

CLOVER: *(Not sure she believes him.)* Uh-huh. Sit down. Eat with me. I made spaghetti.

RIVER: It smells good, but I have work to do.

CLOVER: What sort of work?

RIVER: Can't tell you. It's top secret.

CLOVER: You're kidding, right?

RIVER: No. Yeah. Sort of. *(Starts to go.)*

CLOVER: *(Jumping in front of his path.)* Wait! *(He stops.)* You're not pulling a Mimi on me, right? *(Looking right at him.)* You're not, right?

RIVER: No. But I went to her grave yesterday.

CLOVER: You did? *(He nods.)* Why didn't you tell me? I would have gone with you.

RIVER: I don't know. I wanted to go alone this time.

CLOVER: I miss Mom too, but just because we miss her doesn't mean we want you to be like her. I mean, that part of her. She didn't want that for you either. She didn't like it. She never wanted to be peculiar. Eccentric, flamboyant, dramatic—yes, but not a sick person. Not put away over and over. That's not a happy thing.

RIVER: *(Irritated.)* I know that! So what's your point?

CLOVER: My point is I'm not sure I could do that again.

RIVER: Who says you'll have to? *(Beat.)* Anyway did you hear about that fourth pipe bomb in Chicago?

CLOVER: Who hasn't? It's terrible. You can't know what to expect these days. What makes you bring that up?

RIVER: It was on the news. It's interesting. Wondered what you thought about the kid.

CLOVER: He's sick or just mentally disturbed. What is there to think? The mayor might end up blind over it.

RIVER: Like that would make a big difference. He's blind already if you ask me.

CLOVER: Jesus! What a thing to say.

RIVER: It's the truth.

CLOVER: See this is exactly what I mean. Is there something going on in your head or are you just trying to make me think there is something going on in your head? Bringing up this pipe bomb thing? Is it attention or psychosis?

RIVER: It's research actually. Could you imagine me doing that?

CLOVER: Doing what—research?

RIVER: No, creating a pipe bomb. I have the technology you know? Twenty-one-year-old engineering genius. You'd be all over the papers too. All that publicity.

CLOVER: What the hell are you talking about?!

RIVER: *(Shrugs.)* Nothing.

CLOVER: Are you trying to tell me that you . . . what are you trying to tell me, River?! Are you asking me if you're nuts enough to make a pipe bomb? Yes, I think you're nuts enough—

you win, but tell me that you didn't! Tell me that you had nothing to do with the Goddamn—

CLOVER: There's nothing light about it. And it's *really* not funny because I don't know what the hell you do in that basement. And I don't know what you do with all your time either. But I won't put up with crap, River. I won't let you fall apart on me. If you fall apart, that's it. You're out of here. It doesn't matter if you have a full scholarship to Northwestern or that you can make something great out of yourself with engineering or computers or something. If you fall apart, you can't do anything. Your life is crap. So listen to me.

RIVER: I didn't! God! I'm just trying to make light of the fact that you think I'm crazy.

RIVER: I told you I don't want to be an engineer or work with computers.

CLOVER: Fine. Whatever. That's not at all what I was saying anyhow.

RIVER: So what were you saying?

CLOVER: I'm saying be normal. Please. I know that we were taught that that is the worst thing you could possibly be, but the fact is that you'll be a lot happier. Some people think that we have no control over maintaining sanity, but I think we have a hell of a lot more control than people think. You have to do things. If you need Dr. Roberts back again, please tell me. I'll scrape together the cash. And the other thing is you've got to get out and be with people. Socialize. Are you socializing these days, River?

RIVER: Oh God, not again.

CLOVER: That's what people do in their first year of college. They party a little.

RIVER: That's why I don't sit down with you to eat, Clover. I get a lecture every time. Why aren't *you* socializing?

CLOVER: I did in my first year. I'm not in that place anymore. Now I just want to graduate and make some real money.

RIVER: You never had a date. You never have one now either.

CLOVER: Why are you distracting things? We're not talking about me right now. I'm talking about *you*. I'm thinking you might want to live on campus next year instead of commuting.

RIVER: Why? You want to get rid of me?

CLOVER: No! Absolutely not! But it's hard to get into the social scene having to commute to college. If I get a full-time job this summer after graduating, I could probably help you swing a dorm room.

RIVER: Why don't you get rid of me? I would! So I could have the place to myself.

CLOVER: What are you talking about? This isn't about me.

RIVER: But why isn't it about you?

CLOVER: I'm trying to say that I want you to make more friends. I think it'll help keep you healthy.

RIVER: What about what would keep *you* healthy? Why are none of the choices you make about *you*? Do you ever wonder that? You're asking me about my friends. Well, I never cared much one way or another about friends. Lately, I care a little more, so things might change. But you do. You always wanted lots of friends. You love parties. So where are they, Clover? Why are you always here with me?

CLOVER: It's a little difficult to have friends over all the time while I'm working full-time and going to school full-time. I have to do that if we're going to keep the house.

RIVER: So why keep the house?

CLOVER: Why keep the house?!

RIVER: Yeah. Keeping the house isn't going to bring Mimi back, no matter how much we want that. And the fact is we don't want to bring all of Mimi back. Neither of us do. So why keep it? Why do you fight so hard to keep it?

CLOVER: I don't know. Where the hell would we live? Besides, I thought you—

RIVER: Well, stop thinking for me, Clover! I don't want you to. I want to have my own life now. I may not do what you want me to, but I won't go crazy or, at least, I'll try my best not to.

CLOVER: So if you didn't live in the house with me, where would you live?

RIVER: Share an apartment with somebody maybe.

CLOVER: How would you pay for it?

RIVER: *(Shrugs.)* Job probably.

CLOVER: Oh yeah. Right. And what job could help you afford an apartment? Besides, you're not steady enough with jobs, River. You know that. Howard told me you've missed work six times in the past month.

RIVER: Why did you take it upon yourself to talk to Howard about *my* job?

CLOVER: Because I've been concerned. You seem to have less cash. I was concerned you might lose it.

RIVER: Who cares if I lost it? I hate it. And how is your asking going to change things anyhow?

CLOVER: What's going on, River? Why don't you show up to work?

RIVER: Because he charges too much for toilet paper. Because he has a lot of beer-belly hicks with annoying vocabulary in there. Because it's a convenience store and I've never wanted convenience. And because I hate it!

CLOVER: Why?

RIVER: Because I do! I don't like selling cigarettes and beer and nachos to a bunch of idiots.

CLOVER: Oh, well, too bad. We can't do everything we like all the time. I'm sorry you're afraid of a little hard work.

RIVER: I'm not afraid of hard work. But I'd rather get a job landscaping or cleaning out pet cages. Something else. But *I'll* find the job this time.

CLOVER: Fine. Do whatever you want. By the way, cleaning out cages is no picnic either, believe me. My concern was that you were missing work because of whatever you're doing downstairs in the basement.

RIVER: So? What if that were true?

CLOVER: So I think it's foolish. And I want to know exactly what it is now. It's my basement too. So if something illegal is going on down there, River, I—

RIVER: Illegal?!

CLOVER: I thought I smelled some chemical down there when I was doing my laundry today. If you don't come clean, I'll break that damn padlock and look myself.

RIVER: Oh my God. You *do* think I'm making pipe bombs?

CLOVER: Well what am I supposed to think?! Dr. Roberts said if you had a breakdown, it would happen now or in the next few years.

RIVER: I'm not having a breakdown. I'm stripping that old dresser I bought at the garage sale if you must know.

CLOVER: Really?

RIVER: Really. But that's not all. I'm also creating something. *(Clover looks concerned.)* A novel.

CLOVER: A novel?

RIVER: Yeah. That's why I've been at the library. I got the idea from all those news reports about that kid making the pipe bombs. It's a pretty cool plot idea actually.

CLOVER: Yeah, cool. So where did this novel thing come from all of a sudden?

RIVER: Can you leave your agenda for one second to get in touch with my enthusiasm about this?

CLOVER: Hey, writing is great, but I don't want you to ignore your homework. You have a lot of difficult engineering classes to keep on top of.

RIVER: What if I told you I might be dropping one of those classes?

CLOVER: What?! River, you have a scholarship in engineering. You have a huge opportunity. Dr. Roberts said an artistic field would not be the best choice.

RIVER: I knew you'd jump to conclusions. I knew it. He said, it was not the best choice because it's unpredictable. But if I choose it then it's *my* unpredictable life, not somebody else's unpredictable weirdness affecting me. And besides I didn't say I was changing my major anyway. I'm just excited about playing around with the idea of writing a novel. And I'm tired of taking a million difficult classes at once.

CLOVER: Yes, but it's best to get all the requirements in—all the really tough requirement courses done within the first year.

RIVER: Just like it's best to socialize in the first year. And I should move to campus. And I better never miss work even if it's a job I hate. You always know exactly what's best for me, don't you, Clover?

CLOVER: I'm just telling you my experience.

RIVER: Well, my experience isn't yours. And I know you're afraid I'll blow up just like Mimi if I do something really creative and something goes wrong, but it doesn't work that way. You can't prevent my meltdown. Maybe I won't even have one. Ever think of that?

CLOVER: I know. I hope you don't. But that doesn't stop me from wanting to protect you.

RIVER: You can't! *(Beat.)* You want to know what my novel's about?

CLOVER: Yeah, I got it—a teenager who makes pipe bombs in his basement.

RIVER: No, his sister's the main character actually. They have a mental case mom who's a lot of fun, but loses it frequently. His sister is always trying so hard to keep the family together. She tries so hard to hold onto the control of the situation, that she misses her own life. She doesn't even know what she wants.

CLOVER: What do you want me to say? I get it. It's supposed to be about me I guess.

RIVER: Haven't you ever thought about that, Clover? What you want?

CLOVER: Sure I have! Is this supposed to be more research?

RIVER: No! *(Beat.)* Well, what do you want then?

CLOVER: I don't know. To graduate, and get a job working

as a store manager or something. To make decent money. To be normal. Totally normal. Just that.

RIVER: You say that, but what does that mean? Does that mean you'll get married? What kind of guy would you like? A sensitive type, or a real tough guy? Where would you live if you could choose anywhere to live? What's your normal?

CLOVER: I don't know! I haven't thought about it.

RIVER: That's my point. You've never had a chance to think about it because you're always thinking about me. In my novel, she has to discover her own life—what she really wants or she'll die. Each person in the family has to move on by themselves or they'll die.

CLOVER: Is this story about me or you?

RIVER: Both. *(Beat.)* Have you ever had sex, Clover?

CLOVER: What?! I'm not talking about this with you!

RIVER: Me either. Don't you think that's odd? And neither of us have a best friend. I think we should move out. Both of us to different places. Start somewhere fresh. Maybe I'll want to do more social things if you aren't nagging at me to do them. And maybe you'll get out more if you stop worrying about me for a second. What do you think?

CLOVER: Who am I talking to? Who are you?

RIVER: I won't fall apart if you're not looking out for me. I promise.

CLOVER: I'd feel as if I were letting her down.

RIVER: Why? Mimi always wanted us to be our own people, remember? She "longed" for us to be our own people, even if that means you'll be all irritatingly normal.

CLOVER: But I promised her that I would take care of you.

RIVER: You have been. But I guess if you really want to take care of me now, you have to let me grow up. On my own.

CLOVER: *(Beat.)* So . . . how does the novel end?

RIVER: *(Beat.)* I don't know yet. It's unpredictable I guess.

THE UNFORTUNATE GIFT

Nicolas, 15, and Jennifer, 14, are waiting at a city bus stop. They both attend high school at Marymount High. Nicolas is a sophomore, and Jennifer is a diligent freshman. Jennifer got a late start this morning because she was up until midnight last night studying for her biology class. Nicolas is late because he decided not to take the last bus. He had a strange feeling about it. Nicolas is known at school as an eccentric. For his biology project last year, he deprived himself of sleep for several days and recorded his thoughts and answers to short quizzes. The project was a hit with his teacher, but most of the kids just thought he was weird. Fellow students try to keep their distance from him. Jennifer doesn't know him at all, but she has observed his slightly strange behavior in the hall heading to class. Nicolas looks down the street in search of a bus. Jennifer, who just ran a block to try to catch the last bus, leans against the bench trying to catch her breath.

NICOLAS: *(Looking down the street.)* You sound tired.

JENNIFER: *(Panting.)* I ran the whole block. I thought that was the 71 bus.

NICOLAS: It was the 71 bus.

JENNIFER: Oh. *(Beat.)* That was the 71 bus?

NICOLAS: That one that just left a second ago? Just now?

JENNIFER: Yeah.

NICOLAS: That was the 71.

JENNIFER: It was? *(He nods.)* Shoot! God . . . blessed! I'm so late. I slowed down at the end of the block there because I thought . . .

NICOLAS: You thought it wasn't the 71 because I didn't take it?

JENNIFER: Yeah. Well, no. I mean—I don't know where you're going or anything.

NICOLAS: I've seen you at Marymount. You go there too, right?

JENNIFER: Yeah.

NICOLAS: I'm a sophomore.

JENNIFER: Yeah, I think I've seen you in the hall. I'm a freshman. I can't wait till I'm a sophomore.

NICOLAS: Yeah, sophomore year is a better year. It's a really good year. In fact, this is my favorite year in my whole life so far. Last year was highly depressing.

JENNIFER: Oh.

NICOLAS: No. It's good because I can appreciate how fantastic this year is. It's really fantastic.

JENNIFER: Good. *(Long pause.)*

NICOLAS: I've noticed you before. In the hall outside of Sister Pat's chemistry class. I saw you on the bus too. Normally I do take the 71. And I'm going to take the next one when it comes.

JENNIFER: Good.

NICOLAS: It's the only one that goes by Marymount. Do you wonder why I didn't take the last one?

JENNIFER: *(She shrugs, not at all sure what to make of this.)* I guess.

NICOLAS: It didn't seem right. Something didn't seem right.

JENNIFER: Uhh. Okay.

NICOLAS: You ever meet someone you're immediately uncomfortable with and you have no idea why?

JENNIFER: Yeah. I guess.

NICOLAS: That's kinda how I felt about that bus. It happens from time to time. I hate it. I think it might be a psychological disorder. Luckily it doesn't happen too often.

JENNIFER: Are you trying to creep me out or something?

NICOLAS: No! I'm just telling you why I didn't take that bus. It's just weird—those feelings.

JENNIFER: I mean, not to be rude, but it's not like I majorly care.

NICOLAS: Fine. I wasn't trying to creep you all out. I'm not like that.

JENNIFER: I know. You just think you're psychic right? What was going to happen on that particular bus? Was it going to crash and go flipping over?

NICOLAS: No, no. Nothing like that. But a drunk man was going to be found dead on it.

JENNIFER: Oh, come on!

NICOLAS: I'm serious. I could see the face of an older business woman on the bus—a woman who had not yet got on.

JENNIFER: So?

NICOLAS: So she was to get on the bus two stops down from here. In the picture in my brain, the business woman walks past a man on the bus. As she walks past, heading to a seat near the back door, he, the pale, drunk man, falls from the bus seat to the floor. She screams—says he's dead. The bus driver stops and the man, all pale, is on the floor. He *is* dead.

JENNIFER: You are totally crazy. You're one of those kids who sits in total darkness playing video games all night long, right?

NICOLAS: I don't do that. I only own one video game. Frogger. I hate it. I'd rather read any day.

JENNIFER: Right.

NICOLAS: I'm telling you the truth.

JENNIFER: You're just trying to creep me out.

NICOLAS: In the instant when the bus was heading to stop in front of me, I saw that whole thing in my head. The idea of seeing a dead person has always made me scared. I got a bad feeling, like the feeling you get when someone makes you uncomfortable and you don't know why, and I didn't get on.

JENNIFER: So are you saying that if I contacted the Mass Transit Authority, and I asked them if a drunk man was found dead on a 71 bus, they would most definitely say yes?

NICOLAS: Yes. I'm pretty sure that's true.

JENNIFER: You're so crazy! Okay, psychicdorkalus, so predict when this bus will come then?

NICOLAS: It'll come in a little under 320 seconds. It's a bit delayed.

JENNIFER: Fine. I'll set my watch's timer by your prediction.

NICOLAS: I wouldn't listen to myself if I hadn't predicted things correctly in the past.

JENNIFER: Whatever. You watch too many movies.

NICOLAS: Seriously. I mean, why else would I make myself late for school?

JENNIFER: I don't know. Maybe you didn't feel like going to your first class.

NICOLAS: My first class is Tragic and Existential Drama with Ms. Scudlo. That's my absolute favorite class. She's the only teacher at Marymount that has even a tiny bit of imagination.

JENNIFER: I heard she's a total flake. Told everyone that she spent her summer vacation with an Italian lover who was a famous painter. I heard it was total bull. She had to take care of her sick mother in Cleveland the whole time.

NICOLAS: The lover was when she took a long weekend in July to Italy.

JENNIFER: Yeah, that's not what I heard. She also believes she has a ghost named Hilary that helps her teach Shakespeare and the Tragedy of MacBeth. She also says Hilary, the ghost, eats half her sandwich every lunch.

NICOLAS: What's wrong with that?

JENNIFER: I'm just saying it's totally weird, and she's a freak.

NICOLAS: What's weird? The ghost eating half the sandwich or just the idea of the ghost in general?

JENNIFER: Think about it. We're not in kindergarten. If she thinks "the ghost" helping her teach Shakespeare is some really, really clever way of teaching, it's not. It's annoying. Really annoying. And insulting too.

NICOLAS: I don't think it's annoying or insulting. I happen to think she really sees Hilary. Every day. I think she feels she needs her.

JENNIFER: For what?

NICOLAS: To remain interesting.

JENNIFER: Interesting? Being crazy is interesting?

NICOLAS: Yes. She's not very confident. All she has is her teaching and her potential genius. Name me one genius who wasn't a bit crazy.

JENNIFER: You think Ms. Scudlo is a genius?

NICOLAS: No. But maybe she's striving to be one. Wanting to be one. I'd like to be one someday.

JENNIFER: A genius?

NICOLAS: Yes. I'm writing a book already. My first.

JENNIFER: About what?

NICOLAS: About my secret need to be a genius. On everyone's secret need to be a genius. It's about a fifteen-year-old kid like me who starts to realize that he can predict the future. As time goes on, it seems like he can not only predict the future, but cause certain things to happen.

JENNIFER: Wow. That could be convenient.

NICOLAS: Yes, for a while, but then it's not. I think in the next chapter, he'll even change the future by making people begin to call him a genius, but he'll be very disappointed.

JENNIFER: Why?

NICOLAS: Because it's somehow not as good when you have to magically force people to call you that. Manipulating the future isn't all that fun. Neither is predicting it, eventually. He'll wish away all his powers by the end of the book. He just wants to be accepted for him.

JENNIFER: It sounds interesting actually.

NICOLAS: Do you read a lot?

JENNIFER: Some. A lot of mysteries lately.

NICOLAS: Really? *(She nods.)* You'll be the first to read my stuff then.

JENNIFER: You know, I heard about that special project you did for Sister Pat's biology class last year.

NICOLAS: So?

JENNIFER: So this girl from your class told me it was totally cool. You didn't sleep and you videotaped yourself the whole time. You were all weird and demented.

NICOLAS: That was the point of the project.

JENNIFER: To be all weird and demented?

NICOLAS: No! To show how personalities actually alter with little to no sleep. I forced myself to take these little word puzzles every few hours. I also had to play "Frogger"— the one video game I own. All my scores went down as I got more tired. I just wanted to understand more about sleep deprivation for reasons.

JENNIFER: What reasons?

NICOLAS: I told Sister Pat that anyway. I just wanted to observe the effects. But I was curious if it would affect my psychic abilities—increase them.

JENNIFER: So when did you first think you could predict things?

NICOLAS: Four years ago.

JENNIFER: So what are some big things you predicted, Mr. Nostradomous? You've heard of him, right?

NICOLAS: Of course. Well, I predicted my friend Billy Robins' parents' house being burglarized. You can even ask him. I predicted my mother's friend's pregnancy. You can ask her when you meet her. I predicted that tornado warning we had last summer.

JENNIFER: You can't prove any of them at the moment. Predict something about me. Right now.

NICOLAS: Okay. I predict that I will become one of the most important friends you will make in high school.

JENNIFER: You? But I don't even know you. And what I *do* know of you makes me nervous.

NICOLAS: Yes. And you'll always think that about me, but you'll like me all the same. We'll be friends for years to come. Maybe even romantic someday, but it won't last.

JENNIFER: Why not? I mean, not that I want anything to do with you, but what's that about?

NICOLAS: That's all I know. We'll be friends for many years.

JENNIFER: Okay. Whatever. So what's your name? I remember that girl from your class pointing you out, but I never heard your name? I suppose if we're going to be friends . . .

NICOLAS: Nicolas. I'm Nicolas.

JENNIFER: Good to meet you. I'm Janet.

NICOLAS: Good to meet you, Jennifer.

JENNIFER: How'd you know that my name wasn't Janet?

NICOLAS: *(Shrugs.)* I'm not sure. I just figured you'd try to test me.

JENNIFER: That's creepy. So what else did you predict? Tell me something really big, Nicolas? Something good—totally juicy.

NICOLAS: *(Beat. He shrugs.)* My dad's death.

JENNIFER: *(Beat.)* What?! That's just wrong! Your dad is not dead! This is all bull, isn't it?

NICOLAS: No, it's not. Ask Billy Robins. It happened when I was ten.

JENNIFER: He's your friend. He'll back up your lies.

NICOLAS: I'm not lying! And he wouldn't either. He's not that good a friend. Only so-so. Not like you'll be. Besides, I wouldn't lie about something like that.

JENNIFER: You probably do this kinda thing to tons of girls at school. You two try to creep them out together. It's not going to work on me.

NICOLAS: I wouldn't have brought it up if you didn't ask. I don't even know why I told you. Check with the office. My father died five years ago when I was ten years old. He died in a car accident. He was a sales rep. He had to cover a large territory. He had a problem with insomnia.

JENNIFER: Insomnia?

NICOLAS: He didn't get much sleep, and he drove to New York and Vermont a lot. He was on his way back from New York and he fell asleep at the wheel.

JENNIFER: *(Completely skeptical.)* And you predicted it?

NICOLAS: Not exactly. We were watching TV, and I looked up and out the window for a second. In my mind, I saw my dad falling down a hill. I told my mom what I saw in my head. I was really nervous. I told her it was nothing when I saw the look on her face. So stupid of me. But then we got a call. That was it.

JENNIFER: *(Fiercely.)* You better not be lying! Cause that is totally not funny at all.

NICOLAS: Check the obituary section in the *Boston Herald* or the *Globe*. August, five years ago. I'm not lying. I wish to God I were.

JENNIFER: I'm sorry if you're not lying. I don't know anyone who lost a parent. I don't know what to say.

NICOLAS: There's nothing you can say. *(Beat.)* I just feel sorta down sometimes. I felt like he was the only one who totally understood me. Ya know?

JENNIFER: Yeah. It's so sad. I can't even imagine. I'm sorry.

NICOLAS: It did no good to know ahead of time. It really doesn't help things much to be able to predict. It just makes you uncomfortable. I wish some day that my psychic power would completely disappear like the boy in my book. Like maybe they already have. Maybe I was all wrong about that drunk guy dying on the bus.

JENNIFER: I'm gonna call the MTA, believe me. *(Beeping watch.)* Ah! That alarm is so loud. That's my timer. *(Turns it off.)* Three hundred twenty seconds are up and no bus in the—Oh my God! Is that the bus? That's the bus. Just like you said.

(Nicolas shrugs as Jennifer looks strangely back at him.)

JENNIFER: Creepy.

A GOOD SOLID HOME

After a half a dozen attempts at artificial insemination, Robert, 39, and his wife Monica decided to adopt a child. A private agency put the couple in contact with Angie, an 18-year-old girl who felt unable to care for her expected child. Monica and the pregnant mother quickly bonded via the phone and through letters. After some initial conversations over the phone, the couple arranged to adopt Angie's unborn child. Throughout the remainder of Angie's pregnancy, the adoptive parents asked the birth mother if she was certain about her decision. Angie reassured them, and she signed all necessary papers. It has now been two months since Angie gave birth and handed the baby over to the adoptive couple. Everything had been going smoothly until a week ago when Angie suddenly called them. In this scene, Angie travels from New Jersey to Florida to confront the adoptive parents.

ANGIE: Okay, I know I called ya out of the blue, but I've been thinkin' about this for the whole two months.

ROBERT: Ms. Andrews, I don't mean to be abrupt, but I think we should have a lawyer present.

ANGIE: Why? We're friends. Your wife and I wrote to each other like every week before he was born—about real personal stuff too. I'm not here to do no legal thing. I just want to talk about our, our like arrangement. Besides aren't *you* a lawyer or somethin'?

ROBERT: No, I'm an accountant.

ANGIE: Oh. Well, that's kinda similar, isn't it?

ROBERT: Not really. We'll have to discuss this tomorrow, Ms. Andrews. From our previous discussion, we thought you were coming tomorrow. We already made arrangements with our lawyer.

ANGIE: But I can't do tomorrow. We gotta drive back then. Like at 6:00 A.M. I gotta work. I can't miss like five days. My manager will fire me like that. *(Snaps her fingers.)*

ROBERT: Well, I'm sorry to hear that, but my lawyer has advised me not to engage in a discussion on this matter.

ANGIE: I'm not asking you to *engage* in anything! I just want to talk. I just want to talk about things, ya know.

ROBERT: Talk?

ANGIE: Yeah. About things. About the way I'm feeling.

ROBERT: We're trying to avoid any legal maneuvers. We'd be happy to talk to you tomorrow about whatever you'd like, but it's not a good time right now.

ANGIE: I don't care if it's a good time. I just drove from Jersey City for God's sake. Twenty-four hours in a beat-up sedan with a chain-smoker and no air. So I don't care if it's the perfect timin', I need to talk today. And I'm not doin' any maneuverin' or I woulda brought a lawyer myself. Right? Right?! *(Beat.)* I'd be pretty stupid—totally stupid to drive all the way here and start tryin' to maneuver with you guys. You're college educated and all. I don't even have a high school diploma.

ROBERT: You drove here?

ANGIE: Yeah, that's what I've been tellin' ya. It's not like I could afford first freakin' class on American Airlines. We're stayin' at my cousin's place.

ROBERT: Who's the chain-smoker?

ANGIE: My boyfriend. It's a real bad habit. Worse than picking your nose.

ROBERT: Your boyfriend? Is he new? I don't remember you mentioning him before.

ANGIE: Yeah, that was on account of the fact that he was sorta not my boyfriend at the time. He was in juvie. And I didn't know if it would work out in the end cause he's kinda violent. He got outta rehab recently. He seems better, but . . . He didn't even know I was pregnant.

ROBERT: Are you trying to tell me that he's the real father?

ANGIE: Oh God, no! My boyfriend was in juvie for like a year. No, the guy who got me knocked up was *real* mature, but married. Like I told you and Monica, he didn't want nothin' to do with it.

ROBERT: I see. So this has nothing to do with the father then?

ANGIE: No. *(Looks around.)* So this is a nice place, Robert. Real nice and cheery-like. It kinda looks like one of those interiors ya see in those home magazines. All perfect. Ya know, like the kind ya think nobody lives like that. Nobody is *that* coordinated. You are.

ROBERT: Thanks.

ANGIE: *(Looking out.)* Man, you and Monica got a view too. You're like practically on the beach. I'd kill to live on a beach like this. You probably got to be careful of typhoons and hurricanes blowin' down your house. Course we got beaches too, but they're full of needles and crap. Gosh, I can't seem to stop feelin' nervous-like.

ROBERT: Um, would you like something to drink, Ms. Andrews?

ANGIE: What? Ya mean like a drink-drink?

ROBERT: Oh. Well, if you'd like.

ANGIE: No, I wasn't gonna do a drink-drink. I don't really like drinkin' cause of how it affected my boyfriend. That's why he was in rehab. I had a Slurpee earlier and that made me real sick. They always do. I don't know why I get 'em. They always make me feel bloaty and like throwin' up. Ya know?

ROBERT: I'll be honest with you, Ms. Andrews. Your phone call earlier this week came as a complete shock. We've been worried that perhaps you're considering retracting the adoption. We haven't been able to sleep since.

ANGIE: I'm sorry. I know I feel crazy too. That's why I called, but then you guys seemed so far away and stuff. You were goin' on about lawyers and papers and stuff. It seemed like you just wanted me to disappear into thin air. Like I never existed.

ROBERT: I thought we all agreed that it would be less painful if we didn't have contact.

ANGIE: Maybe we agreed to stuff. I guess I changed my mind or somethin'. I mean, ya know sometimes how ya *think* you're gonna know how you're gonna *feel* about somethin' and then *(Slaps her head.)* WHAM it actually happens? And you don't feel the same way ya thought you were gonna. And ya gotta make peace with it. Ya know what I mean?

ROBERT: To a certain degree.

ANGIE: So where's your wife? Where's Monica? I'd like to talk to her too.

ROBERT: Visiting her parents. They live . . . not too far away.

ANGIE: She's tryin' to avoid me, huh?

ROBERT: We decided it was best for her to stay with her parents until we knew what you wanted.

ANGIE: I'm not tryin' to disrupt your life or anything. I like you guys. I really do. You're like family. It's just . . . Is Ricky there too?

ROBERT: Yeah.

ANGIE: Is he still as cute as when he was born?

ROBERT: You know, I really don't feel like talking, Ms. Andrews. I'd like you to leave.

ANGIE: Geez! I just asked a little question.

ROBERT: We thought everything was perfect until you called this week. For two months our lives have been about lacking sleep, changing diapers, and feeding schedules and it's all been absolute heaven. And now . . . well . . . you would hesitate *yourself* to launch into a casual conversation. Especially given the capricious circumstances. Wouldn't you?

ANGIE: Um, yeah. I guess. I don't know exactly what ya said. I just want to talk about my son.

ROBERT: Your son? *Your* son?

ANGIE: Yeah. Ricky. The one I gave birth to like two months ago. You scooped him up and brought him off to "perfect homes and beaches"?

ROBERT: I know who you mean. I'm commenting on the *my* part.

ANGIE: Oh. You think he's not mine just cause I gave him to you?

ROBERT: No, he's not. Legally, he's not.

ANGIE: He came out of me. He's made up of my genes and crap. I had it explained to me like this: If I bit off my fingernail and gave it to you and told you you could keep it, even if you told everyone it was yours, it's still really *my* fingernail. Ya know?

ROBERT: You had it explained to you like that? By whom?

ANGIE: Never mind that. My point is he's mine.

ROBERT: Are you honestly equating our son to a chewed off fingernail?

ANGIE: No, no! I'm just tryin' to do this anthology thing that someone explained.

ROBERT: *(He stops, shakes his head in disbelief at her, but doesn't bother to comment on her misuse of words.)* Yes, biologically, he's yours. I agree. But we've been caring for him for two months now. We're his parents. He's bonded to us, and we love him. He loves us. It's not as if you weren't aware of the fact that this was going to happen. You signed the papers. We planned, as parents do, for more than seven years to have a child. Seven years!

ANGIE: Well, it's not *my* fault you couldn't do it! *(Robert looks stung.)* I didn't mean nothin' by that. A lot of good people can't do it.

ROBERT: That's true. And a lot of irresponsible, miserable people can.

ANGIE: So what's that supposed to mean?

ROBERT: I don't mean that about you. It's just, it's difficult to explain how hard it is. And I don't feel it necessary to describe the details to everyone. Suffice it to say that it's full of hospitals, and incredible amounts of time, and money, procedures, and discussions, and decisions, and heartbreaks. We are all taught that having a child is a natural occurrence—anyone can do it. Anyone . . . but *you*. Each attempt gets your hopes up. And worse, you carry the hopes of all your friends and family with you. Each time it fails, you feel like a deficient human being. You feel that God is against you. That you don't deserve what others receive so naturally. It keeps, it keeps making you feel less than you are over and over.

ANGIE: I know what you mean. I always kinda feel that way about myself. I didn't know you guys went through that much. Monica told me you did that test tube thing a couple times.

ROBERT: I'm sorry to go on about it.

ANGIE: No, I don't mind. I like that a whole lot better than you being so formal, calling me Ms. Andrews. It's not like you guys don't know me as Angie. I like it better when you're being real. Cloudy talk and big words always make me nervous. I got people in my life who do that cloudy talk thing. They act like I can't see through it. Like I'm dumb, but I'm not, ya know? I just screwed around in school. If I had my way now, I'd get my GED in a second, so I could go to college.

ROBERT: You could, Angie. It's a lot easier to get work when you have an education.

ANGIE: You're just saying that so I don't even consider takin' back Ricky.

ROBERT: Was that your intention? Because you told me your intention was *just* to talk.

ANGIE: I don't know. I'd like to see Ricky. And Monica.

ROBERT: His name's not Ricky. Please stop saying that. It's Joshua.

ANGIE: What? Joshua? But . . . I thought—

ROBERT: We never signed an agreement concerning that. This is infuriating. He's our son.

ANGIE: But Joshua sucks. Ricky's a much better name. It sounds like a singer or a race car driver. Joshua is like a snotty kid who thinks he knows everything.

ROBERT: He's named after my father.

ANGIE: No offense. *(Beat.)* Maybe you could call Monica. Get her to come back here for a few hours with him?

ROBERT: I don't think that's a good idea. What good will it do? You'll just long for him all the more when you leave. Why would I facilitate that?

ANGIE: You guys just acted like my friends till you got him. Now, it's like—"See ya! Bye!"

ROBERT: We did not mislead you, Ms. Andrews. You agreed all along. It's all signed, sealed, and delivered. We agreed to pay for all your hospital bills and be as supportive to you as possible, and afterwards sever ties. Not because we wanted to, but because it would be confusing and difficult for everyone involved.

ANGIE: Well, I know, but sometimes people change their mind. You know I still have time to change my mind. I talked to people, and I can still take Ricky back

ROBERT: Okay, and this is where this conversation ends because I am very angry. One—because you said you just wanted to talk and weren't planning any legal maneuvers. Two—because you are obviously attacking our rights to *our* legal son. And three—I told you I didn't want to discuss this without a lawyer present. I want you to leave now, Ms Andrews!

ANGIE: I'm not attacking you! I've just been real sad. Like there's a hole in the middle of my gut since I gave him away that day. I always had sort of a hole in me, but it's bigger now and more noticeable. Even my boyfriend noticed it first thing when he came home. I told him I was pregnant and gave the baby away. He was like, "That's so strange cause I could see there was a hole in you. It's so obvious."

ROBERT: A child can't fill that void, Ms. Andrews. I felt empty when I was eighteen years old too. Everyone does. I didn't know what I wanted or who I was.

ANGIE: I don't think that's it. I don't know. Maybe. *(Pause.)* Okay. Maybe you're right!

ROBERT: We have so much to offer your son, Angie. And I don't mean just material things, although that makes life easier, but I mean a solid home, a wealth of experiences, and a sense of who we are. Things you haven't even given yourself enough chance to develop yet. If you only knew how much of a family we are already, you wouldn't even consider this.

ANGIE: *(Pause.)* A kid makes you feel like ya did somethin'. Like you accomplished somethin'.

ROBERT: Yes, but what a kid needs is for you to give *him* a sense of accomplishment, which only happens after *you've* accomplished things you're proud of in your own life.

ANGIE: I know you don't think I've done anything in my life. I haven't. Havin' Rickie made me feel like I did somethin' so good, I wanted to hold onto it. I know I ain't got a lot to give him like you do. I mean, you live so close to Disney World for one. And you're both real smart and nice. Even when you use big words. I kinda wanted to see the place. Ya know? Check it out. Make sure it looked right. I get afraid some times. I get afraid that I won't have another chance.

ROBERT: You're so young, Angie. You'll have another chance. Plenty of them. I know it. And by that time, you'll have so much more to share.

ANGIE: You think? I don't know. *(Beat.)* Ya know, you're kinda encouragin'. The way a father should be. *(Beat.)* I was on the bus the other day and this old drunk lady fell over on the seat behind me. Dead. I felt sad. Like no one would even know or care. Cause maybe she never did nothin' in her whole life. I got a flash ahead like that would be me if I didn't change. Since then, I've been thinkin' about school and goin' back.

ROBERT: Why don't you?

ANGIE: Yeah, like I have the money. Big joke. Just like my life. *(Looking out the window.)* I gotta go get Tommy, my boyfriend. He's sleepin'. He told me he'd whip my butt if I didn't get him outta the sun, so he don't burn up like a lobster. *(Pause.)* So I ain't ever gonna see my son again, am I?

ROBERT: I think it would end up being very painful.

(She nods.)

ANGIE: I guess Monica and I can't be friends either. *(He nods gently.)* This really sucks.

ROBERT: I want you to have something. *(He pulls out a checkbook and hands her a check.)* Here.

ANGIE: *(She takes it.)* I didn't come here for no money! I don't care about money!

ROBERT: I know.

ANGIE: Don't be thinkin' I did! *(Looks at check, holding her chest.)* Holy Sh—geez! That's a lot. Too much! *(Handing it back.)* I can't take that. I can't even hold it without getting all shaky. And I never came here for that!

ROBERT: Angie, you gave us the most incredible gift we could have asked for. Please let us give you something in return. *(He tries to hand it back to her. She puts up her hand to say no.)*

ANGIE: No, it's not right. Look, I didn't come here for money, but, honestly, and I feel real ashamed about this, but my boyfriend did. He convinced me that you guys owed me somethin' for my sufferin'. Not just for the hospital bills. I don't agree with him. And truth is he'd probably steal the money away from me anyhow. He told me it would be easy to come here and sorta pretend like I wanted Ricky. Thing is, I do. At least, to see him. I was pretendin' before but I kept gettin' distracted by the truth when we were talkin'. I don't know. It's so messed up. I mean, you're right, what kinda life could I give him? But you, you're good people. You got a nice house, and you're married. Me, I don't even know if I'll be with my boyfriend next week. I—he'd be better off with you. You're smart and real good. I see that in you. It's just hard, ya know? So much for me bein' a good liar.

ROBERT: I appreciate your honesty. *(Hands it back.)* And I still want you to have it. Just promise me you won't tell him. Okay?

ANGIE: No. Like I said, I'm not good at lyin'. And he'd just blow it on nothin'. But I could use one favor.

ROBERT: Anything.

ANGIE: Send me a picture of him? Send it to me by mail. I want to look in his eyes, so I can see how happy he is. Ya know? I just want him to be happy.

ROBERT: *(Nods.)* I promise.

ANGIE: *(Angie starts to leave. She stops without turning.)* And Robert? *(Beat.)* All that crap about filling in the hole in my gut and being able to make it through school. And telling me that I will have lots to share with a kid some day. Tell me honestly. Don't lie, okay? Did you mean those things for real?

ROBERT: *(Beat.)* Every word.

ANGIE: *(She looks right at him.)* You be a good father, okay? *(Points at him.)* Treat him right or I'll be back! Give him a kiss good-bye from me. Will ya?
(He nods. She exits in a rush.)

HIT-AND-RUN

When Evie and Neil, both 18, accidentally hit a home-less man in a deserted portion of Montana, a clash of morals and values ensues. Their future and their relationship begins to unravel from the moment Evie slams on her brakes.

EVIE: *(Shocked and panicked, but not screaming, Evie gets out of the car to look.)* I never even seen him. It's like he came outta nowhere.

NEIL: *(Standing next to the body.)* Get in the car, Evie!

EVIE: *(Seeing the man on the ground, covering her mouth.)* Oh my God. I'll stay with him. I'll stay with him. You get help. I'll stay with him, and you get help.

NEIL: *(Yelling, and grabbing her.)* Get in the car, Evie. Now.

EVIE: What are you doin'?!

NEIL: Please. I want you to get in.

EVIE: *(They get in.)* Oh God! Oh God, oh God. I can't believe this is happenin'! I didn't see him. Did you see him? We should do somethin' about his bleedin' right away.

NEIL: *(Touching her arm.)* It's okay. It's okay, hon.

EVIE: No, it's not okay! He looks really bad! You've got to drive! I can't.

NEIL: Drive where? We're in the middle of Montana, Evie. There isn't anythin' for miles.

EVIE: There was a . . . there was a house a couple miles back. I don't know where exactly, but—but awhile back. Where we stopped to eat, remember? Just back there. They'll let you call an ambulance.

NEIL: Now, hold on, Evie. Let's just talk about this first.

EVIE: Talk about what, Neil?! What's there to talk about? I hit him! I can't drive back. I'm too scared to drive. You drive back there. It's not that far.

NEIL: He's a homeless guy.

EVIE: So! So what does that have to do with anythin'?

NEIL: Well, he's okay I think. He just looks like he has some bruises.

EVIE: Bruises? That's all? I hit him hard enough to throw him off the road.

NEIL: Oh I don't know about that. He may have dived off the road. I'm not going to lie to you. He is knocked up a bit, Evie. But I don't even know if he got that from your car. He mighta been banged up anyway.

EVIE: Yeah? *(Beat.)* I can't believe that. You saw him fly up like that. And that noise when he hit the car. He's not just bruised. I don't think so. That's not possible. Don't try to soften it like you do, Neil. This time you can't soften things like you do. *(Beat.)* You drive, okay? You aren't too freaked out right?

NEIL: Drive where?

EVIE: To go get help! Why are you bein' so stupid?!!

NEIL: I'm not sure you're thinkin' this through, Evie.

EVIE: No, I don't think *you* are! We're not goin' to leave him here for God's sake.

NEIL: *(Beat.)* I'm just sayin' that it may not be all that bad for him. I mean, he could be just banged up. And you and I— well, if we go get help for him, they'll call the police. We could get in a lot of trouble for this.

EVIE: What in the hell are you talkin' about?! We could get in a helluva lot more trouble for leavin' him here.

NEIL: He's a homeless guy, Evie.

EVIE: So. I don't think that makes a bit of difference.

NEIL: All I'm sayin' is no one is gonna go lookin' for him.

EVIE: And anyway, how are you so sure he's homeless?

NEIL: The rags he's wearin'. He stinks like alcohol and sweat. His face is all leathery from the sun. He's definitely homeless. There's no doubt. There's nothin' out here for miles and miles.

EVIE: I think maybe we should take him with us if you think the hospital's far.

NEIL: Do you mean move him?

EVIE: Yeah. I mean, I know you're not supposed to move people, but maybe we could find something hard to move him with—something stiff to put him on.

NEIL: I'm not movin' him. He looks like he's violent.

EVIE: Violent? How would you know? He's lyin' there in pain.

NEIL: His knife fell outta his pocket. It was on the ground a few feet away from him.

EVIE: *(Beat.)* Okay, even if he is homeless and violent. Even if no one will come lookin' for him. He's still a person. He deserves to live, Neil. I can't believe your attitude. I think you're kinda sick. *(Beat.)* Geez, he's cryin' out there.

NEIL: The thing is Evie, they could put you in jail for this.

EVIE: What?! It was an accident. You saw the road. Plus it's raining. It was so dark. Those curves are crazy difficult. I'm not from here. I don't know this road. They'll understand that. Especially if we go for help right away.

NEIL: Bein' not from around here doesn't give us any advantage, Evie. The cops in these small towns love this crap. And it doesn't mean that they give a good damn about the homeless guy out there. They'd probably throw him in a ditch and forget about him. They just love to bust kids from big cities. The cops'll hear we're from Dallas and he'll be all over us. They'll do the Breathalyzer. And you aren't goin' to pass it. Okay?

EVIE: But I only had four beers. I don't even feel drunk, Neil.

NEIL: It don't matter. It'll show up positive. And listen, if he's hurt in the least, they'll try to get you put in jail for somethin'. They could even go for somethin' like attempted manslaughter or murder or somethin'.

EVIE: Murder?!

NEIL: I don't know. But you can kiss gettin' into college goodbye or gettin' a job.

EVIE: But you could tell them. You could be my witness. He came out of nowhere, right?

NEIL: I could say that. And he might have. I mean, we don't

know. This guy could be a major con artist who likes to get money out of innocent people. I remember when I worked at the movie theater. This guy—this homeless, drunk guy used to fall in front of cars as they were movin' around the parking lot.

EVIE: Are you serious?

NEIL: He did it all the time. He brought like four different customers to court. Took a butt load of money from them for injuries. That's all I know. He was a total con man.

EVIE: Okay, but that guy is bleedin'. I don't think he's a con man. And honestly, I don't think I was completely watchin' carefully. I mean, we were jammin' to that song.

NEIL: Maybe he was intendin' on being a con guy but he got a little too in the way of the car. Maybe the accident was totally his fault. He is drunk. He smells all the way to Ohio.

EVIE: Right. So if he did that, we'd have a case. You could say that the homeless guy jumped outta nowhere. You can confirm that it was like pitch-black and then I heard this hard noise and his body went flyin' into the air. I had no time to stop. He was maybe tryin' to pretend to get hit and—whatever—and he really got hit in the process.

NEIL: There's only one problem, Evie. I'm obviously your stupid boyfriend. I would say anythin' to try and get you out of it. You think his lawyers don't know that? They'll think I'm worse than you by far. They won't believe me worth a good Goddamn. They'll think I got you drunk. Shoot. When they give you the Breathalyzer test, they're gonna give it to me too. And how's that gonna look? I'm drunker than you. And I'm testifyin' that the guy came outta nowhere? I can just see it now. "Well, no wonder. You were drunk, too. Right?" Plus these conservative-type people out here ain't gonna like that I took you outta town for this road trip. Neither is your mom. Trust me, they are not gonna like that our parents don't even know where we are. Or that we lied about where we were goin'.

EVIE: It's not like we're that young.

NEIL: We're still under drinking age. The deal is that I'm not like the best character witness for you right now. Okay?

EVIE: Okay. So maybe it won't look great, but I don't think I could live knowin' that I hurt someone. And if I have to pay for it by doing some time, I will.

NEIL: After they do the Breathalyzer, Evie, they'll test you for drugs too.

EVIE: I don't do drugs. *(Beat.)* It was just a little weed. Two puffs.

NEIL: That's not how they'll see it.

EVIE: My mom can help. She would help me get out of it.

NEIL: Yeah? What she'll do is break us up first. She'll break us up and pay for this real expensive lawyer, which she doesn't have the money to do, right?

EVIE: This is all just guessin'. We don't know what'll really happen. We don't even know how hurt he is.

NEIL: You honestly don't think she'd make us break up?

EVIE: *(Beat.)* Yeah, she might. But we're talkin' about a man's life here.

NEIL: Yeah, and we're talkin' about our lives and future too. Do you know how much money your mother will spend on a lawyer? She'll want to get the best lawyer she can find.

EVIE: I don't know. But she doesn't need to do that.

NEIL: Yes. She does! This will look bad. You were goin' about fifty miles an hour down a thirty-five mile zone. You're drunk, according to the Breathalyzer. You've done drugs. You and your crazy boyfriend have been out on a road trip for a couple of days doin' God knows what. That's what the other lawyer'll say. You will do some time for this Evie. You can kiss college and me good-bye.

EVIE: He's hurt that bad, huh?

NEIL: Didn't you just hear anythin' I just said?

EVIE: Yes! That's why I'm sayin' that. I wouldn't go to jail if he walked away with a couple of bruises. He's hurt bad. How bad?

NEIL: *(Shrugs.)* I don't know. I'm not a doctor. But his head and legs look bad.

EVIE: We'll drop him off at the emergency room. We won't stay.

NEIL: That could be worse. There'd be people all over. There'd be witnesses. We'd be seen. We'd have left the scene of a crime with all those witnesses.

EVIE: We could dump him off in one of the small towns around here. Everybody would be asleep. At least someone would find him in a few hours when the sun comes up.

NEIL: You want to put him in your car? They'll be blood all over the back seat. How are you gonna explain that?

EVIE: How am I goin' to explain the dent in my hood or the blood all over that?

NEIL: Car wash. Nothin' more than a car wash and a fender bender.

EVIE: Who are you? It's like you're a monster or somethin'. Geez, a few months ago we picked up a dog who was hit on the highway and you called the driver a killer. This is not right, Neil. I think we should at least try to take him to a hospital. We can dump him off in the distance . . . away from people.

NEIL: If he's got back injuries, movin' him could kill him.

EVIE: And, what, leavin' him here's gonna heal him?!!

NEIL: He has a chance. It's all a fate thing. If someone comes by, he'll be taken for help. He'll be taken to safety. Just like we did with that dog a few months back.

EVIE: I can't believe you. I can't believe how cold you can be.

NEIL: I'm not cold, Evie. I just want to have a happy life with you. I love you. We had plans for school. And I just know kids like us and cops. Kids who don't come from money . . . families like us who they call white trash. We'll never get a fair trial. Look, we both have plans and this is goin' to ruin them. Maybe forever. That's how my old lady went down.

EVIE: I know.

NEIL: She did a little coke. Got caught. Everythin' was down hill from there. She thought she'd get out and get a new job, but she's never recovered from what she's been through. If anything she became more of an addict being in there. Neither of us needs a setback like this. Not before we even begin.

EVIE: Let's make an anonymous call about him. Could we at least do that?

NEIL: *(Beat.)* Sure. If we're careful. It'll be okay. Someone will come by and find him after we call. I promise. It'll all be good. *(Hugs her.)* I love you, baby.

EVIE: We could stop at the first gas station we find—call and then hang up suddenly.

NEIL: I'm so glad you agree, baby. If you were in jail, I would be miserable. I couldn't stand it. I don't know if I could wait.

EVIE: *(Pause.)* What?

NEIL: Nothin'. Just may not've been able to wait for you to get out is all.

EVIE: Yeah, I'd feel the same way. You won't have to wait for me though, Neil.

NEIL: I'm glad. Now, let's go.

EVIE: You won't have to wait because I'm dumpin' you. Here and now. Get out of my car.

NEIL: What?!!

EVIE: You're disgustin'. Get out of my car, Neil!

NEIL: You're not serious.

EVIE: Like hell I'm not.

NEIL: It's rainin' out there.

EVIE: Aww. See how it feels? Well, we'll leave it up to fate. Maybe someone will help you—it's a fate thing. In the meantime, I'll get help. Get out! Now! Or I'll tell the cops it was you drivin'! *(He looks at her in awe.)* Who would know? There ain't no other witnesses. Right?

THAT'S ALL FOLKS

Through the years, Peter, 16, has been given the daunting challenge of taking care of his autistic younger sister, Shelly, 14. Shelly is a high-functioning autistic teenager who attends a special program in the local high school. Peter watches out for Shelly every day. He protects her from other kids, eases her tantrums, and makes sure she makes it to and from school. In the past few months, Peter has started to notice girls more. He is particularly interested in the new girl at school. He'd like to talk with her, but each time Shelly embarrasses him or comes between them. To make Peter's life worse, Shelly and Peter's parents have been fighting for weeks now. The word divorce *has even come up. Peter knows that Shelly's autism has played a part in the tension. When Peter arrives home from being out with a friend, Shelly is sitting in his room. This is the last straw!*

PETER: What are you doing in here?! Get out of here!

SHELLY: I watch Bugs Bunny. Five minutes till "Bugs Bunny and Friends."

PETER: You don't belong in here, Shelly. It's *my* room.

SHELLY: Next stop Wilson.

PETER: Go downstairs and watch whatever you want.

SHELLY: Doors closing. Doors closing. *(Makes a realistic sounding ding.)*

PETER: Get out, or I'm going to throw you out!

SHELLY: *(Flapping her hands, upset.)* T-t-t-that's all folks!

PETER: Come on!

SHELLY: *(Waving her hands a bit.)* No. Loud. Loud. *(Touching ears.)* Looooud.

PETER: Yes, I'm being loud, Shelly, but it's *my* room. I can be as loooooud as I want.

SHELLY: *(Rocking.)* Yeah.

PETER: You don't think I have a right to be loud in my own room?

SHELLY: Yeah. *(Beat.)* Lawrence is next.

PETER: You don't think I have a right to do anything if it doesn't involve you. Or at least Mom and Dad don't.

SHELLY: Priority seating is intended for the elderly and those with disabilities.

PETER: You embarrass me. Do you hear me?

SHELLY: *(Turning in another direction.)* Priority seating is intended for the elderly and those with disabilities.

PETER: You looked like an idiot today, ya know? Why can't you be like a normal autistic kid who doesn't like to touch? Do you know how weird that looks to come running at me—hugging me? It's weird. I'm your brother. You don't do that in front of other people.

SHELLY: Your cooperation is appreciated.

PETER: But you don't care. You just keep going on with your own little thing. I know everybody thinks you can't stop, but I know you can.

SHELLY: *(More quietly.)* Your cooperation is appreciated. Your cooperation is appreciated. Your cooperation is appreciated. Your cooperation is appreciated. Your cooperation—

PETER: Stop it!!

(Shelly stops. She even briefly looks up at him.)

PETER: I'm sorry, Shelly. I just . . . hate this. I sorta have a thing for that Donna girl, ya know? That new girl. So when you came . . . at me today, well, it scares other kids. I mean, you scare other kids. I was really pissed off even though I know you don't mean to scare anyone. I got really angry. I even had to go to the Y with Josh to blow off some steam. It's like I get angry all the time now. I hate it. I don't think it's fair to be in this position. It's just I told you I'd pick you up from your classroom. Why didn't you wait?

SHELLY: *(Quietly.)* This is Lawrence.

PETER: I know you were just being you. I'm just tired, and I want my own space tonight. Okay?

SHELLY: Doors closing. Doors closing. *(She makes the ding sound.)*

PETER: I know you hear me . . . Sooo. Go. Down. Stairs.

SHELLY: Who directed most of the Looney Tune Cartoons?

PETER: I don't want to play trivia. The TV is free down there.

SHELLY: Try again. Who directed most of the Looney Tune cartoons?

PETER: Fine. I'm gonna get Mom then.

(Shelly shakes her head furiously and makes a humming noise.)

PETER: What's wrong?

(Shelly begins flapping her arms. In between, she starts to bite her hand.)

PETER: *(About her biting.)* No. No.

SHELLY: *(Still biting.)* Gone. Gone. T-t-t-that's all folks.

PETER: Stop it!

(She lets out a cry and stops biting.)

PETER: Okay, Mom's gone. That's okay. She'll be back.

(Shelly lets out another hum noise and plunks into the chair.)

SHELLY: *(She folds her legs, leans forward, and rocks herself. She imitates a famous Bugs Bunny cartoon. Blankly, without emotion.)* Would you like to shoot me now or wait till you get home?

PETER: It's practically six. Are you sure she's not here?

SHELLY: *(Continuing.)* Shoot him now. Shoot him now.

PETER: Did something happen?

SHELLY: *(Touching her ears.)* Loud.

PETER: A fight?

SHELLY: You keep out of this. He doesn't have to shoot you now. He does so have to shoot me now. I demand that you shoot me now.

PETER: Dad and Mom had another fight?

SHELLY: *(Quietly singing, mumbling the words to the Bugs Bunny theme song "Overture.")* Overture . . . light the

lights. This is it. The night of nights. No more rehearsing
and nursing a part . . . we know every part by heart.

PETER: He left?

SHELLY: T-t-t that's all folks.

PETER: *(Reaching out to her.)* Listen. Did he leave?

SHELLY: *(Imitating Woody Woodpecker and Porky.)* H-h-h-ha-
ha. H-h-h-ha-ha. T-t-t-that's all folks. T-t-t-that's all folks.
H-h-h-ha-ha.

PETER: *(As if to say enough already.)* Okay! *(Beat.)* Do you
know why?

SHELLY: *(Imitating her father.)* I am so sick of this! I am so
sick of you and everything! It's enough to have to deal with
Shelly every day. Everything we do is with autistic kids—
autistic events. I'm tired of the obsession. I don't want my
life based around this! Do you understand this?

PETER: Where's Mom?

SHELLY: I am so sick of this! I am so sick of you and everything!

PETER: He didn't mean it, Shelly.

SHELLY: *(Biting her hand in between, not ever looking at him.)*
I am so sick of this! I am so sick of you and everything! It's
enough to deal with Shelly every day. It's enough to deal
with Shelly every day.

PETER: It's not your fault. This is not your fault.

SHELLY: *(Does perfect imitation of father's emotion without
adding her own.)* Do you understand this? Do you understand this? Do you understand this?

PETER: Yes, yes. I understand. I understand how you feel, and
he's just using you as an excuse. It's not your fault. Now,
where's Mom?

SHELLY: Doors closing. Doors closing. *(Making the ding
noise.)* Doors closing. Doors closing. *(Makes the ding
noise.)* Doors closing. Doors—

PETER: She just wants to be left alone then. She'll come out of
her room soon. Don't worry.

SHELLY: Closing. *(Makes the ding sound.)*

PETER: It's not right what he said, Shel. It's not even true.

SHELLY: *(Begins singing again quietly, rocking.)* Overture. Light the lights.

PETER: They just fight. They can't seem to get along.

SHELLY: *(Singing, rocking.)* This is it. The night of nights.

PETER: We could try to help them though.

SHELLY: *(Singing.)* No more rehearsing and nursing a part.

PETER: You could try to get better, Shelly. It would make things easier maybe.

SHELLY: *(Singing.)* We know every part by heart.

PETER: I know you're in there. I understand you. Look at me. The first step is more eye contact. Look at me.
(He steps in front of her and tries to make her look. She turns away.)

SHELLY: *(Singing.)* Overture.

PETER: I'll work with you every day. I promise.

SHELLY: *(Singing.)* Light the lights.

PETER: I'm talking to you, Shelly. Tell me how your day was.

SHELLY: *(Singing.)* This is it. The night of nights.

PETER: I know you're sad. So talk to me directly now. I'm your big brother. Why don't you talk to me?

SHELLY: *(Singing.)* No more rehearsing and nursing a part.

PETER: You have to talk directly, not through TV stuff anymore.

SHELLY: *(Singing.)* We know every part by heart. Overture—

PETER: *(He forces her to look at him.)* No, no. What's going on with you, Shelly? What's going on?
(She pauses, quietly. She avoids his eye contact.)

PETER: *(He feels her calm down. She's with him.)* That's good. Look at me now. Come on. You can do it. Tell me.

SHELLY: *(Pause.)* Doors closing. Doors closing. *(Makes the ding noise.)*

PETER: Come on, at least try. At least try to look at me for once!

SHELLY: Priority seating is intended for the elderly and those with disabilities. Priority seating is intended for the elderly and those with disabilities. Priority seating is intended for the elderly and those with disabilities.

PETER: Don't you see what you've done to us?!

SHELLY: Doors closing. Doors closing. *(Makes the ding noise.)* Doors closing. Doors closing. *(Makes the ding noise.)* Door closing. Doors—

PETER: *(Slapping her hard across the face.)* Stop it!

(Shelly cries out and throws herself off the chair.)

PETER: Oh God.

(Shelly begins biting her arm hard.)

PETER: Oh God. Please, Shelly. I'm sorry.

(He moves toward her but she squirms away from him making a whining sound and biting her arm.)

PETER: I didn't mean it. I don't know what I'm doing, Shelly. I'm an idiot. Please stop. Stop hurting yourself. Please.

SHELLY: *(She begins banging her hand hard against her head.)* Do you want to shoot me now or wait till you get home? *(Peter moves down to the floor with her, trying to stop her hand. She fights against it.)*

PETER: I didn't mean what I said. Please . . . stop. I'm stupid. I'm just a kid. I say stupid things I don't mean half the time.

SHELLY: *(Still biting her hand, mumbling.)* Do you want to shoot me now or wait till you get home? Shoot him now. Shoot him now. You keep out of this. He doesn't have to shoot you now. He does so have to shoot me now. I demand that you shoot me now. *(She keeps repeating, whispering more.)*

PETER: *(Trying to hold her hand back away from her teeth.)* I know I'm a rotten brother. And I know if I could get through to you, Dad wouldn't be so angry so often. *(She pulls her hand away.)* Okay. Fine. But whatever happens, we're gonna need each other now more than ever. And it doesn't matter if you keep biting yourself or not, the pain will still be there. So go ahead if you want to. Go ahead. I'm obviously not helping you any. I'm just making things worse. I can't believe I hit you. I'm sorry, Shelly. I'm sorry.

(He moves away from her.)

SHELLY: *(She stops struggling and curls up in a ball. Very quietly.)* It's not your fault. This is not your fault.

PETER: What did you say?

SHELLY: It's not your fault. This is not your fault.

PETER: *(Pause.)* We communicate—you and I. Probably better than other brothers and sisters. We just connect in a different way I guess, you know?

SHELLY: Yeah.

PETER: It'll be all right. You know? Maybe he'll be back. He'll be back. I'm sure of it.

SHELLY: Yeah.

PETER: If he doesn't, he's pretty stupid. Cause we're pretty good kids.

SHELLY: Yeah. I knew I took that wrong turn in Albuquerque. Should have zigged when I zagged.

(Peter smiles.)

PETER: Should we get Mom?

SHELLY: Yeah. *(She reaches out her hands to him.)* Hug?

PETER: *(Beat.)* Sure.

(They embrace.)

PETER: I love you, kiddo. Don't ever forget that. 'Kay?

SHELLY: *(Beat. Nods.)* Um.

PETER: We'll make it through this. Okay?

SHELLY: Yeah.

PETER: But no huggin' me at school, all right? Okay?

SHELLY: Yeah. *(She lets go.)* Who directed the most Looney Tune Cartoons?

PETER: *(Playing along.)* Umm. I don't know. Thomas Jefferson?

SHELLY: *(Makes bad buzzer noise.)* Wrong answer.

PETER: Maybe, humm, let me think . . . Mel Blanc.

SHELLY: Ding! Correct. Ding!

PETER: Come along, Rabbit. Doors opening. Doors opening. Priority seating is intended for Bugs Bunny and his pal Daffy. Ding! *(She takes his hand.)* Ding. *(Thinking a moment before they leave.)* Ding. *(To her.)* He'll be back. He's gotta come back, right?

SHELLY: Ding.

(Peter gestures for her to move ahead.)

A WOMAN'S CHOICE

Luke, 24, discovered recently that his 18-year-old wife was several months pregnant and considering an abortion. He was shocked. Despite the fact that the child was unplanned and their relationship was tense, he desperately wanted this baby. He spent a lot of time convincing his wife, Kat, that this would rebuild their relationship. He took on a second job so they could save money for the baby and put a down payment on a house. It seemed he had convinced her that having the baby would be the best for everyone. But, last week, with no warning, Luke's wife went into a Planned Family Center and aborted it. When Kat told him, Luke went crazy. Kat took off to stay with her sister in Florida. Luke made several threatening phone calls to the abortion center, angrily accusing the counselor of coercing his wife. Luke impulsively decides to confront the counselor in person when he sees her leaving the center late this evening. Jessie, 27, is struggling to break free as Luke pushes her into the lobby.

LUKE: Ow! *(Suddenly pulling his hand away.)* Stop it! *(Pushing her into the room.)* Relax! I just want to talk to you. I'm not going to do anything.

JESSIE: *(Fearfully.)* Please, please. Please don't—

LUKE: I'm not going to hurt you. I just wanted to talk to you in person. That's all. I swear!

JESSIE: Well, then let go of me. *(He does.)* I know you're upset. I can see that. But if you just want to talk, why are you pushing me?

LUKE: I'm not going to do anything but talk to you.

JESSIE: Okay, okay. But the facility is . . . What's your name?

LUKE: Luke.

JESSIE: Okay, Luke, I was just going to say that the facility is closed. I'd be happy to talk to you tomorrow.

LUKE: But on the phone you said you couldn't talk to me. Or maybe you just wouldn't. You couldn't tell me anything you said. That made me so angry because my *wife*, won't talk to me either. She's suddenly in Florida with her sister.

JESSIE: Look, I'm sorry that you and your wife are having problems, but we don't get involved in our clients' personal lives.

LUKE: You tell her to kill my child and then leave me? You call that not getting involved in our personal lives?

JESSIE: I can assure you that no one here told her any such thing. And while it is true that I am not at liberty to discuss individual cases, I can clarify what we do here so there's no misunderstanding. I see how upset you are. And I'm sympathetic. I can arrange counseling for you if you'd like. I'd be happy to help you tomorrow.

LUKE: Not tomorrow! Tonight! I want to get some peace on this tonight. Do you know how crazy I've been at the shop? I may lose one of my jobs because of all this. I've been working all hours, trying to get the cash together. And I don't need counseling from you! I see how you people counsel. Last week my wife tells me she loves me and agrees about our baby, and the next thing I know, she talks to you and my child's dead.

JESSIE: The security guard will be here any minute. He must be running late. He'd have called the police by now. But I won't. I won't call the police, and I'll convince him not to as well. As long as you go quietly back through that front door, and come back tomorrow to discuss this rationally with me.

LUKE: I'm not coming tomorrow. I want to talk now! And the security guard isn't late.

JESSIE: What do you mean?

LUKE: I mean, he's in my van. He's in my van as we speak.

JESSIE: What?

LUKE: Don't get all crazy on me. He's fine. I have him in my van. He's not dead or anything! *(She looks horrified. He reacts.)* I put the radio on for him. Don't act like that! I had to tie him up. He's fine. He's not hurt. He stopped me in the parking lot. I had no choice. I needed to talk with you face-to-face. That's all. Is that too much to ask? To try to understand. To tell you how wrong you were. How you've ruined my life!

JESSIE: Look, I know you're furious and hurt about this situation, Luke. But you are making a terrible mistake. This is going to get you in a lot of trouble. You could wind up doing time.

LUKE: What did you say to her? Just tell me what you said to her that day. I need to know. And then I'll let you both go.

JESSIE: About what specifically?

LUKE: About me. About keeping the baby.

JESSIE: I didn't say anything to her. I just talk to them about their options.

LUKE: You're the main counselor here, right?

JESSIE: This is not a counseling center. I'm not a therapist. I'm studying to be a nurse. This facility is for women's gynecological care, birth control, and abortion.

LUKE: I know what you do here. I'm not stupid.

JESSIE: We counsel by giving facts and options prior to the procedure. We also help with referrals afterwards if a woman would like one-on-one counseling. But I don't get to know these women. I meet them for only a few hours in a group.

LUKE: So how can you tell them what to do then?! How dare you!

JESSIE: I don't! I don't make their decisions. I don't tell anyone what to do. I deal with a lot of women here every day. *(Cringes.)* I, I don't even know who your wife is exactly. I think I have an idea, but I'm not entirely sure.

LUKE: Well that's even worse! You don't know who she is, but you tell her to have an abortion? To leave me? Did she describe me as some crazed guy who flies off the handle? I don't know what happened. Everything changed suddenly. She got so cold. I have a bad temper, yes. But I've never hit her!

JESSIE: I can't discuss this as I told you. All I can say is that I'm here to give the women the facts. That's all.

LUKE: Yeah? The facts? Did you tell her that at seven weeks, our baby was sucking his thumb? He drinks too and sleeps and wakes up and gets bored. I've been reading a lot these last few weeks. I've been doing lots of things to prepare. A baby is responsive to pain at seven weeks . . . to touch and cold and sound and light and stuff. That baby would feel the pain of it. Did you tell her all that?

JESSIE: Yes. Sort of.

LUKE: Sort of?

JESSIE: They watch a film. They can see the development of the fetus at several stages.

LUKE: That's how you get out of it, right? You call it a fetus instead of a baby. Fetus sounds so inhuman, like an alien or a fish.

JESSIE: I discuss their options, the possible outcomes, emotionally and physically, of the procedure. Then we leave them alone in a room to decide.

LUKE: But there's a kind of pressure in that room, isn't there? Especially if the woman's young, like my wife. There's a kind of stuck-up-ness if the girl hasn't gone to college. Or if she has any doubt about her husband. I know I get angry, but I'm a good man. I wanted this child. I loved this child. But you people made her scared. Made her think we couldn't handle it. Pressured her into thinking I couldn't handle it.

JESSIE: If there's any pressure, it's the other way around. There's more pressure to convince them *not* to have an abortion. They are given a lot of other options.

LUKE: Well, if that were true, then why is it that Planned Family is performing more abortions in the U.S. than any other facility? It's commercialization. It's the money. That's why!

JESSIE: No, I couldn't disagree with you more. It's safe here. And affordable. Planned Family's been here for the last thirty to forty years when other places haven't. Maybe it's because it's a place where women can be treated fairly and with dignity no matter what their choice. A place where their wishes are respected.

LUKE: Wishes? Dignity? Someone opens you up and pulls out the pieces of your living child. That's dignity?

JESSIE: *(Gesturing to the door.)* Why don't we go see how the security guard is doing? I don't think this conversation is getting us anywhere.

LUKE: *(Blocking the door.)* I'll be the judge of that. *(Beat.)* Are you a lesbian or something?

JESSIE: What?!

LUKE: I said are you a lesbian or something? Do you hate men or something?

JESSIE: No, I don't hate men.

LUKE: But you're a lesbian?

JESSIE: No, I'm not a lesbian! And why would that make any difference?

LUKE: Because you don't seem to understand that it's not *just* the woman's choice. You don't see any reason to talk to the father about this, do you? Morally? Asking him? Giving him a choice? It was part of my body too! And I'm her husband. Not just some random guy. Her husband. This was my child, my body, my future. But I have no say. I don't even have to be notified, right? I don't even have to be notified that it is going to happen. That you'll kill him. Right? *(Beat.)* Answer me. Right?

JESSIE: *(Beat.)* That's right.

LUKE: I took on a second shift at the factory to try to save up for a house for us. I started to build a baby bed. *(Pause.)* See, I don't have a family. My mom died last year. She was never much of a mother. I thought this would be my family. That we would be a family.

JESSIE: Look, the longer he stays out there, the worse the situation will be for you.

LUKE: You keep acting like you're thinking of me, but you're not. You're a liar.

JESSIE: I'm not lying. You will be put in jail for this. And they won't be sympathetic about what you've done. Why don't you call the police now and apologize? *(She gestures, heading for the door.)* Come on, why don't we just go out and check on him?

LUKE: No! *(Grabbing her tightly.)* I don't think you understand.

JESSIE: *(Frightened.)* Ow!

LUKE: You're not listening to me. I'm trying to talk to you here.

JESSIE: What is it you want me to understand?

LUKE: I called you this afternoon to make you uncomfortable. Nowhere near the pain I'm feeling, but at least some guilt or regret. But it's too easy here. You don't understand the pain you cause. You hand women the papers. Sign away. And rip out another life. Just work. Just routine, right?

JESSIE: No.

LUKE: Even if you don't believe in God or a soul, you must admit that this glob or mass or fetus, as you call it, is unique. He's got eyes and a nose—he's human. Did you know that nothing new will be added from the time of the fertilization until the death of the old man or woman except that he'll grow and the mind will develop? But nothing new will be added? How is this "fetus" not human?

JESSIE: It's not that I don't understand your position, Luke. I can see your point of view, and you have every right to it. But what you're doing here, to me, to the security guard is not just disagreeing. It's fanatical.

LUKE: Is it fanatical to stop people from killing people? Then I guess I'm a fanatic. I just have this really stupid idea that life is precious.

JESSIE: You don't think anyone here agrees with you? I think life is precious!

LUKE: Then act like it!

JESSIE: The women who become pregnant are just as precious as the unborn. It's not some easy, snap decision they make. Some mothers just can't do it.

LUKE: So put the child up for adoption.

JESSIE: I knew you'd say that sooner or later. But what if they don't get adopted, which happens all the time? Then the child's left to this random system of ours that sucks them into foster care where they never escape.

LUKE: But they could escape. Some escape. Some get past their upbringing, creating things in this world. Building things, making masterpieces, music, changing the way we see stuff.

JESSIE: Yes, but some of these women are physically unable to carry a child. They may be suffering from dangerous addictions or diseases. They don't want to pass that on. Others find it too painful—physically or emotionally. They just can't do it.

LUKE: Oh, well fine then! Let's kill it by all means. It's really inconvenient. People find their aging, sick parents inconvenient. Should we kill them too?

JESSIE: Don't be ridiculous! I'm talking about complex situations.

LUKE: Like what?

JESSIE: Like rape for instance.

LUKE: Well, that has nothing to do with my situation! That has nothing to do with my child.

JESSIE: So you agree with abortion in instances of rape?

LUKE: I don't want to argue with you anymore! I want to know why you told her I'd be a bad father! I want you to feel pain for what you've done!

JESSIE: *(Snaps back angrily.)* What have I done?! Huh?!

LUKE: *(Grabs her hard.)* I could kill you with my bare hands for what you've done.

JESSIE: Then kill me. Do it. Go ahead. *(He's shocked by her behavior.*) I will not be a victim anymore. I promised myself that. So if you want to kill me, go right ahead.

LUKE: I didn't mean . . . I don't . . . I'm angry, but I . . . *(He starts to let go of Jessie's arms.)* I don't want to hurt you. I just . . . I just don't understand how Kat could do this to our baby.

JESSIE: Kat? That's her name? *(He nods.)* I just remembered who she is. *(Beat. Sighs.)* Luke, did it ever occur to you that your wife may have had a difficult reason for wanting to abort her child?

LUKE: What are you talking about?

JESSIE: Things you weren't supposed to know. Things I know all too well myself.

LUKE: I don't understand. What are you saying? Look at me.

JESSIE: *(Turns.)* Some women who are raped get ashamed. They don't tell right away. *(Beat.)* I know. I was young when it happened too.

LUKE: You were . . . ?

JESSIE: *(She nods.)* A frat boy. From my college. We had been drinking, so even though I said no repeatedly, it had to be my fault. I went to his place after all. Right as I was starting to bury the incident, I realized I was pregnant. I went to some local place that advertised help for young pregnant women. It turned out to be a front for some pro-life fanatics who kept telling me I'd turn into a Hitler-type if I murdered my baby. I told my two best friends and they just assumed I would definitely abort. Get rid of that filthy thing. So I could go on with school and forget it. *(Beat.)* It wasn't until I came to a place just like this one. The woman there just told me the facts. Told me the potential outcomes, gave me a lot to read, and left me alone to decide. On my own.

LUKE: Why are you telling me all this? What are you trying to say?

JESSIE: When someone violates you, you have to take control of things. Sometimes you shut out the people you love the most. Out of shame. You can't bear to have any reminders of what happened, even if that means that you must suffer great losses.

LUKE: Are you trying to tell me that my Kat was raped? *(Pause.)* By who? *(Beat.)* How? She never . . . but she never . . .

JESSIE: You talk about how precious life is to you, but isn't she precious—your wife? Don't you trust her to know what's best for her? Or would you prefer to force and pressure? You say life is precious but you grab an innocent man and throw him in your car because he gets in your way. You threaten a woman who you don't even know because she doesn't agree with your point of view. What is your moral responsibility? Do your actions have consequences? Were you showing us how precious we all are? Did it ever occur to you that your wife was hurting?

LUKE: I didn't . . . know. She never . . . that's why . . . *(Beat. Quietly.)* I'm sorry.

JESSIE: Then you'll get help for your temper. And you'll talk to her gently. And when you see her again, you'll hold her because she's been through a lot. But you won't let on what you know. *(He nods.)* In time, she may tell you. *(Beat.)* Now, if you don't mind, we have to call the police so we can file a report on this. I'll go to the station after I pick up my son. But you have a man to untie first. Right?

LUKE: *(He nods.)* Yeah. *(Beat.)* Did you say you have a son? *(She nods.)* Do you mind telling me if he was . . . if he was conceived from your—

JESSIE : Yes. I mind. It's none of your business. Besides, what does it matter?

NO-FAULT

Keith's father died three days ago of a heart attack. He had taken his son, Keith, out driving so the boy could get in enough practice hours to get his license. Keith's father was always a bit nervous about being a passenger. On every turn, his father would give Keith advice as he gripped the arm rest tightly. A few nights ago though, Keith's father was unusually quiet as Keith drove. When asked what was wrong, his father told Keith that he had some pains in his chest. Once he heard this, Keith suggested they go to the emergency room right away, but Keith's father brushed it off, saying he was fine. Keith really did want to keep driving. He wanted to practice parallel parking in the lot behind the church. It wasn't until they were on the way home that the pains got worse. Soon Keith's father slumped over. In an absolute panic, Keith stopped the car and flagged down help. By the time the EMS arrived, Keith was sobbing. Though they tried repeatedly to revive his father, he was pronounced dead that night. Since then, Keith has barely spoken. His mother and sister were devastated and shocked. It is now the first day of the viewing at the funeral home. Keith stands outside of the doors afraid to look at his father's body in the open casket. He sits in silence when Jude, his 18-year-old sister, approaches him.

JUDE: *(Long pause.)* So . . . How ya doin'?
KEITH: *(Quietly.)* All right.
JUDE: Liar. I don't know why I'm asking you that. People have been asking me that all day, and all I feel like screaming back is, "How the hell do you *think* I'm doing?!" *(Sighs.)* This dress is ugly. I look like a saggy immigrant, don't I?
KEITH: You look fine.

JUDE: Come on, all I need is the babushka on my head and the rotting teeth. There weren't a lot of choices. Black dresses come in four styles: tacky-sleazy, gothic sleazy, snotty-sleazy, and saggy-immigrant. So that's why I'm Gretal Vanschnop tonight. It looks terrible, doesn't it?

KEITH: It's okay.

JUDE: Gee, thanks.

KEITH: What?

JUDE: Nothing.

KEITH: I didn't mean anything—

JUDE: I know. I just know what he would say.

KEITH: Oh.

JUDE: *(Beat.)* He'd tell me I looked great even if I looked horrible. Remember the prom last year? A beauty school girl got all pluck-happy on my eyebrows. I looked awful. My face was frozen in a state of constant surprise. *(She does the eyebrow look.)* My dress sucked. Dad just beamed when he saw me. I always thought he was lying when he said I looked great, but I'm not sure he ever was. I think he *really* believed Mom and I always looked great. You know, you might want to remember that kind of thing when you start dating girls. Girls love that crap. You're real cute. Girls are gonna go for you if you don't act like a dweeb. So you interested in any yet?

KEITH: *(Annoyed.)* I don't know.

JUDE: I'm just trying to give you a word of advice, Keith. Start early. Don't want my bro turning into some loser computer freak.

KEITH: I'm not a computer freak. I just happen to like them. And I don't feel like talking about this stupid stuff right now.

JUDE: What's your problem? I just don't want you to turn into one of those freaks, who hides in his basement, hacking away, crashing e-mail systems, building bombs, avoiding deodorant—that kind of thing. You know what I mean?

KEITH: Why are you talking about this? It's like you have to joke about everything. Who cares what you look like? You looked awful going to the prom—so what! Who cares? Dad died three days ago. Our dad. We have to come to this stupid funeral home and look at him and talk to people. I mean, at this very moment what sane person gives a care whether I am interested in girls yet or not?

JUDE: What are you trying to say there, Keith? That I'm insane? I'm just trying to make conversation. Can't we talk? It's better then not talking at all.

KEITH: Is it? *(Beat.)* And why do *you* care about my dating anyway?

JUDE: I don't really. I guess it's the only thing we could potentially have in common.

KEITH: Yeah? Well, you bring it up all the time. Why do you have to make me out to be some weirdo? I like programming—so what?! I'm only fifteen years old. Dad says he didn't start dating till he was like—old. He was like . . . eighteen. *(Beat.)* I mean . . . said . . . he *said* he didn't start dating till then.

JUDE: Yeah. I guess. Boys start later with everything I guess. I wasn't trying to insult you, Keith. It's cool that you're into programming. I was just talking to talk to you, okay?

KEITH: Okay. *(Beat.)* I'm sorry if I don't happen to say the right things, like Dad. You're right, he always made me feel better too. You look great, okay? Real nice.

JUDE: Thanks.

KEITH: What did the funeral director say?

JUDE: Mr. Creepyola? I don't know. We're early. They're still arranging the flowers in the room. Probably still arranging Dad as well.

KEITH: *(Disgusted.)* Jude.

JUDE: Well. Am I wrong? Aunt Alice peaked in at him. She says he looks good—like himself. Course she's a moron. I'm sure he doesn't look like himself. I mean, I'm glad he doesn't look like anyone else. But when you're dead, you rarely look like yourself. It's insulting to even say. You look like a heavily made-up wax version of yourself. Remember Grandpa? *(Keith nods.)* We'll be able to go in in a few minutes.

KEITH: Is that dress one you picked out today with Mom?

JUDE: Yeah.

KEITH: How is she doin'?

JUDE: I don't know. About the same as us I guess. Less than perky.

KEITH: Did she say anything?

JUDE: About what?

KEITH: About everything.

JUDE: Not really. Why don't you talk to her yourself?

KEITH: No. I just wondered if she happened to mention things.

JUDE: She's sad, Keith. She feels lost. She's concerned about us. She doesn't know what to say to you because you seem to be avoiding her. She's giving you time.

KEITH: That's all she said.

JUDE: Basically.

KEITH: Is she mad?

JUDE: Mad? No. Wait. Now, what are you talking about?

KEITH: I don't know. Nothing really. It's just . . . people get angry. I remember that from psychology class.

JUDE: Yeah. Sure. *(Beat.)* Do you think she's angry with you?

KEITH: This seems to be taking a long time. I could use some water. You want some?

JUDE: No! Wait a minute. Look, Mr. Dweeb, I hope you don't have some retarded delusion that you're responsible for this, because—news flash—Dad died of a heart attack.

KEITH: I know, but he happened to be with me.

JUDE: The paramedics and the doctors both said there was nothing you could have done.

KEITH: Well . . . besides getting him to the hospital.

JUDE: He didn't want to go. He barely complained.

KEITH: He complained some.

JUDE: Okay, so what could you have done?

KEITH: Taken him to the emergency room as soon as he brought up his chest.

JUDE: Didn't you insist on him going?

KEITH: I didn't insist. I suggested it.

JUDE: And he said no.

KEITH: I should have known something was wrong, Jude. You know Dad. He always reminds you to watch for oncoming traffic and stupid morons coming out of nowhere every time you make a lefthand turn. He's always gripping the door handle too. He was silent at Nine-mile Road when I turned. Totally silent. And his hand was in his lap. He even yawned. I should have known something was wrong.

JUDE: *(Sarcastically.)* Oh yeah, he yawned—that really makes you guilty. What did he say when you asked him if you should take him to St. John's ER?

KEITH: He said, "I'm fine. Keep driving." Then he was talking about when we'd go to get my license and he told me to head over to the school to practice parallel parking.

JUDE: See? There's nothing you could have done. He refused to go. He didn't want to.

KEITH: I didn't either.

(Jude looks strangely at him.)

KEITH: I wanted to practice parking and then get home to hang out with Jeff and Sam and look at used CDs.

JUDE: So?

KEITH: So maybe he could tell I didn't feel like it. That I didn't feel like waiting around all night.

JUDE: Maybe he could. So what? *(Beat.)* You didn't know. He had no history of heart problems.

KEITH: That's not all.

JUDE: What do you mean?

KEITH: I mean, I left out things when I've told some people. I told Mom everything when she first got to the hospital, but afterwards, to others, I left out parts.

JUDE: Like . . . for instance?

KEITH: Like after, when we were practicing parking, he brought up that he felt tired and kinda weak . . . like maybe he was getting a chest cold. He thought that's why his chest hurt. So I asked him what he wanted to do.

JUDE: You told us that. I remember that part. He wanted to go home.

KEITH: No, that's the thing. I didn't tell you exactly what he said. That's not exactly how he said it. He said, "I'm not feeling so good, Keith. I think we ought to even head home now or . . . "

JUDE: Or what?

KEITH: He didn't finish the sentence.

JUDE: Okay, so he said he wanted to go home.

KEITH: He wanted *me* to finish it . . . to say . . . "Do you want to go to the hospital?" But I didn't finish it. I just told him I'd take him home right away.

JUDE: Umm. Well then, that's conclusive. You are guilty.

KEITH: Yeah, I am. I am guilty. I know that.

JUDE: I was kidding. Exaggerating to make a point.

KEITH: No. I should have known he was playing it cool. That's what Dad does.

JUDE: I don't feel like talking about this anymore.

KEITH: Why not? Because you know I'm right? Because you know you would have realized it and done things differently?

JUDE: No.

KEITH: What would you have done? *(Pause.)* Come on, what would you have done? I'm curious.

JUDE: I don't want to talk about it. You did all you could. Now, let's drop it.

KEITH: What does Mom think?

JUDE: She doesn't blame you in the least. *(Beat.)* I don't know why people always have to wear black for funerals. Why not white? It's pure. It's serene. It's more heaven-like. Dad even had the forethought to die at the right time of year to wear it. Or red is good. Red was his favorite. Why couldn't we just wear red?

KEITH: I think she does blame me.

JUDE: If she does, she doesn't want to and won't in time. Instead of sympathy cards, people should send you lottery tickets or tickets to good comedy shows, and plane tickets to exotic islands and money. All the "sorries" of the world won't make up for anything.

KEITH: And money and tickets will?

JUDE: Hell no, but they couldn't hurt. And baskets full of chocolate, not flowers or fruit. The last thing you need is an apple or pear. God, I hate pears. They're the most boring fruit in the entire world. Don't you think?

KEITH: I'm not only afraid to lose him, Jude. I'm afraid because I don't know how to live and always be responsible for this.

JUDE: You aren't responsible.

KEITH: You don't understand then. Even if it's a complete accident, and it was, I'm still always responsible for what happened.

JUDE: Remember Grandpa? Aunt Frieda could not stop going on and on about the holy water that was blessed by virgin saint somebody and how she should have christened Grandpa and he probably wouldn't have—

KEITH: Anointed.

JUDE: Huh?

KEITH: Anointed Grandpa.

JUDE: Yeah. Whatever. It was so ridiculous. Like she could have changed anything. Like any of us have control? I was scared to go in the room then too.

KEITH: Me too.

JUDE: I was glad you were with me. I was glad I had you.

KEITH: But I didn't do anything.

JUDE: Yes, you did. You remembered all the important moments you had with him. We remembered them together.

KEITH: *(Closes his eyes.)* I just wish we weren't here. I wish to God we weren't back here again, Jude. I'd do anything to take back these past three days.

JUDE: When I die, cremate me, Keith. I just don't want to be remembered as a waxy figure with formaldehyde freezing my veins. I'd rather swallow glass or be hung by my eyelids or swallow glass while being hung by my eyelids and forced to listen to Christian rock music.

KEITH: Wow.

JUDE: Promise me.

KEITH: I promise. *(Beat.)* So why didn't you want to answer my question, Jude? What would you have done?

JUDE: *(Sighs.)* What do you want to hear?

KEITH: The truth. I just want to hear the truth.

JUDE: Fine. I probably would have taken him to the hospital.

KEITH: I knew it.

JUDE: Wait. I would have taken him because I had a class in health this year at Columbia, and I would have remembered how tight chest pains could be the only sign of a heart attack. But I don't know for sure that I would have taken him if he said he wanted to go home instead. And more importantly, I don't know if taking him there would have made a bit of difference in things. It's as if you want to feel responsible for it, but you can't. Things happen, Keith. Things happen that we can't control. If your theory of responsibility was true, Dad might have killed Mom three years ago when he put off taking her to the emergency room when her stomach ached.

KEITH: Her appendix?

JUDE: He gave her a heating pad. The worse thing you could possibly do for an inflamed appendix. And it burst. The doctors couldn't find anything when she arrived. Was it their fault? You didn't know this, but she would have died if the surgeon on duty didn't insist on opening her up immediately. So she didn't. But Dad waited. He kept telling her it wasn't serious enough. Do you think he was to blame? If she died, would he be to blame? Would he?

KEITH: *(Shakes his head.)* No.

JUDE: Don't look now, but Mr. Creepyola is opening the door.

It's time for us to go in. You'll talk to Mom tonight when we get home, right? About all this?

KEITH: Yeah. I guess. Sure.

JUDE: She'll set you straight. *(Beat.)* Dad loved you so much, Keith. He was very proud of you. He always wanted someone around as dweeby as him. And he got it. The last thing in the world he would want is for you to think you're responsible. You know if he were here he'd be cracking jokes about the funeral director's nightlife and telling us not to chew gum and showing us the photo albums of the deceased.

KEITH: Yeah. Proudly showing us the picture of him as the president of the debate team in college and the first time he went skiing. He looked so nerdy. Those checkered pants.

JUDE: He was a ladies man, right? Those pants were frightening. *(They laugh.)* You'll hold my hand when we go in? Stop me if I start telling inappropriate jokes.

(Keith nods. He takes her hand.)

JUDE: We'll remember the most important moments, right? The funny and the sad?

KEITH: All of them. *(They begin to walk.)* Apples.

JUDE: Huh?

KEITH: I think apples are more boring than pears.

JUDE: *(Smiles.)* Probably. You're probably right. You sure I look all right?

(He steps back and takes her in.)

KEITH: You look great. You look really great, Jude. Let's go.

ROMANCE

A few days before Christmas, Miriam, a depressed history professor, 30s, walks into a small Boston chapel in the evening to contemplate her failed marriage. The snow has been falling hard since early morning. Somehow Miriam manages to lose track of time and stays long after the janitor locks up. An intoxicated mailman named Mick, 30s, bursts into the same chapel that night to talk to God. Given the time of night, both end up startling each other. Eventually Miriam tries to flee the scene and head off toward the bus station for the night, but the snow has gotten worse. Mick persuades her to wait until the snow clears up a bit. While she's there, he takes the opportunity to ask her opinion about God and the afterlife.

MICK: Do you believe in an afterlife?

MIRIAM: No. I believe we live on in the hearts of those that love us.

MICK: Oh, don't give me that crap! I guess that means you figure when we croak, that's the end.

MIRIAM: I think it's pretty egotistical to assume we go on forever.

MICK: So what? Is it egotistical when we don't walk in front of a car or that we stop someone from stabbing us with a knife? We want to go on, live. We don't call that egotistical. It's called self-preservation. And all us healthy ones believe in it.

MIRIAM: I really don't know the answer.

MICK: I do. I believe in anything that keeps us goin' on after this lousy life. Reincarnation, heaven, any of that stuff. Of course, I'd like to be reincarnated with the same name. Then you're used to answerin' to it. *(He holds out hand.)* The name's Mick. You got a cigarette before you go?

MIRIAM: *(She hands him the suitcase. Then goes through her purse.)* Miriam. Sure.

MICK: You don't have a clue of how to get to the bus station, do you?

MIRIAM: *(She continues to look through purse.)* A little clue. It's okay. I'm used to having no direction, literally and figuratively.

MICK: So stay, at least, until it quits snowin'. I couldn't hurt a flea. I hang out in chapels all night. I light candles for my mom. And she wouldn't think it was very nice if I killed somebody.

MIRIAM: Yeah, and I'm sure that's what Norman Bates said to his mom too.

MICK: I like you. I trust you. That's rare.

MIRIAM: *(Pause.)* I'm sorry I've been abrupt. I know you mean to be nice. But talking isn't . . . well, it's not easy. *(She hands him the pack.)* Here.

MICK: Could have fooled me. *(Looks at pack.)* Lucky Strikes? Wow. *(He offers her one.)*

MIRIAM: I know. I hate smoking. I just bought them for the rough neighborhoods.

MICK: What does that do? Relax you as you get pulverized?

MIRIAM: No. They make me look intimidating.

MICK: Intimidating? Right . . . okay.

MIRIAM: I also thought it would be dramatic to offer them on occasion. I guess I've been looking for drama in my life.

MICK: *(Sarcastic. Lighting cigarette off a candle.)* And look how cheaply you got off. Two bucks for Dr. Æma. Some of us aren't even looking for it, and we end up payin' a lot more.

MIRIAM: I'm married.

MICK: And what does that have to do with the price of eggs in Iowa?

MIRIAM: I just thought you should know. I mean, I heard you before when you were talking to God. I mean, *accidentally*, I overheard you mention that you were sad because some *her* was leaving and that you'd never forget *her*.

MICK: Wait? You thought I was talking about you?

MIRIAM: *(Pause.)* No. No! Did I say that? Don't be ridiculous. We've only just met. I only meant that—that whoever the her is I might be able to offer some advice about her. Being a married woman and all. *(Pause.)* So what happened to her if you don't mind answering?

MICK: *(Takes a drag.)* Where's your ring? *(Coughs.)*

MIRIAM: Pardon?

MICK: If you're married, where's your ring?! *(Mick coughs.)*

MIRIAM: Well, I'm not sure I'm technically anything right now. I'm in the midst of a separation. I think. Though my husband doesn't know it. I imagine.

MICK: And I'm coming to you for advice? *(Touches his head.)* Oh, boy. *(He puts his cigarette out.)*

MIRIAM: What's the matter with you?

MICK: I think I'm gonna be sick.

MIRIAM: The drinking?

MICK: I didn't think it would still have this effect on me.

MIRIAM: Still? You mean this has happened before?

MICK: Only a few times. Maybe a dozen or so.

MIRIAM: Oh my God, you really are sick. Take off your tie. Wow, you're all dressed up.

MICK: Yep, you can dress me up, but I still puke everywhere. *(Cough.)*

MIRIAM: Don't be contemptuous. Here, put your head down. *(She puts his head gently on her shoulder.)*

MICK: Ow. Not so rough.

MIRIAM: Breathe deep. *(Pause.)* So what was the occasion?

MICK: *(Adjusting on her lap.)* When were you gonna tell your husband you split?

MIRIAM: Why don't you just relax for awhile? Close your eyes.

MICK: When he started posting signs up for your whereabouts? After he poured millions into search helicopters? After he quit his job, worried sick, exhausted and half-dead? Were you gonna wait till the very last minute?! Till it causes him the most pain and embarrassment?

MIRIAM: You've got the wrong Morris. I don't even think it will disrupt his patient's appointments.

MICK: *(Sits up.)* How do you know? *(Touches his head.)* Ow.

MIRIAM: Maybe you ought to lay your head down again.

MICK: No, I'm fine. Answer. How do you know?

MIRIAM: I pick up his hair follicles in the shower. I know.

MICK: So what! What does that prove? You don't know his every thought. People are surprised every day to discover mysteries and secrets about their lovers. Nothing is set in concrete. Especially when the day comes that they are put on the spot. Wham! *(He slaps his hands. Touching his head.)* Ow. Anyway, that's when the truth comes out. That's when you really know.

MIRIAM: I didn't mean he wouldn't be concerned. He's not that cold. He'd probably assume that he'd forgotten that I had one of my Literature Conferences. After a day, he'd figure out that the lovely sweet smell in our room comes from my powder spray, and he'd discover that he has to put his own tea on in the morning. By the second evening, he'd begin to miss the sound of Beethoven's *Moonlight Sonata* playing over and over with the taps of my typewriter. He laughs at the primitiveness of me still using one. And then he'd get a case of heartburn, but he wouldn't know why. He'd feel as if he'd lost something, but wouldn't know what. And then he'd remember that he'd felt as if I should be home by now. After which, he might feel a slight pang. A pang of longing. Longing for only me. But he'd brush it off quickly. So quickly. Too quickly. Finally, he'd call my mother. *(Pause. Laughs sadly.)* And she'd get the helicopters out.

MICK: You can't think like that. You can't make all those assumptions. It's not fair not to give him a chance to respond.

MIRIAM: Oh, but I have!

MICK: No, you just think you have! You've never laid it on the line. You never came right out and said, "Do ya love me, or don't ya?! Cause if you don't, I'm leavin'!" Never since you've been married, right? *(Pause. She goes back to her suitcase.)*

MIRIAM: But why should I have to? If you love each other you know.

MICK: Oh, it's just like a woman to think like that! You assume mental telepathy. You say, "I've been so upset. How could you not know?! My hand was on my hip like this all night." We're supposed to read hand gestures?

MIRIAM: You ought to. I read yours—I mean his.

MICK: No, you just *think* you do.

MIRIAM: When he's angry he puts his head back, his shoulders tense a bit, and he strokes his hair out of his eyes.

MICK: Maybe he had a crick in his neck, his shirtsleeve was wrinkled wrong, and his hair was buggin' the hell out of him.

MIRIAM: He seems so angry with me. But it all remains polite. Civilized. Just like a doctor.

MICK: Maybe he thinks you don't want him anymore. Maybe that's what makes him angry. Makes him furious to think you don't love him anymore. *(She moves away from him.)*

MIRIAM: You don't know. You've never been married!

MICK: No. I haven't. *(Pause.)*

MIRIAM: I didn't mean that insultingly.

MICK: It must feel powerful to be so beautiful.

MIRIAM: *(Pause.)* Beautiful? Are you talking about me?

MICK: Yes, you and . . .

MIRIAM: It's been a long time.

MICK: So remind him. Be blunt.

MIRIAM: He used to say it all the time when we first got married.

MICK: When was that?

MIRIAM: Seven years, and about thirty-three hours ago. But who's counting?

MICK: Did he forget the anniversary?

MIRIAM: No, he bought me a new briefcase. One I had admired. It was lovely.

MICK: But . . . ?

MIRIAM: That was all.

MICK: All?

MIRIAM: Well we didn't . . . I mean, I expected . . . Where are those cigarettes? *(She begins rummaging through her purse.)*

MICK: *(Pause.)* Would you dance with me?

MIRIAM: *(Looking around.)* I don't think that would be appropriate.

MICK: And sitting in here smoking at three in the morning is? *(He takes her hand.)* Besides, who would know? Other than God, you, me, and Santa Claus. Come on.

MIRIAM: *(She stands.)* Why?

MICK: Because I want to. It was something I wanted to do. *(He takes her gently.)*

MIRIAM: Sorry that my hand's so cold.

MICK: Well, you know what they say about that.

MIRIAM: And it's true. *(He twirls her a bit.)* This seems really silly.

MICK: I don't feel silly.

MIRIAM: I don't keep rhythm so well. No music.

MICK: Here's one you might know. *(Mick hums "Jingle Bells.")*

MIRIAM: *(She laughs, humming along.)* When we went on our honeymoon, my husband, Morris, told me he had a great Christmas present for me. And I was guessing like a necklace or some real big thing . . . Oh, I can't tell this. I'll be embarrassed. *(She stops dancing.)*

MICK: Don't be.

MIRIAM: Okay . . . Oh, I can't!

MICK: Don't worry. You'll probably never see me again.

MIRIAM: *(Pause.)* Why?

MICK: I don't know. Does it matter?

MIRIAM: Yes. *(Pause.)* Well, he wrapped himself up in Christmas paper, he was nude, and he tied a jingle bell on his . . . well, you know. And it was great. The best—I mean, not the jingle bell. We took it off for safety reasons.

MICK: And now . . .

MIRIAM: And now . . . what?

MICK: No more bells?

MIRIAM: You could say that. You know I just realized that I still haven't finished my Christmas shopping yet. Isn't that weird?

MICK: Why'd you stop?

MIRIAM: *(Pause.)* The day I was supposed to get it done, I bought this red dress instead. Perfect. Low cut but sophisticated. The kind that shows my legs off just perfectly. I have nice molded calves, the thighs aren't so fine.

MICK: That's exactly how I'm built too.

MIRIAM: Ha. Ha. I was so anxious. I waited for him. I felt so, so red in it. So voluptuous. You know? I wanted him so bad. I didn't mean to have him be uncomfortable. I never intended that. This red dress was supposed to cure his problem, OUR problem. So I tried to remain hopeful while he seemed both humiliated and terrified. I knew it was a problem, but we both figured it would go away. But it doesn't. And he blames me. Like I cause it. Like maybe, I don't want him bad enough. Isn't that crazy? And the months go by and it becomes harder to talk about. I thought the dress would . . . I gave it away to a friend. I couldn't look at it. It reminded me of our failure. My failure. I try, I try to get him to talk about it. To go get help. But he shuts down. And I can't take it anymore. I'm so lonely without him. I'm so, so lonely. God, I'm lonely. *(Mick hugs Miriam. He slowly begins dancing with her again.)* I can't, I can't do this with—

MICK: Shhh. For a few seconds close your eyes and dance with me. You can be anywhere you want, with whoever you want. Just dance.

MIRIAM: You smell nice.

MICK: Thanks.

MIRIAM: *(Touches his breast pocket.)* What's this in your pocket?

MICK: *(Stops.)* Nothing.

MIRIAM: What's the matter?

MICK: Nothing. Just . . . nothing.

MIRIAM: You never answered why you were all dressed up in a tux. Was it a wedding?

MICK: No. The weather must be clearin' up out there.

MIRIAM: Did you have to go to a wedding and just broke up or something?

MICK: No. The car's down the street.

MIRIAM: So where are your first-class tickets to?

MICK: Look, no one got Goddamned married today!

MIRIAM: Men don't often dress in tuxedos, looking so hand-some.

MICK: It was a funeral.

MIRIAM: Oh God. Why didn't you tell me?

MICK: I liked having my mind off of it. So how did you plan to tell Morty?

MIRIAM: *(Pulls out letter.)* I wrote him a letter.

MICK: A letter? A lousy letter? Letters are for love, Miriam, not for ends.

MIRIAM: What makes you an expert on love?

MICK: I don't claim to be. Just on mail. Just correspondence. Mail carrying actually.

MIRIAM: So if you don't mind telling me, who died?

MICK: I suppose you'd want us *(Referring to mail carriers.)* to deliver your nasty little note?

MIRIAM: I've poured out my whole heart to a complete stranger. And you don't even trust me enough to tell me who died?

MICK: She got letters. Mushy ones. And white roses. I even took her to all the classic romances. Took her to *Casablanca, It Happened One Night, Philadelphia Story, Rocky*, on and on. I did everything you're supposed to. Everything!

MIRIAM: Oh my God, is that who . . . ?

MICK: No.

MIRIAM: But I thought you said there was a funeral?

MICK: There was. The family was spread over the pews. He isn't Catholic exactly, but close enough. The brothers and sisters, all married, sat right here. And there . . . *(He points.)* There sat Mom, hair done up high. So they do the whole walk down the aisle, everything's smooth. Everybody's pretty. Until they get to the part where ya got to, where ya gotta . . . *(Slaps his hand.)* Wham! You know, tell it like it is. And he gets to askin' her if she wants to spend the rest of life with him and there's this pause. And he thinks— "Wow, she's makin' this dramatic!" But the pause goes on. He looks over at her and she doesn't move. She stands there. Still. Only he can hear her breathing. He tries to catch her eye to see if she's just nervous, but she ignores him. He looks over at mom and her forehead's all wrinkled, tense, and her hair starts unraveling. And then, this knot forms in his throat—like a lump, but kinda twisted, and it gets real dry. And he thinks, he can say something, do something, tell a joke, he can stop this. But the only thing that comes out of his mouth is a little moan. A little cry—a noise, so small. You can barely understand that he's sayin' "Marie, Marie." She turns to him with a face so full up of sorry. His sisters, his brother keep tellin' him that it was cold feet—cold feet. But in that instant, he knew she didn't love him. She wanted, wished, hoped to, but she just didn't. She wanted to, but she didn't. Didn't love him. And the whole thing turned into a Goddamn funeral. *(Pause.)* So don't tell me about lonely.

MIRIAM: *(Pause.)* Okay, you win. *(Beat.)* But do you really think that's your last chance?

MICK: Who's gonna want me? I mean, look at me.

MIRIAM: *(She looks at him.)* I'm looking at you now. And I think you're very attractive.

MICK: *(Embarrassed.)* You do not.

MIRIAM: *(She moves in closer.)* Yes, I do. You are a very attractive man, and if I weren't married, I would be after you in a second.

MICK: Noooo.

MIRIAM: *(She nods.)* Yes. *(Reaching her hand out to him.)* Yes.

THE JOURNAL

Anne, a single mother in her late 30s, recently discovered her teenage son's journal, which revealed that he had been having an affair with his high school English teacher, Mr. Randy Thurber, late 20s. Randy was a comfort to the 17-year-old Tad when he needed to talk about difficult things, like growing up "different." Unfortunately, as the two got to know each other better, they both started to develop romantic feelings. Innocent hugs progressed into small kisses and more recently into make-out sessions. In the last few weeks, Randy has decided that they should slow things down. Tad has been in a deep depression. Anne, concerned for her son, decided to read his journal. She was horrified to find out that one, Tad is gay, and two, he's involved with his English teacher. This evening, Anne has shown up unexpectedly at Randy's house. She is prepared to confront him directly.

ANNE: *(Holding two cups of hot cocoa.)* Hello, Mr. Thurber.

RANDY: *(Startled.)* Ms. Roberts? Hello. I, I—Is everything all right? *(A bit panicked.)* Is Tad all right? He's not—

ANNE: He's fine or as fine as he can be. He's staying with his uncle for the weekend.

RANDY: Oh. Good. Well . . . Is everything okay with you? Would you—would you like to come in?

ANNE: No. No, I'd rather not actually. I thought you might come out here since you have this big porch and all. I'd like to speak to you.

RANDY: Um, uh, okay, sure. *(He closes the door.)* I'd—that's fine. I love the porch. It's my favorite part of the house.

ANNE: You seem pretty young to own your own home. You look like you're barely out of school yourself. High school teachers must be making more than they used to.

RANDY: My mother died last year, and she left the house to me.

ANNE: Oh, that's right. I think Tad had told me that.

RANDY: I moved back from going to school in Chicago to, to—

ANNE: I'm sorry—about your mother.

RANDY: It's okay. She'd been fighting cancer for a long time. That's why I came back to care for her. She got tired. *(Beat.)* I hope you won't be too cold out here—with this breeze. You want me to get you a sweater?

ANNE: No. I can't even feel it. I'm too angry. *(Handing him cocoa.)* I brought you some hot chocolate.

RANDY: Oh. Thank you.

ANNE: I don't know why. I'm actually furious. I'd like to dump it on you actually. *(Beat.)* I guess I figured I should bring it since I was going to force you out in the cold. I had this half-idea I'd use it to bribe you if you were difficult.

RANDY: I appreciate it. Difficult?

ANNE: Yes. I think you might have a good idea about what I'm here to say. I hope you won't make this difficult.

RANDY: Well, I—at the moment I don't really have any idea what you're about to say so if that's difficult then . . .

ANNE: Really? Well, I'll give you a guess then. It has to do with my son. Your student, Tad, my son.

RANDY: I know. I noticed he's been different lately. Maybe a little depressed.

ANNE: Depressed? Listen, Mr. Thurber, that's an understatement.

RANDY: Randy, please.

ANNE: No, I'd rather not. I'm not here to make you think we're friends or to make you comfortable in any way. Tad's been a good deal more than depressed, Mr. Thurber. He's been downright suicidal for the past two weeks. It's a major ordeal to get him to go to school. Tad has never been like that. You'd think he'd be in a great mood—most kids are as seniors. But no. Something has him so down. And you know what? He hasn't told me one thing about it despite my asking over and over. But he does seem to talk to you a good deal. Or at least he told me it was talking. All those after school hours working on the school paper.

RANDY: *(Looking down.)* Umm.

ANNE: Ummm? Would you have any insight into his depression?

RANDY: No. I don't . . . know. I suggested that he go to the school psychologist several times.

ANNE: Well, no offense there, but I doubt he'll go to your school psychologist for anything.

RANDY: Why not? He's uh, he's uh good with the students.

ANNE: Because Tad's protecting you, you idiot!

RANDY: What?

ANNE: You know exactly what I'm talking about. How dare you stand there and act as if you don't?!

RANDY: *(Pause. Looking down. Touching his hand to his head.)* Oh God.

ANNE: What's "Oh God"? I thought you couldn't possibly imagine what had Tad so depressed?

RANDY: It wasn't intended.

ANNE: *What* exactly wasn't intended?

RANDY: I, uh, I just . . . Here he is a very talented writer in my Advanced Essay class . . . and I already suspected that Tad might be . . . *(Clears his throat.)* and then he came to write some things in his papers that made me quite sure he *was*, and suffering because of it.

ANNE: But you didn't know for sure he was gay, did you? He might have been just thinking about things. Exploring things in his mind. He's a young man. Young men and women do that. Did you ever think that?

RANDY: Uhhm, well, he seemed pretty clear and concrete in his writing. And I know all too well how it is to grow up "different." I was sympathetic to him. And he must have trusted me—

ANNE: Wrong person to trust.

RANDY: *(Beat.)* He'd come to me to talk about it. I thought . . .

I thought . . . I could help him. I could give him my two cents and keep him busy—tell him to join the journalism club and write for the paper.

ANNE: To be near him? To lead him on? Did you like him from the start?

RANDY: No! So he could do something constructive. I just thought I was going to help him.

ANNE: And this is how you do it?! He's a suffering gay boy! So let's have an affair with him?!

RANDY: It's not an affair! I mean, it's—it's . . . not sexual. It hasn't gone that far.

ANNE: Well how far has it gone exactly, Mr. Thurber?

RANDY: Not too far. I mean, too far—yes, yes but, but—

ANNE: Spit it out! I deserve to know what I'm dealing with.

RANDY: Well, we've, we've kissed a little.

ANNE: *(Pause.)* Kissed? I wonder what that means. Or if I can believe you. How long ago?

RANDY: End of last year things started to get a little romantic. But we only kissed two months ago.

ANNE: A little peck or long make-out sessions? I wish it were the peck but frankly I doubt it. Because you are all over my son's journal. In graphic detail. In fact, Mr. Thurber, you *are* my son's journal. It made me sick to read it. I just, I just wanted—what were you thinking?!!

RANDY: I wasn't! I don't know! I don't know! Never in my wildest dreams would I think something like this would . . . I know this is all wrong, but I just . . . sometimes you can't help how you feel, Ms. Roberts. Your son is so talented and mature.

ANNE: I don't want to hear this from you! It's wrong!

RANDY: I didn't mean to have feelings for him.

ANNE: Oh good God. You didn't mean to so it's all okay? I know you're young yourself, Mr. Thurber, but you're an adult. And you have dangerously decided to commit your life to teaching children.

RANDY: He's not a child. He's seventeen years old. He's going to be in college in less than a year.

ANNE: Well, he's *my* child. And seventeen is not an adult yet. Besides, you don't see the abuse of power you have in this situation? You're the wise teacher to him. The teacher of his favorite subject and you understand the gay thing on top of it. Of course he's going to fall in love with you. Not for you—for the freedom you represent! He's not capable of loving you.

RANDY: I think you underestimate Tad.

ANNE: I think you underestimate me and my anger right now, Mr. Thurber. I have half a mind to go to the principal and the board about this. Maybe even the papers.

RANDY: Oh no! Please, please don't—

ANNE: That would cause quite the ruckus. Can you imagine the scandal? I'd think you'd be booted out of your job right quick! We'd have quite a conversation chain going for the next couple of years in this dead town.

RANDY: I don't care if you feel you must destroy my career.

ANNE: Oh you don't care? I thought you loved being a teacher?

RANDY: I do. It's all I've ever dreamed of my entire life. But I would resign tomorrow if you asked me to. Just please, please think of Tad in all of this. He'll be devastated and humiliated if you go and tell people.

ANNE: And you didn't already devastate and humiliate him?

RANDY: I never humiliated him. I think if anything I made him feel accepted and normal. I do wish this never happened for both our sakes. But I can't help what I feel.

ANNE: Yes, but you can control yourself! Do you think this is the only student to have a big crush on his teacher, Mr. Thurber? My God, you're an adult. If you started to feel something, you should have backed off immediately.

RANDY: I know. That's why I slowed things down before they went too far.

ANNE: Oh, it went way too far already, Mr. Thurber! And

slowed it down? That's what really eats at me. That's what really got me when I read it in his journal. You've slowed things down. What does that mean exactly? Let's keep him hanging?

RANDY: I know it sounds strange to you, but I've gone over and over it. I really believe my feelings for him are genuine. I think if we wait until after he graduates . . . after a bit of time—

ANNE: What?! You intend on continuing this thing?! Stay away from my son!

RANDY: Things will be different when he's out of high school.

ANNE: Oh, and then everything will be hunky-dory, will it? You'll put him through college? Take care of him in your little house? Where will he go to school—at the community college? Our little town will love this. I'm sure he'll be loved and accepted. And when I see him strung up in a cornfield, it's you I'll have to blame for this.

RANDY: That is not going to happen. And I didn't say any of those things. I don't know. That's in the future. We'll have to see.

ANNE: No, we won't see. Do you have any idea what you've stripped my son of?

RANDY: I guess you'd say I've stripped him of his opportunity to find someone his own age. To find someone in school. Maybe you think he could have been straight and found a nice girl in your estimation.

ANNE: Yes. Maybe. For high school. Some nice girl to go to the prom with. To fit in and feel right about. He can laugh later about it. You see, I'm not a closed-minded idiot, Mr. Thurber, as much as you'd like to think. I mean, I'm not happy about my son being gay, no, but I suspected it a long time ago. And it doesn't matter. I just wish he would have waited until college to discover it. I just wish he could have waited till he was out of this high school. In a place where he could fit in. Where things might be more natural. Where he wasn't manipulated and controlled into—

RANDY: I'm not manipulating or controlling anything. If Tad wants to end it, we will. But I think he loves me too.

ANNE: What difference does that make?! It's a crush. He doesn't know what love is yet! He's too young.

RANDY: I think he does. He's old enough to know what he wants.

ANNE: Look, I've lived this, okay?! Don't give me the bull. Tad's father was five years older than me when I was in high school. He told me we should wait until after I graduated. Sound familiar? He'd marry me—he said. I could have the baby and then he'd put me through school. Sounds good on paper. He kept me hanging on to him. Meanwhile, I didn't make friends my own age or plan to go away to college. Every night I came home to talk to him on the phone, and made sure I went to bed early for the baby. When I did graduate, I had to take classes at the community college while I had a toddler in toe. And Tad's father . . . well, he couldn't marry me or put me through college because things had changed. He wanted to go to Europe for grad school. And he had fallen in love with someone else. I don't regret having Tad for one minute—he's the joy of my life, but I do regret not having my youth. And I will not let you strip my son of his senior year and his life to come! He is too young, and you are too old! It is as simple as that!

RANDY: What do you want me to do?

ANNE: Break it off completely. I mean, no possibilities of anything.

RANDY: Just because your life worked out like this doesn't mean necessarily that—

ANNE: What were you doing in high school, Mr. Thurber? Were you contemplating long-term relationships and mortgages? Or were you imaging all you could do with your life—all the different possibilities and people you could be with?

RANDY: *(Pause.)* He may go into a deeper depression if I just break it off.

ANNE: Are you worried about him or you? Cause now that I know what's happening, I'm going to be ready for that. I'll take care of him and listen and support him.

RANDY: He may not let you in.

ANNE: I can be very persuasive. And I don't expect him to totally let me in—he's seventeen for God's sake. Why would he? That's why I'll get him a counselor for now.

RANDY: I've already promised him we'd talk about our possibilities this summer.

ANNE: So unpromise him. It's not the first time life will disappoint him. Any pain he feels now will be ten times worse if it's three years later. There is no way for this to really work and you know it. Somewhere in your heart or mind you know that.

RANDY: I know you think I'm crazy, but I do love him.

ANNE: I love him more, Mr. Thurber. And if you really love him, you'll do the right thing. Not the thing easier for you at the moment. *(Beat.)* My son can't go back. He can't go back.

RANDY: *(Pause.)* I'll call him tomorrow.

ANNE: Good. I'll expect it. And I'll be there to clean up afterwards.

RANDY: *(Beat.)* It's strange. He was so frightened to tell you. Not about us—he thought we should keep that a secret for years. About his being . . . He thought you'd kick him out or disown him completely. But I think you're taking it quite well. *(She nods.)* I don't think he'll be too thrilled that you read his journal however. Sometimes, I wish my mother knew, but she was too sick to . . . Anyway, it doesn't matter now. I'll make sure that Tad knows that this breakup is coming from me and me only. As far as he's concerned, we've never spoken.

ANNE: Thanks. I'd appreciate that. In return, I will never mention this to a living soul. But if I ever catch wind of you doing this with another student—*ever*, I will immediately go to the board, the principal, and every journalist I can find in this vicinity. I'll have you dumped from the school so fast you won't be able to see straight. And then I'll hire someone to shoot you. Do you understand?

RANDY: Completely.

ANNE: *(She starts to leave. Stops.)* Oh, and I did know your mother. We got friendly at a couple of church functions a few years back. She did know. And she still thought you were the best thing since sliced bread. *(Shrugs slightly.)* Just so you know.

TO THOSE WHO WAIT

Two weeks ago, Ron, 25, and Jill, 26, whose families were friends and neighbors growing up, announced their marriage engagement. The couple started a whirlwind romance nine months ago when they bumped into each other in London. Each was studying abroad. Neither one told their families about their relationship in case things didn't work out. Jill's father was surprised at the announcement, but not unhappy. Jill's older sister, Val, however, has been sharp—even downright rude—to Ron ever since the declaration. Ron takes this opportunity to confront Val's inexplicable behavior. The scene takes place in Val's father's house.

VAL: *(Jumps at the sight of him.)* Oh! Geez, you scared me. I thought you two were out.

RON: I hoped you would emerge from your cocoon. It's a gorgeous day.

VAL: Law school is difficult, in case that needed any clarification, and it's not exactly easy living with one's father while doing it.

RON: So why don't you live in the dorms at Columbia?

VAL: Money. I'm trying to avoid sinking myself further into massive debt. Noise level. Besides, I like Astoria. It's about as quiet as New York gets.

RON: Can I make you some coffee?

VAL: No thanks. So how is the potential son-in-law enjoying his old stomping ground?

RON: Potential? A bit perplexed.

VAL: Perplexed? Hmm. Where's Boo Boo?

RON: She's up taking a shower. She cringes at that nickname.

VAL: I know. I've been her sister for many, many years now. She both hates and loves it. But it's an established formality. I don't like Yogi either, but to change it now would propose that *we* had changed, grown up, and neither of us are ready for that yet.

RON: I understand that. We're meeting your dad at the Barolo tonight.

VAL: Barolo? Hmm. How nice.

RON: Want to come? Their porcini risotto is amazing. The best in Soho. I'll even go out on a limb, better than mine. And that aside, the view is magnificent.

VAL: What are you talking about? Barolo doesn't have a view.

RON: No, not a typical one, but it does have a garden. Models, artists, actors among the Japanese cherry trees.

VAL: Oh geez, give me a break, Ron. Talk about ruining your appetite. Jazz greats and *(Gestures to him.)* Jazz-great-want-to-be's as well.

RON: Yes, on occasion. Stunning characters. More spectacular viewing than a bunch of old skyscrapers anyday.

VAL: Right. You know, my father would rather walk over to Ditmars Avenue and eat at Lou's diner. Real characters there too. And much less pretentious.

RON: So are you coming?

VAL: I think not. For several reasons, but the main one being money.

RON: Oh, but I'm the one paying.

VAL: I don't think I'd feel comfortable about that.

RON: Why? We're practically family.

VAL: Not if I can help it.

RON: *(Stung by this.)* Oh. That hurts. I was feeling an icy sort of current coming at me since your sister and I announced things, but I didn't think it was so arctic. I certainly didn't think it was this exacting.

VAL: Well, forgive me for my less-than-welcoming attitude, Ronnie.

RON: Oh no! Please don't call me that. It makes me think of my chubby period.

VAL: You were always charming, even when chubby. And lots of fun too.

RON: I hear an elongated *but* coming.

VAL: You had such an imagination. And so talented. Girls loved you.

RON: You're confusing me. Is this the rotten jazz musician speech?

VAL: Yes. I'm not thrilled that you plan to leave my sister here in New York right after the wedding.

RON: Hey, I don't have any choice. This is a chance of a lifetime. Rodney Waters is asking me to play with him for the next eight months. Do you realize how big this is? His sax player is not going to take time off again. This is a chance I can't pass up.

VAL: Fine. So why aren't you taking her with you?

RON: She's eager to start her PR job. She wants to get an apartment and decorate. She really doesn't like traveling. She only said she liked London because she found me there.

VAL: I don't think it's a good idea to start your relationship away from each other. And the fact that you're willing to do it, makes me a little wary.

RON: Well she's willing to do it too.

VAL: Only because she needs to be close to home. She gets homesick. In fact, I bet that's the reason she fell for you so quickly in London. You were her only connection to home.

RON: I barely knew your kid sister when we were growing up. I think we exchanged two words. We moved away to Boston before she was even fifteen. She doesn't connect me to home, to Astoria.

VAL: We lived next door to each other for eight years.

RON: Anyway, Jill's an adult. She knows her mind.

VAL: She's a baby!

RON: She is old enough to tell the difference between a relationship built of pure loneliness and homesickness and one based on mutual love and respect.

VAL: *(Laughs.)* But how can you have mutual love for each other? You've only been dating nine months. You barely know each other. You practically said it yourself.

RON: I think you can know someone after three months, especially if you spend all day and every single night together—

VAL: *(Covering her ears.)* Ehhhh. In the category of do not need to know.

RON: It'll almost be a year by the time we get married. I grant you it would be ideal if we could date longer, but I have to go to Paris.

VAL: So put off the wedding. Let her wait awhile. Till after you get back.

RON: We don't want to put it off. Why should we? I don't understand. Are you still sergeant Val? Telling me what to do?

VAL: Yes, actually. If necessary. Am I going to have to make you fall in line?

RON: Last time I did that, as I remember, you made me crack my head on the sidewalk.

VAL: It was an accident. Sort of. Look, I've always protected her and ever since Mom died, even more so.

RON: I don't understand. We were kind of like best friends, and now you think I'm such a bad choice.

VAL: I don't think you're bad, Ronnie, but I do think you are a bad *choice*.

RON: Bad choice? What's this about? Oh God, this isn't about a certain July night of adolescent fireworks?

VAL: Oh geez, don't act like that just crossed your mind just now? You always do that. You'd find out that some girl had fallen madly for you after a school concert and you'd act all miffed, as if you hadn't been aware of it the whole time.

RON: You had fallen madly for me?

VAL: I didn't say that.

RON: But it is about that night I kissed you?

VAL: No, you're wrong.

RON: It's not?

VAL: *I* kissed *you*, Moron. You were leaving. I was just going to miss you.

RON: I did think about you a lot after we moved to Boston.

VAL: I hope Jill's preoccupied. You're creeping me out now.

RON: What's creepy? I just wanted you to know that I thought of you.

VAL: Oh what kind words you have bestowed upon me, sir.

RON: I thought we'd be dead wrong for each other.

VAL: I agree totally. But why?

RON: Because you're impossible.

VAL: I am not!

RON: You need someone who will always make you feel really loved. You'd be miserable chasing me down, but we'd be doing that because, because you'd always be playing hard to get.

VAL: That doesn't make me impossible. That makes you impossible! *(Pause.)* I don't want to give you the opportunity to leave her.

RON: I would never leave her, but even if things didn't work out between us, she would handle it a lot better than I would. You know, she's lot stronger than you think. *(Beat.)* I love her, Val. I love everything about her. I love the way she bites her lip when she drives. I love when she bosses me about when I'm making omelets. I love the way she *chews* her pizza—all chompy-like. I really, truly love Jill.

VAL: I believe you, and I, of all people, know why she is loveable, but I just don't trust you Ron.

RON: Why? Because I said I'd write and call when we left for Boston?

VAL: Are you kidding me? No. Of course not. But I don't think you've changed from that insecure little boy who pretends that girls aren't looking at him. Always pretends he has no idea that he's attractive and desirable.

RON: Is it so bad to be humble? I would think that might be a good quality.

VAL: You're not really humble. You just pretend to be because you know it's charming. You thrive on attention. You *need* it. Constantly. Look at yourself, the month you're marrying my sister, you're leaving. For Paris! Ron Zarre will be sexy, charming, and fun. He'll have women chasing after him. But a safe wife at home. And he'll love it. And one day, he won't resist. He'll forget the wife.

RON: What are you basing this on? You haven't seen me in nine years, Valerie. Nine years! I'm not that stupid little kid you bossed around or the hormonal fickle teen that kissed you once. I'm sorry that you have no one in your life. If you stopped being so hard and controlling, maybe some guy would be interested.

VAL: We're not talking about me!

RON: Exactly! This has nothing to do with you. Nothing! It's none of your business. I know you're jealous of Jill. You've always been. She's the baby of the family. Well, I'm sorry it was *her* and not you. Okay? I'm sorry!

VAL: Uhh! You are so totally full of yourself! It's unbelievable. I know I'm right now. It's not like you to resort to character insults.

RON: No matter what you do, I'm going to marry her.

VAL: No, you won't.

RON: I need some air. *(Ron starts to go.)*

VAL: My friend met you a couple of weeks ago.

RON: *(Stops.)* I'm sorry?

VAL: A friend of mine. Met you.

RON: Really? What was his name?

VAL: Elizabeth. She's quite striking. It must have been before Jill got back from London. She met you at a bar in the village. You played a set with some band there.

RON: I meet lots of people.

VAL: Elizabeth told me about meeting you right before you and Jill made your engagement announcement.

RON: *(Turns toward her.)* And what did she tell you?

VAL: Oh that you talked until three A.M. Then you invited her to some after-hours bar. Eventually you took her home. Acted like the perfect gentleman. You even gave her a nice kiss when you reached her door. Funny you never mentioned

Jill the whole time. You told her you'd call in the next couple of days. And, surprise, you didn't.

RON: Of course I didn't. Okay, I was a little tipsy. It was my first night back in New York. I was impressed with her. She knew a lot about jazz. I just, I got carried away. I didn't sleep with her for God's sake.

VAL: No, but I'm sure you thought about it. And I bet you never told Jill a thing.

RON: I'll tell her. Is that what you want? I'll just tell her. She'll understand. It's no big deal.

VAL: I think you're very talented, Ron. I think you'll go far. I'll even buy all of your records. But I don't think you should marry Jill. She wants to settle down. She wants a home and children. You want to play music all over the world and have fans. It just doesn't fit together. You *will* cheat on her. You can't help yourself. (*Beat.*) Don't just tell her about Elizabeth, break it off, Ron.
(*Pause.*)

RON: What? You think you can still call all the shots?

VAL: You think she won't fall apart by your leaving? When someone you love cheats on you, you can't help but hurt immensely. And if you think differently, you're wrong. I won't let you damage her. So are you going to tell her, or am I?

RON: *I'll* tell her about the mishap with Elizabeth, and also how you don't want me to marry her. And maybe I'll even tell her about *our* history. She'll think you're jealous. She'll probably end up hating you!

VAL: She might. If you really love her, Ron, like you say, wait until you come back. If it's true love, it can wait. What's a year or two? Maybe by that time, you'll be ready.
(*Long pause.*)

RON: I was looking forward to when I returned to New York after the tour . . . fantasizing about it. Coming home to Jill, my wife. She'd be making spaghetti and repainting one of the walls in our fixer-upper. I need her, Val. I love her. And I am ready.

VAL: We'll see about that. *(She starts to leave.)*

RON: I'll talk to her too, Val. I'm as bullheaded and stubborn as you are. We love each other. I'll prove you wrong!

MY LIFE IS PROOF

Alicia, a 24-year-old graduate student in theater, is suing her grandfather for sexual, emotional, and physical abuse. Harry, 40, her attorney, called her this week to try to convince her to take an offer of forty thousand dollars made by her grandfather's lawyer. Alicia outright refused and has made an unexpected trip to Harry's office to confront him.

HARRY: Alicia, please calm down.

ALICIA: I'm calm, I'm calm. I'm waiting. I'm listening.

HARRY: Look, I am not the enemy, all right? I'm here to help you.

ALICIA: By telling me to settle?

HARRY: Forty thousand dollars is a lot of money.

ALICIA: Not when we're suing him for over a million.

HARRY: You said he didn't have a million.

ALICIA: He might, if he sold everything. But that's not the point, Harry.

HARRY: What is the point?

ALICIA: He's not admitting he's guilty. He'll just say that his poor granddaughter is deranged. He's just a loving grandfather, helping her out by covering some of her psychiatric expenses.

HARRY: Alicia, first of all, perpetrators like your grandfather almost never admit their crimes. I've been doing these kinds of cases for eight years and in all that time maybe three have come clean.

ALICIA: Well that's not good enough. That's why I want to go to court.

HARRY: Secondly, for someone who is not a millionaire, forty thousand dollars is a lot of money to just be "helping out."

ALICIA: He gave my mom thirty or forty.

HARRY: What?

ALICIA: My mom got breast cancer and he gave her like thirty thousand dollars. To help with her medical expenses.

HARRY: I'm sorry to hear that. *(Beat.)* Alicia, just because he gave your mother money doesn't mean . . . cancer is a very serious life-threatening disease.

ALICIA: So is incest! A lot of people die from abuse, ya know!

HARRY: I didn't mean to belittle what happened to you.

ALICIA: Then what did you mean?

HARRY: If anything I've said seemed to indicate that I didn't think what you suffered was traumatic, I apologize. My wife and I . . . we aren't rich. I'm not a wealthy lawyer out to buy a yacht with your money. You know that. I take all of my cases on contingency—if I lose, I get nothing. *(Beat.)* So why do I do this? Because someone has to get the rotten bastards. What I'm saying is I care. Very much. However, as I've told you before, this is never easy. It's messy, it's ugly, it's exhausting. Most lawyers won't even touch these types of cases. Because they know, in court, they'll lose.

ALICIA: Why? How can you be so sure?

HARRY: We have to prove your grandfather is guilty beyond a reasonable doubt. That would be hard enough to do if it happened yesterday and you had wounds and bruises. To prove *he* was the one who did it. But now, years later, it makes witnesses and physical evidence—all of it—that much harder.

ALICIA: Exactly. Harder, not impossible.

HARRY: Alicia, the chances of winning a case like this in court are . . .

ALICIA: Then why did you take it in the first place?

HARRY: I didn't want to take it to be honest with you. The last sexual abuse case I had practically put me out of business. You do realize I have to front all of the expenses myself.

ALICIA: And I repeat, then why did you take it?

HARRY: Because nobody else would.

ALICIA: You know what I think? I think you chickened out, Harry.

HARRY: What are you talking about?

ALICIA: The new lawyer. The "hotshot." He moved it from state to federal court and you got scared. Suddenly, you're in the big league—and you caved.

HARRY: I didn't cave.

ALICIA: The day you called me and told me about the federal court thing. That was the same day you asked me how much my expenses were, without any money for emotional duress.

HARRY: Because he also made me an offer that day, and I wanted to counter it.

ALICIA: But initially when we talked, *you* were the one who added one million dollars for emotional duress.

HARRY: You think one million dollars is too much for what you've suffered?

ALICIA: No. There is no amount that could ever make up for what he did to me. My point is, you were confident enough to up my figure 600 percent. And you meet with this lawyer and he says "federal court" and you drop down to 45 percent. Admit it, you're scared.

HARRY: Of course. But not in the way you think. I told you day one that 99 percent of these cases settle out of court. If this went to court, I would be scared that, one, it would be detrimental to your well-being, and two, that you'd come away with no money at all.

ALICIA: Or that *you'd* come away with no money.

HARRY: That's ridiculous. If I only cared about money, I'd have pursued corporate law. Let me tell you something, Alicia. On my last two cases, I worked my tail off doing research, finding records, footing the bill to have witnesses flown in for testimonials. And you know what happened? We lost. I lost. Both defendants made offers to settle, but we hung tough. In the end it wasn't me I was concerned about. I mean, obviously I would like to make some money at this.

But those women . . . They couldn't afford the treatment they needed. I should have just given them the money I spent on their cases. Because we all wound up worse than when we started. I'm not caving. I'm just trying to be realistic.

ALICIA: I'm sorry.

HARRY: So am I. *(Pause.)* You're a tough cookie—and smart. You should have gone to law school.

ALICIA: My dad would have loved that. He lost it when I told him I was going to be an actor. "Ninety-nine percent of actors are unemployed. You'll wind up in the streets."

HARRY: Alicia, I really think you should take the money. Pay your bills, get the counseling you need. And I won't even take my third. How about a quarter? What do you think?

ALICIA: I can't do it. I want to go to court.

HARRY: We'll get creamed. We have no proof.

ALICIA: My life is proof! I want him to admit what he's done!

HARRY: Someone who can rape his own granddaughter is certainly capable of lying under oath.

ALICIA: So the jury can find him guilty. He can't just do what he's done and have it be okay!

HARRY: What he did is not okay. He should be punished—

ALICIA: Don't you get it? I need to stand up for myself! And for everyone else who this has happened to who can't stand up. I need to show him that I'm taking my life back! You can't imagine how many times and ways I've gone over confronting him. Making him admit it, torturing him the way he tortured me. I locked myself in the closet one day because I was afraid I would go buy a gun and kill him. I was in the fucking hospital on his birthday because I wanted to kill myself. And where was he? Kicking up his heels in his cushy house in Florida celebrating. That is not justice. There is no justice!

HARRY: You're right. Our system is faulty. But it's the best we've got. It shouldn't be called the Justice System. It should be called the "trying-to-do-justice-system."

ALICIA: Then *try* with me for God's sake.

HARRY: You just said you were suicidal. That lawyer will kill you, Alicia. He's a shark.

ALICIA: I'm not afraid of him!! It can't be any worse than what I've already lived through!

HARRY: Fine. You think you can take it?

ALICIA: Yes.

HARRY: Okay-okay! *(Moving with a new energy that we have not seen.)* I'm him. You're in the witness stand. Everybody's watching. Your mom, your sisters, and your grandfather.

ALICIA: I'm ready.

HARRY: So Alicia, you say that your grandfather forced you to have oral sex and intercourse with him, is that right?

ALICIA: Yes.

HARRY: Umm-hmm. And you were how old?

ALICIA: Four to six years old.

HARRY: You don't know how old you were?

ALICIA: I meant it happened from the time I was four to the time I was six.

HARRY: How old are you now?

ALICIA: Twenty-four.

HARRY: Well, you must have an amazing memory.

ALICIA: It's hard to forget something like that.

HARRY: You're not allowed to speak unless I ask you a question. Now, you also claim that your two sisters were with you on certain occurrences of this supposed abuse. Is that right?

ALICIA: Yes.

HARRY: And you claim they were abused by your grandfather as well?

ALICIA: Yes, that's right.

HARRY: The court has heard both of their testimonies and they don't seem to remember any—

ALICIA: Because they're too scared to remember. Their bodies won't let them until they're able to handle it.

HARRY: I see. So *you* can "handle it"?

ALICIA: Not well.

HARRY: Can you please tell the court what you do for a living?

CARLSBAD HIGH

ALICIA: I'm finishing up graduate school. I'm working on an internship.

HARRY: In what? What are you studying?

ALICIA: Theater.

HARRY: And what do you do in the theater, specifically? Do you make costumes? Sets?

ALICIA: I'm an actor.

HARRY: You're an actor! So you make things up for a living?

ALICIA: No. The playwrights make it up. We just help tell the story.

HARRY: I see. But you pretend a lot. In telling their stories. Pretend to be someone you're not, to say that things happened when they didn't—to act as if they did? Is that right?

ALICIA: We try to portray other characters, yes.

HARRY: It's kind of like lying for a living, isn't it?

ALICIA: You should know.

HARRY: So you claim your grandfather sexually abused you in his former house in Brooklyn and in your parents' former house in New Jersey. Something strikes me as odd. Your parents both testified that they weren't aware of any abuse. Yet you say it happened in their house. How would you explain this?

ALICIA: I don't know.

HARRY: You don't know? Uh-huh. Tell me, Alicia, do actors make a lot of money?

ALICIA: It depends. Hollywood film stars do.

HARRY: Let me rephrase this. People in the theater like you. Do you make a lot of money?

ALICIA: No, I don't.

HARRY: Do you have a lot of bills? Student loans?

ALICIA: The usual.

HARRY: How much would that be in student loans? The usual?

ALICIA: I don't know exactly. Maybe twenty or twenty-three thousand.

HARRY: Twenty-three thousand dollars? And then you have your living expenses and your car and unforeseen emergencies and you don't make much money as an actor. That must be rough on you.

ALICIA: I'm getting by.

HARRY: Scraping by with bills piling up. Wouldn't it be nice to have those bills paid off so you can be free to do your acting?

ALICIA: Lots of people have student loans. It's common these days.

HARRY: Answer the question. Wouldn't it be nice?

ALICIA: Yes.

HARRY: Would you say your grandfather has a lot of money?

ALICIA: I guess.

HARRY: Yes or no?

ALICIA: Yes.

HARRY: So let's review here, your grandfather has a lot of money. You're at least twenty thousand dollars in debt and not making much at all working as an actor. You claim that your grandfather sexually, physically, and emotionally abused you and your two sisters. They don't recall any abuse. You say the abuse happened in the homes of your grandfather and your parents, but you don't know where your parents were while it was supposedly happening. Your father stated that he did not know of any abuse. Your mother said the same thing. You agreed that it would be nice to have your bills paid off. It's a lot of debt. And in your daily work, you pretend that things happened to you that didn't actually really take place at all. Would you agree with all of that?

ALICIA: Not what you're insinuating.

HARRY: Would you or would you not agree with the statements that I have made?

ALICIA: *(Beat.)* Yes.

HARRY: Of course you would because you made all of this up, didn't you, Alicia?

ALICIA: No!

HARRY: You've been diagnosed with major depression on several occasions, have you not?

ALICIA: Yes, and post traumatic—

HARRY: You've been in more than one hospital because you overdosed on medication. Is that correct?

ALICIA: Yes.

HARRY: You're not exactly a stable human being are you?

ALICIA: If I'm not, it's because—

HARRY: Answer the question!!

ALICIA: No.

HARRY: Your grandfather never laid a hand on you! Did he?!

ALICIA: Yes!!

HARRY: He never fondled you, he never raped you, he never did those sick, demented things that you're accusing him of!! Did he?!

ALICIA: Yes!!

HARRY: You are under oath, Alicia! You're depressed and unstable and broke and you want to blame someone for your life and make them pay for it and you picked him! Didn't you?!

ALICIA: *(She suddenly curls inward, protecting herself. Her eyes are filled with terror and she looks like a little girl. Her speech is broken, like she's somewhere else. She makes a fearful, whining sound.)* Mmmmmm. No.

HARRY: Say it!

ALICIA: Go away. Get away from me. *(She breathes heavily through her mouth and watches him with hyper-paranoia.)*

HARRY: *(Dropping the character.)* Alicia?

ALICIA: Mmmmm. Stay away from me. You stay over there.

HARRY: Alicia, it's okay.

ALICIA: *(She jumps at a tiny sound.)* I'm not bad. Uhh. *(She lightly touches her forehead with apprehension.)* You're gonna hurt me.

HARRY: No, no. Alicia? You're safe now. It's me, Harry. You're in my office. It's safe here. *(He moves toward her but she recoils.)* I'm sorry. I'm sorry. Can you hear me? *(She still looks terrified but she's silent now and she nods yes.)* It's okay. It's all going to be okay. *(She stares at him and starts to rock.)*

LIBERTY AND JUSTICE

Carla, a 30-year-old social worker from Brooklyn, questions a 34-year-old Northwestern medical residency student in a darkened New York jail cell. Dr. Rahman was brought to this undisclosed location due to his suspected involvement with terrorists who, more than a week ago, caused bioterrorism. When he willingly left his condo with FBI investigators eight days ago, Mohammed told his wife he'd take her out to dinner that night. He had no idea that he would endure hours of interrogation in the county jail. He thought that the FBI would quickly discover their error. After all, he had a wife and two small children and worked very hard to pass his medical boards. The gravity of the situation came into full focus when he was flown from Chicago to a darkened cell in New York City. An armed convoy escorted him there. Carla, a social worker, has been assigned to his case. Since the attack on the World Trade Center, she has suffered her own personal losses. Carla tries to put aside her feelings in order to do her job—which has expanded far beyond its original description—but she is not happy about the assignment.

CARLA: *(Peering into his cell.)* I'm here to ask a few quick questions, Dr. Rahman. My name's Carla Spinelli. Is it okay if I come in? *(He nods. She gestures for the guards to open the cell door and enters.)* You speak English, right?

MOHAMMED: *(He nods cautiously.)* Are you my lawyer?

CARLA: *(Chuckles.)* No. *(She pulls up a chair.)* I'm a social worker turned civil liberties spy. *(Mohammed looks puzzled.)* Confused? Everybody is. I used to work full-time in the Brooklyn Correctional Facility. Handled family problems, drug rehab, made sure inmates got dental care . . . things like that. But because of the terrorism—recent changes in laws concerning detainment, due process—all that, some social workers in government facilities are assigned to check out conditions. Ask a few questions.

MOHAMMED: May I ask you one? *(She nods.)* Do you think I'll be out in time to take the medical boards? I'm here studying to be a trauma surgeon. I'm on a grant. It's very important—

CARLA: *(Stunned.)* Doctor! You've got a lot bigger things to worry about than your medical boards. You do realize that you are in an FBI holding cell? A cell used to detain potential terrorists?

MOHAMMED: But I'm not a terrorist! I need a lawyer to discuss this with, but no one tells me anything. I don't even know my guilt.

CARLA: Feeling a little like Kafka?

MOHAMMED: Who's Kafka? Is he involved in this last attack?

CARLA: No. He's a novel—doesn't matter. Basically I'm here to make sure civil liberties don't go to hell. Not that it's in my job description. But then again it's not in a mail carrier's job description to wear latex gloves. I guess we're all crossing lines.

MOHAMMED: Did you say Brooklyn facility? Am I in New York?

CARLA: State. Yep. That's right. But I can't tell you where exactly. I'm here to ask a few questions. I can't explain anything to you in full detail, and I don't expect you to defend yourself in any way. Save it for the authorities, the FBI, and your lawyer.

MOHAMMED: Why did they bring me here? Why couldn't they hold me in Chicago?

CARLA: Don't like the accommodations, Doctor? I'll tell you. It's better food here than at the big city hospitals. Food supplies in twenty-three hospitals have been contaminated. Isn't that cute? So on top of the disease and sickness we're facing, we also have food poisoning. Yep, I'd say you have it pretty good. *(Beat.)* They brought all of the suspects in this last contamination incident to New York. I'm sure they have their reasons.

MOHAMMED: Does my wife know where I am?

CARLA: Your lawyer will notify her.

MOHAMMED: When? I have not met him. Or her. I asked for a lawyer from the start.

CARLA: Well, they're working on it.

MOHAMMED: With all respect, ma'am, it's been days.

CARLA: Doctor, do you know what's going on right now?

MOHAMMED: Of course I cannot know. I've been locked away.

CARLA: Smallpox was released in Chicago, New York, and Washington D.C.—

MOHAMMED: That is all I had heard when the FBI arrived at my door eight days ago.

CARLA: Well, it wasn't contained. It's everywhere. They quarantined 50,000 people last week. Emergency units are going all day long. We had the public schools and the federal buildings shut down. There have been threats and information leaks that say more hijackings, more contamination, threats of the nuclear kind. Do you understand the situation? Nothing's working like it's supposed to. So if you gotta wait a couple extra days for a lawyer, I don't give a damn. At least you aren't in a hospital bed trying to hang on to your life like thousands of people. Like some of my closest friends in fact.

MOHAMMED: I'm sorry. I didn't know. I can't imagine how this . . . how is my wife, my children?

CARLA: They're quarantined, like everyone else. They're fine. At least, I haven't heard otherwise.

MOHAMMED: I don't mean to be difficult, Miss, but it is my right to have a lawyer when I'm questioned.

CARLA: Who told you that?

MOHAMMED: (Beat.) Well . . . I . . . I heard. I mean . . . I've seen it on television. It's one of my rights.

CARLA: (Chuckles.) Well, Dr. Rahman, I wouldn't believe

everything you see on TV. Of course you would be entitled to a lawyer if you were an American citizen. But you're not. You're allowed a lawyer if you can afford one. But nobody's going to rush to get you one. You're not all that popular thanks to what the papers are calling you. If the authorities have any evidence at all that you are connected with these terrorist attacks, and even if they aren't certain, they can detain you for days.

MOHAMMED: How many days?

CARLA: Public opinion is growing in support for drastic measures. They'll probably make sure you have a lawyer once exact charges are drawn up against you. However, you still could continue to be detained even afterwards. Do you understand?

MOHAMMED: Are you saying that there have been charges made against me?

CARLA: Not exactly. But let's get to the questions first.

MOHAMMED: What is my guilt?! I told them. I only came here to study to save lives. I could be in the hospital now, helping these people. Look at me. I'm not the type to hurt anyone.

CARLA: How are we supposed to know that?

MOHAMMED: I weigh one hundred pounds. My wife jokes that she could conquer me. I don't know how to make these, these contaminates. I did not study this in my country.

CARLA: But you could have connections—chemists in Saudi Arabia.

MOHAMMED: Who? I know no one who studies this. Who says this?

CARLA: Just me. I'm just guessing why they might think you're involved. Like I told you though, I'm not here to determine your guilt. I just know what I read in the papers.

MOHAMMED: And these papers are ruining my name! My reputation! I did not do this. I need to speak to friends, and to a lawyer. Can you help me?

CARLA: How do you know this chemist in Saudia Arabia that they report about?

MOHAMMED: I explained that to the FBI. He is a distant friend of one of my old professors. I met him once. And once only. I wired him a great sum of money from Saudia Arabia because I bought a house from him through this connection.

CARLA: And your brother who hijacked the plane from Boston last year?

MOHAMMED: I have no brother! I explained this too. My name is so common there. It's like John Smith here. People who have my name go by their second name because it's so common. I don't know that man at all. Never did. This should have already been looked into.

CARLA: Maybe it has. I'm not in on the big information distribution list. I shouldn't even be talking about this with you at all. *(Taking out a pen.)* Now, let's get to those questions.

MOHAMMED: Will you help me with getting a lawyer? I just want to protect my wife and children.

CARLA: First things first.

MOHAMMED: I am a religious man, Miss Spinelli.

CARLA: Well, I wouldn't use that as an argument. It's religion that started all of this.

MOHAMMED: I mean that I pray for peace. I'm religious, and I pray for peace.

CARLA: Well, you can pray for peace all you want. I pray for peace too. But the fact is, some guys came over here and killed 5,000 innocent people just heading to work.

MOHAMMED: I'm sorry. I mourned those people too. I had nightmares over and over about a man falling from the sky. I ran to try to catch him, but I run out of time. No matter how I tried. I wanted so bad, as a doctor, to save him, but I couldn't. Would a terrorist have that sort of dream?

CARLA: You could be an angel or a devil for all I know. You know how many guys I've met in the correctional facility? The ones that made me think, "Wow, that guy actually seems nice, really polite and sweet." I come out of the cell and his guard says, "Yeah? That guy stabbed his mother sixty times in the chest." I'm not naïve anymore. I know I can't tell the bad from the good.

MOHAMMED: And that is true of this war too. The enemy is not a nation. You can't know who is the bad one. It's individuals.

CARLA: Individuals in countries and in nations that allow them to hide there. We're looking at contamination of 50,000 people. A lot of good people have died already. I lost my uncle in the train bombing. He lived to "save lives"—as you like to say. He was a fireman. These countries and nations must pay for who they harbor. If you want to pray for peace, aim it in their direction. Because we have to react. We have no choice. *(Beat.)* I think it's best if we just get to my questions now.

MOHAMMED: I think it is horrible—all of it. But do you think there is only unfair suffering here?

CARLA: The first question on my list is if the FBI clearly identified themselves when they arrived at your doorway, Dr. Rahman?

MOHAMMED: There are innocent women and children who are dying in many Arab countries. There have been thousands and thousands of Palestinians who are killed for defending their own land.

CARLA: Did you hear my first question, Doctor?

MOHAMMED: Even my people in Saudi Arabia are denied rights because of the government there—an intolerant government of the elite that your country supports.

CARLA: Well then complain to your government or create a new one. Hell—declare war on us, but don't send some lunatics on a suicide mission to kill innocent citizens. You do see the difference, don't you? If you don't, you're an idiot.

MOHAMMED: Of course I do. We do complain to the government, but we are not in a democracy. We have no real voice. How do you overthrow an aristocracy? My people come into the tents of the royalty. They hand slips of paper to royalty begging for medical assistance for their mothers. The royalty then chooses who they help. This is the only voice they know. Do you understand? It's no voice at all. *(Long pause.)* Yes.

CARLA: Yes?

MOHAMMED: They clearly identified themselves as FBI.

CARLA: Good. What happened from there?

MOHAMMED: I let them in. My wife was terrified. I made a point of being calm even though I felt nervous. They asked me about plane tickets. All I explained. They told me that I needed to come with them. I asked for a lawyer. The oil company, Saul Armo's, has sponsored me here. They would have provided money for a good attorney. Or my family.

CARLA: That was your mistake.

MOHAMMED: Mistake? Isn't that what anyone here in the United States would have done?

CARLA: You're not from the United States. It slowed down the process. There is some gray area about your rights. The FBI had to back off on questioning. You could have been questioned and potentially released immediately.

MOHAMMED: But that doesn't make any sense! You said I have no rights because I'm not an American. Then why did they back off? Why not question me? Why does this slow things down?

CARLA: Just answer the question. Did anyone abuse you in this process?

MOHAMMED: What does that mean? I thought denying me a lawyer for days or keeping me in chains in a very cold cell was abuse. But then if we were in a really dirty country, I couldn't even speak of this. I'd be tortured or dead in minutes.

CARLA: That's right. In China they put you in a cell not much wider than your body. Chop off your hands when they even suspect that you stole something. No proof necessary.

MOHAMMED: Yes. And some governments put you in a cell forever. Never to be seen. But I guess I thought this was a free country.

CARLA: Free? I don't know. Free-er, Doctor. No place is totally free. There's always class and race and religion to get in the way. But I'd forgo some freedom for safety. For my niece at St. Luke's Hospital. I'd forgo some freedom for her. Wouldn't you for your daughter? Give away some presumed innocence?

MOHAMMED: Maybe it's easier to say because you are sitting there.

CARLA: When you arrived here in this cell? *(Quietly.)* Did any of these gentlemen harm you?

MOHAMMED: No. They screamed, "Zero tolerance!" They put me in chains and moved me so fast— faster than I could go, so my feet dragged down the hall. It was uncomfortable. But abuse? No. And I understand if they thought I was guilty of these crimes. I understand.

CARLA: And the agents that questioned you here?

MOHAMMED: All seemed fair but one. *(Carla looks questioningly.)* Do you know when I arrived here three years ago, me and my wife were so happy? The surgeons I met were geniuses, full of knowledge. I kept looking around at young students and people who felt they could do anything. *(Gesturing to her.)* Women who are policemen. Poor men sometimes make a lot of wealth. Religious interests—your choice. All choices respected, even appreciated. A man doesn't go to jail for his thoughts, for speaking his beliefs. And I thought—this America—it's a good place. All men are equal—all men have a voice. Liberty and justice for all.

CARLA: Wow, you pile it on thick, Doctor. The *New York Times* has been editorializing about this for a year. Which freedom do we give up? I say, whatever freedom we need to at the moment to get the devils. Not very liberal-God-like of me. But, ya know what? You do what you need to when your family's dying. Right, Doc?

MOHAMMED: When he stood behind me, he asked me my name. The last FBI agent who came in last night. I respond to all questions slowly. I'm like that. I'm not uh . . . quick to—

CARLA: Impulsive?

MOHAMMED: Yes. Cautious. When I didn't answer quickly enough, he kicked me hard and knocked me across the room. I asked him about my wife and children. He said nothing.

CARLA: Would you like to file a complaint? I have the forms. But it tends to slow down the process.

MOHAMMED: No. No complaint.

CARLA: If it's any consolation, Dr. Rahman, I think you will be free in the next month or so.

MOHAMMED: Thank you. Now will you tell me my guilt, please?

CARLA: Sign this. *(She hands him the pen.)* It confirms we had this conversation. *(He reads and begins to sign.)* You know most of their suspicions. They haven't been formally addressed yet.

MOHAMMED: May I ask you something, Miss Spinelli? *(She nods.)* Will you help me with the lawyer? It sounds like a your word will help. *(He writes a name on the paper and rips it off.)* Here's my brother's number. He will get me a lawyer here. Please. I know this is not your job. I know you haven't time to worry about me when your family is suffering, but I have no voice here. The good and the bad you have no need to decide. Your good system decides. Will you help me?

CARLA: I can't.

MOHAMMED: My wife will be persecuted by people who hear of your government's suspicions. Eight Muslims in Chicago have already been shot for no reason. I can't protect my family here. My daughter is four years old. She has done nothing. She is innocent just like your niece.

CARLA: Hey, don't bring my niece into this.

MOHAMMED: I pray for her. *(Kneels.)* Please, please. I beg you. One phone call only.

(Carla takes the phone number from him.)

CARLA: Fine. Now I've got others to see.

MOHAMMED: *(Bowing.)* Thank you. Thank you for your kindness.

CARLA: *(Carla starts to go but stops suddenly.)* Hey, hold on. I thought you said you didn't have a brother?

MOHAMMED: What? Of course I have brothers. *(Beat.)* Oh. No. I said I have no brother *here*. None in the U.S. I meant.

(Carla looks suspiciously at him and nods.)

MOHAMMED: So you'll help me?

CARLA: *(To the guards.)* Give him a blanket. He's freezing. He's got no body fat.

MOHAMMED: *(Calling out to her as she leaves.)* Miss Spinelli. I just want to be home with my family. Please! I will show you! I am a man of faith!

CARLA: *(Under her breath.)* That's what scares me.

HYSTERIA

Rich's wife and one of his two children were sent to a hospital last week when a subway car they were in was contaminated with Pyrexia, a man-made disease. Though it looks promising for both his wife, Sandy, and his youngest daughter, Christina, they have been quarantined. Due to his growing concern about their safety in their Manhattan high-rise, Rich, 40s, contacts his sister, Carla, 30s. She agrees to let him and his oldest daughter, Jill, stay with her in her Brooklyn flat until the hospital release date. The relationship between Carla and her brother is strained at best. Rich, a conservative, high-powered financial consultant is the complete opposite of Carla, a liberal social worker for the New York City Correctional Department. Both have good intentions and high ideals. In the last year, terrorist attacks have become far too common. The U.S. economy has been hit hard, but worse than the financial strain is the emotional strain. Carla enters with a load of groceries.

RICH: Jill was out with Ali again.
CARLA: *(Carrying in groceries.)* I got a great deal on pre-cooked lasagna noodles.
RICH: I just got off the phone with Sandy. I had to tell her about Jill.
CARLA: Did you know you could get them pre-cooked?
RICH: They were at the library—Jill and Ali.
CARLA: Your wife's got enough to worry about. How are they by the way?
RICH: Okay. Good—no signs of the disease yet. All negative. They'll be released from the hospital by next week if all keeps testing negative.
CARLA: Hey! That's great, Rich.

RICH: It is. This Pyrexia scare has been all over the media.

CARLA: What hasn't been? You know, I'd even prefer the usual celebrity garbage about so-and-so's affair over the constant panic spreading.

RICH: It's not just merely panic. It's the truth. It's just been pumped up a bit. Pyrexia's fatal.

CARLA: I know, and I'm not underestimating that. I'm just saying that they told us 30,000 or more were exposed and probably half that number would suffer the disease. Nobody we know has a full-blown case. And we know like . . . six people quarantined?

RICH: I guess.

CARLA: I'm thankful, believe me. I just think they scare us way too much.

RICH: Well, if they didn't scare us, we'd complain that it wasn't covered properly.

CARLA: I just think the panic spreading causes irrational behavior.

RICH: Now, I think *you're* blowing things out of proportion.

CARLA: Am I? I'm in the FBI holding cells every day. Half the people being held aren't even involved.

RICH: How do you know? Besides, if it were any other country, those folks would be thrown into prison and tortured for suspicious behavior. So civil liberties are screwed a bit?

CARLA: Yeah . . . anyway . . . I stopped at the Kosher Corner. I love that bread. What's that stuff called?

RICH: I would be careful over there, Carla.

CARLA: Yes, I may end up converting to Judiasm. That would piss Mom off, huh?

RICH: Yes it would. You were always the rebellious one. Are you sure Jill isn't your daughter? I told her a million times not to go to the library in the last few weeks.

CARLA: Used to be drugs. Now, it's checking out a book. Never know where diseases may lurk.

RICH: You think you're so funny, but it's dangerous. Any public place.

CARLA: Hum, well, that eliminates . . . ohhhh, all of New York. So . . . you and Jill feel like helping me make lasagna tonight?

RICH: Didn't you hear anything I just said about Jill and Ali?

CARLA: Yes. *(Beat.)* I'd like to be an Italian Jew. I think that would be an interesting combo.

RICH: Sandy said I should have sat down with her.

CARLA: What did you say to Jill exactly?

RICH: I told her she should never see him again.

CARLA: Well that was a dumb idea.

RICH: Thanks a lot.

CARLA: Well, she's *fourteen*, Rich. She's going to do the opposite of what you say.

RICH: She said they were just friends. So what's the big deal?

CARLA: Well exactly. They're friends, Rich. My niece, God forbid, has integrity.

RICH: Integrity? His family's supporting terrorists.

CARLA: No, he's not. His father happens to be a lawyer. He's defending people's constitutional right to have representation. You can see the difference.

RICH: Yes, but I don't want him to put her in danger. I've already had to deal with half of my family being hospitalized in the last week. I don't want to worry about her too.

CARLA: Then don't. Jill really likes this kid. He helps her in physics. They bonded while in a school play. I mean, what is more American that that? You met him. You said he was a great guy.

RICH: Yes. And he was a good kid but that was before things got out of hand with the attacks. That's before I understood who his father was associating with.

CARLA: He's not associating with them. He's defending them. As a lawyer. That's what he does. That's his job. And who's to say those men are guilty anyway?

RICH: Oh come on, Carla.

CARLA: Oh come on? My God, you of all people should

understand how easily people jump to conclusions when things seem suspicious. But often they can be explained.

RICH: Why me of all people?

CARLA: Oh come on, Rich.

RICH: Oh. That was different. I mean, it was totally different. We're talking misappropriating some funds, not murder. And Roger was the only one who went down for it.

CARLA: Yeah, and a lot of people suspected you.

RICH: Fine. I don't know if they are part of the terrorist network or not. And maybe Ali's father is incredible. A really good guy. And I'm unfairly judging his work.

CARLA: Now, you're talking.

RICH: But it doesn't matter. Jill told me there were rumors all over the school and that kids don't trust him.

CARLA: All the more reason he needs a friend.

RICH: It's not just Ali I'm worried about. It's all the people he associates with religiously. And it's the other kids at the school who might harm Jill because of her association.

CARLA: You say "association." We're talking about friendship . . . maybe even more than friendship.

RICH: Do you know something I don't?

CARLA: No.

RICH: What do you know? What did she tell you?

CARLA: Nothing.

RICH: I don't believe you.

CARLA: I'm just responding to the way she looks when he calls.

RICH: Do they talk often?

CARLA: I don't know. You lived with her for the last fourteen years.

RICH: I don't know. I guess I didn't pay much attention.

CARLA: Maybe you *should* pay attention. She's growing up fast. She'll be out of the house before you know it.

RICH: I don't need a lecture.

CARLA: Yeah, and you know what I don't need? I don't need my brother to suddenly thrust me in the middle of his family ordeal and then expect me to say nothing.

RICH: I didn't want you to say nothing, but I don't need a lecture.

CARLA: Well, I don't need to walk into my place after a long
day and be confronted with conflict. This is my place. It
isn't the high-rise on the Upper East Side with the doorman,
but it's all mine. All day long I do conflict, Rich. Prisons
tend to be like that. Social workers catch hell. So when I
come home, I veg. I joke. I like to eat. It would be nice if
you'd greet me with a "Hey, how are ya, Sis?" or "We
cooked you dinner!" I mean, it's not perfectly easy to share
my place, ya know? Though I'm happy to do it.

RICH: *(Beat.)* We'll get a hotel tomorrow.

CARLA: Uhhhh! So now I get the guilt trip. You did not hear
a single thing I just said. No wonder Jill doesn't talk to you.
(Beat.) Look, you are *not* staying at a hotel, okay? Not with
Sandy and Christina in the hospital.

RICH: So you think I'm a bad father?

CARLA: No, I don't. I didn't say that!

RICH: Yeah, but you *think* it.

CARLA: No. I don't think you're a bad father. I think you gen-
uinely love your kids, but I don't think you're very available. Hell, I don't think you've been available to me all these
years either.

RICH: Like you'd care.

CARLA: Yeah, I do. I don't have any family of my own, Rich.
I mean, I don't have a husband and kids. I have Mom, you
and your family. That's it.

RICH: You could meet somebody.

CARLA: Yeah, I could, maybe, but I haven't.

RICH: That's cause you're too wrapped up in being a social
worker. Working for the slime of the world.

CARLA: Okay, that pisses me off. I mean, that's what pisses
me off about you. I can understand your passion for competition, for wheeling and dealing your days away, but you
can't seem to get your arms around mine. You can't seem
to accept the fact that I love what I do. Yes, I cater to the

slime of the world sometimes, but criminals have families, and families have needs. *(Beat.)* You probably see that very clearly now, being apart from Sandy and Christina for this past week.

RICH: I miss her. I miss them both like nobody's business. The thing is . . . I feel like I can't protect them anymore. I've never felt so helpless.

CARLA: All of us are feeling vulnerable.

RICH: Yeah, but I don't like it. I'm thinking I should just shove aside this damn job, love it or not, and move out to a safer place.

CARLA: And live in some homogeneous suburb or take up the quiet life? It's not you. It's not either of us.

RICH: What would keep me here?

CARLA: Me, ya stupid idiot. I just confessed that I don't have anyone but you and Mom.

RICH: I'll take you both with me.

CARLA: You're not serious?

RICH: I don't know. It's . . . it's the lack of control that I can't stand. I'll spend more time with Jill. I will. Like you suggested. I know you're right . . . I'm unavailable . . . a little too much like Dad.

CARLA: I didn't say that.

RICH: No, no, but I am. I know Jill's growing fast and I know I've been out of the picture more than in . . . and I'm just coming down hard all of a sudden saying, "No, Arab kids . . . No, Arab kids like him."

CARLA: Wow, now you sound like Archie Bunker. Wanna move to Astoria and start calling blacks colored folk?

RICH: I just, I can't get it out of my head. I think Ali is dangerous to her. It's a premonition.

CARLA: So you told her not to see him, but you didn't happen to mention it's because you're scared for her life? Even if it's unreasonable, you should have told her why you're so set on this. That way, even if she were mad, she could understand it's because you care about her.

RICH: I feel I have to control things more now. I told her I'd pick her up from school from now on too. I'll drop her off too. She can go out on the weekends with a few friends that I know about. We can't be too careful. We should move out to some place safer, in the country. Some place where her associations or *friendships* won't put her in danger. Where we don't have to be worried about diseases being spread like crazy everywhere. Where we don't have to be afraid to ride the bus.

CARLA: Where is that place, Rich?

RICH: I won't force you to come. I won't force Mom either, but I do wish you would. I know you guys love Brooklyn, but I cannot do this anymore!

CARLA: You've got to. We all have to. Get up and do the routine. Make breakfast and go to work and laugh with friends. You can't run from shadows. We're all scared. Even us folks who like to act like we're tough guys are scared.

RICH: I can't do the routine! This is not routine! My wife and child in the hospital is not routine. I just want to protect us, Carla. I don't want any of us to die. *I* don't want to die. Please. I don't want to die!

CARLA: Okay, okay. *(Quietly, holding him.)* I know.

RICH: *(Pulls away a bit.)* I can't believe this has gotten to me so much. I haven't told this to anyone. Not even Sandy. I mean, about the dying part.

CARLA: Well, maybe you can say it to me. Maybe you don't feel like you have to protect me as much.

RICH: Maybe. That doesn't mean I don't, ya know, love you as much.

CARLA: I know.

RICH: The big financial consultant with the perfect life falls apart in his sister's flat.

CARLA: And then he goes on anti-anxiety medication or at least takes up yoga. Not so horrible. *(He smiles.)* So you'll think twice about moving out of here? You'd miss the Broadway openings and the beggars' patter.

RICH: I'll think about it. You think about moving too. *(Beat.)* So how do you tell your daughter that you're scared for her life without taking away every ounce of her security?

CARLA: *(Beat.)* I don't know, Rich. I don't know.

BELDON PARK

Luna and Marty, two high school teens, have been best buddies for years. Unfortunately, they've always been in the "out" crowd. Recently, Luna has been revamping her appearance to change this situation. She's becoming a little more stylish and, in the process, a little more revealing and sexy. She feels this might be a good way to attract Josh, one of the more popular boys in her class. Marty is aware of her crush on Josh and is particularly upset about it because, one, he has a thing for Luna and, two, he's overheard Josh dishonor Luna's reputation in the locker room. At the top of the scene, Luna is whooping it up with a group of Josh's friends about heading to the beach this Saturday night to party. Marty vehemently objects to this potential get-together with Josh and his pals.

LUNA: *(Waving.)* Yeah! Yeah-hah! We can party like crazy. You bring the stuff. *(Winks.)* See you guys tonight. *(Coyly, waving.)* See ya, Josh. *(She smiles. Beat. Turns. Sees Marty looking disgusted.)* What? What?! What is your problem?

MARTY: Nothing! I didn't say anything. Though I probably should.

LUNA: You don't have to. You're looking all narrow-eyed and witchy at me.

MARTY: No, I'm not!

LUNA: Well, you looked like you were going to lose your lunch or something just now.

MARTY: I'm not feeling well for your information. My stomach is killing me.

LUNA: Maybe you ate too much. Or maybe God is punishing you for being such a pain to me.

MARTY: I didn't say anything. *(Beat.)* Do you want me to say something?

LUNA: No! God, not like you need to. You're sitting there all contorted and retarded or somethin'. I know you don't like them.

MARTY: No, I don't like them if that's what you're asking.

LUNA: I'm not asking you anything, Marty. You're obviously all moody over your physics final.

MARTY: It has nothing to do with that.

LUNA: Well, ring, ring. *(Marty looks annoyed. She continues.)* Ring, ring. Rinnnng, Rinnnng!

MARTY: Hello?

LUNA: This is the get-a-clue phone. Calling you to remind you this is not your business.

MARTY: I thought we were friends. Is that not my business?

LUNA: Well, I'm not so sure . . .

MARTY: You're not so sure we're friends? Fine! *(Pushes back from the table. Grabs his side.)* Ow! *(Recovering.)* I can't believe what a total loser you've become Luna. Screw— *(He starts to grab his books.)*

LUNA: Hey! Wait. Don't start on me. I only meant that sometimes you act like we're more than friends.

MARTY: *(Looks down.)* No, I don't. I don't feel that way.

LUNA: You seem like it sometimes. And besides, just because we're friends doesn't mean you're the only one I want to hang around with. Ya know? I'd like to meet a few more people in high school. You and Lumpy and Anne are great, but you all could branch out a little more.

MARTY: You make us sound like the royal losers. If you don't like hanging out with us, don't. Fine. Meet some more friends. But those guys are not your friends. They're after something else.

LUNA: *(Flirtatiously in his face.)* Oh yeah, Marty, what are they after? *(She blinks her eyelids.)*

MARTY: You know exactly what I mean.

LUNA: *(Seriously.)* Oh, yeah, they'd have to be after that because why else would they hang with such an ugly girl, right? It wouldn't have anything to do with the music I play or that I'm a good dancer. Well, I'm not ugly anymore, Marty. Not like that anyway. I've grown, I've changed a lot this year.

MARTY: Yeah, right, it's not like you got all cool and philosophical, expanding your mind. You got all bulimic first semester and now you wear a lot of tight clothes. If that's what you call growing, yeah, you've grown and changed.

LUNA: God! You are . . . I'm just one big ole slut to you. At least I'm not a lard-butt sitting around in my puddle of depression, watching scrambled porno on cable all day!

MARTY: Oh gee, thanks a lot. *(Beat.)* I'm sorry. I didn't mean you're a slut. I meant, some of your clothes look slutty, but not all your clothes. And believe me I know I'm a lard-butt, thank you very much.

LUNA: Look, I'm just going out with those guys and a couple of girls to hang out by the beach tonight. I thought it sounded fun. I'm glad they invited me. I'm going because I want to dance and party by the beach. Is that all right with you?

MARTY: Those guys will bring Ecstasy.

LUNA: So? So maybe I'll try it once. It's no big deal once.

MARTY: Do you know what that does to the neurons in your brain?!

LUNA: I don't know. Maybe it'll make me even more slutty than you already think I am. A total slut monster. Whoo-hoo! Won't that be fuuuunnnnn?!

MARTY: No offense, Luna, but Josh is not interested in you romantically if that's what you're thinking.

LUNA: Where did that come from? Who said I was interested in Josh?

MARTY: I just don't want you to get the wrong idea.

LUNA: You have nerve, you know that? I think this friendship is on its way out. You are way out of line. And Anne is too. First of all, because I told Anne explicitly that I didn't want anyone else to know. I told her that, and she promised. See how much that means.

MARTY: But I—

LUNA: Don't! I know she told you, so just shut up. And secondly, because it's none of your business if I want to hang out with some cool people. Some maybe, popular people. It's so totally surprising to you that some popular people might find me half-interesting? That's what's insulting! Your assumptions are insulting.

MARTY: It's not that.

LUNA: If you're jealous, then you're jealous. That's not my fault! You don't know what I think or feel. You really don't know what Josh Michaels thinks and feels. You don't know him. You don't even know what you feel because you pack it in and push it down to the bottom of that huge stomach of yours! *(Pause.)* Anyway, I'm gonna go. And don't wait for me after school. I won't be carpooling with you guys tonight. I'd rather walk. *(She gets up to leave.)*

MARTY: You're right, Luna. I do pack it in so I don't feel.

LUNA: I'm really angry at you at the moment. I didn't mean to make that crack about your stomach. I have a big stomach too. I'm sorry. I just think . . . we shouldn't talk for a couple of days. *(Starting to leave.)*

MARTY: *(Beat.)* Wait. I know Anne shouldn't have told me anything. Though I figured it out already. You drool when he walks in the room. A puddle gathers around your feet.

LUNA: Whatever.

MARTY: And this is absolutely none of my business. You're right.

LUNA: At least you got that right.

MARTY: But it was hard for me to ignore what he told me.

LUNA: What? I'm not talking to you. Okay? Do you understand?

MARTY: And he didn't just tell me. He told every guy in the locker room.

LUNA: What are you talking about, Marty?

MARTY: The park. Beldon Park?

LUNA: *(Pause.)* What about Beldon Park?

MARTY: Him and his buddy Matt. They're jerks. We always said that. And this afternoon made me sure of it. What happened to you? You didn't like them at all last semester. It's like you lost your mind.

LUNA: I didn't lose my mind. So what exactly did Matt say? He probably was just bragging.

MARTY: It wasn't Matt who said stuff. It was Josh. And he definitely wasn't bragging. Those guys are not cool. They're total jerks, Luna.

LUNA: Lump them into a whole sum, why don't you?

MARTY: They are a lump sum. Or maybe just a lump of crap.

LUNA: How would you know?

MARTY: They don't think individually for one. And for two, I've been going to school with them for eleven years. They're like mob mind-set. And no offense, because I'm not trying to hurt your feelings, but they're using you.

LUNA: Okay, then. What did Josh say that was such a big deal to you?

MARTY: Well, he . . . he kinda said . . .

LUNA: I know. He told you that I showed him something at Beldon Park. That I showed him and his friend Matt my boobs. So what?! It's not that big of a deal. Get over it. He was just bragging like guys do.

MARTY: He said you were a whore.

LUNA: *(Beat.)* No, he didn't. He didn't. You're lying.

MARTY: Yes, he did. And he said you did things, Luna.

LUNA: What things?

MARTY: He said you let him do things to you . . . some things—I don't want to say, but they were kinda, ya know? And it was in front of other guys.

LUNA: What do you mean? What are you talking about? What did he say?

MARTY: Ya know, stuff that . . . touching and groping kinda thing. Things girls don't generally let guys do in parks.

LUNA: Well, he's a liar if he told you that!

MARTY: Exactly! That's what I'm saying.

LUNA: Or maybe *you* are.

MARTY: What?

LUNA: You could be a liar. I mean, you hate Josh so much. Maybe you're just trying to turn me against him.

MARTY: What?!! Are you serious?!

LUNA: I don't know. I just can't believe he told you those things.

MARTY: Not just me! Everybody! What the hell?! You are— Yeah, yeah, I'm just trying to turn you against them. That's all, Luna. *(He starts to go.)*

LUNA: Wait!

MARTY: *(Stops.)* Why should I? Why would I want to talk to someone who thinks I'm a liar? We're obviously not even close to good friends if you'd think I'd lie about something like that.

LUNA: I didn't say for sure you were.

MARTY: If you think it's going to be all fun tonight, Luna, you're wrong. There aren't any girls invited tonight. Do you get it? You're the only girl invited. One girl and eight guys. Got it now?!

LUNA: *(Beat.)* How do you know?

MARTY: I know what I'm talking about. *(He lifts up his shirt, revealing a huge bruise.)* Is this proof enough?

LUNA: *(Seeing the bruise. Pause.)* Oh my God! What did they do to you?

MARTY: *(He puts down his shirt.)* I don't know why I even bothered. You aren't worth it.

LUNA: What happened to you? What did they do to you?

MARTY: I just stuffed my face with too much food and my stomach got all purple from expanding too much. From being such a lard-butt.

LUNA: Oh God, Marty. You defended me, didn't you?

MARTY: It's really interesting to see the inside of a toilet bowl up close and personal. Of course, I would have had a clearer view had the toilet been flushed.

LUNA: Oh my God!

MARTY: I didn't even want to defend you. But I couldn't stand what they were saying. I know you're not like that! I know you're—

LUNA: Yes I am!

MARTY: No, you're not! I know you're—

LUNA: Yes!! I am. I was like that. I just . . . I let him. *(Fighting tears.)* I don't know why.

MARTY: *(Pause.)* Well . . . I called him the "A" word, Luna. I slammed his head into a locker hard too. He was all stunned. It was so great. I wish you could have seen it.

LUNA: I'm sorry, Marty. I'm sorry for what I said to you. About everything. Does it hurt bad?

MARTY: They didn't hurt me. It'll heal. We're friends. What I did was no big deal.

LUNA: But it is a big deal. It's a big deal to me. It means a lot. *(Pause.)* I'm so embarrassed. It was so stupid. He said he wouldn't tell anyone. He said he really liked me a lot, wanted to take me out this weekend. He only wanted to see what it felt like. His friends watched. He told me they wouldn't tell anyone. It was a secret. Forever.

MARTY: It's okay. I understand.

LUNA: No! It's not okay! I knew he was using me. But I just . . . I'm an idiot. And a big slutty—

MARTY: You're not a slut!

LUNA: I just . . . I just . . .

MARTY: Wanted him to like you. *(Nods.)* It's okay. *(He hugs her.)* We all feel like that sometimes. Do stupid things so people will like us. It just means, it just means you're human.

LUNA: And what if you didn't talk me out of going tonight? What would have happened to me then?

MARTY: Nothing. We would have been there. Lumpy, Anne, and I would have killed them. We would have killed them. Plain and simple.

(She looks up to him, not sure what to say. She suddenly hugs him.)

CRESCENDO

Alexander, 21, returns home to care for Helena, 63, his grandmother, who is sick with cancer. Helena is a flamboyant, energetic older lady who has always exaggerated Alexander's talent. In this scene, Alexander confronts his grandmother about her overstated view of the world and, in particular, her distorted view of his talent for the piano.

HELENA: Oh my goodness, let me look at you! Let me look at you, Alex!

ALEXANDER: Grandma, I—

HELENA: Bite your tongue, sir. *(Hits his arm.)* And shame on you for not writing or calling for six months. You can forget the inheritance now.

ALEXANDER: Helena, can't we just skip the whole look-me-over routine? It seems kinda too grandma for you anyway.

HELENA: I'll be the judge of that. *(Beat.)* What did they do to you in Las Vegas?

ALEXANDER: What are you talking about?

HELENA: Your eyes are all bloodshot. Shoulders are saggy. And you've a down inflection in your voice that I *do not* recognize. What did they do to you there?

ALEXANDER: Nothing. It was just a long car trip.

HELENA: The car? You should have taken a train. Trains are so much more romantic. Your grandfather loved trains, remember?

ALEXANDER: Yeah, sure.

HELENA: He took me on a lovely, long train trip through Siberia. The food and service was primo—absolutely artistic . . . roasted duck, little tea sandwiches, bittersweet chocolate puff things. All served by total gentlemen in crisp white coats. And the view, well—simply breathtaking, Alexander.

ALEXANDER: I remember. I was seven. I thought *you* took *him*. He was broke and drinking again as I remember.

HELENA: Well I don't remember everything. The point of the story was the romance of the train.

ALEXANDER: Somehow I don't think the train from Las Vegas to Vermont would be all that romantic. Last time I was on a train from Boston, the toilet broke and the smell of it kept wafting into the car.

HELENA: Alexander, there are some details one need not elaborate upon.

ALEXANDER: So how have you been, Helena?

HELENA: I will respond fully and completely once you have answered my question, which is, what did they do to you in Las Vegas?

ALEXANDER: Nobody did anything to me. I worked there is all.

HELENA: Yes, I understand you entertained at one of the casinos there.

ALEXANDER: No, I didn't entertain at the casino. I was a security guard.

HELENA: A security guard? I thought you were playing for patrons.

ALEXANDER: I did some street performing.

HELENA: Ohhh!

ALEXANDER: Like I told Mom.

HELENA: I don't think she told me that exactly.

ALEXANDER: I highly doubt she got that confused, Helena.

HELENA: My understanding was that you were playing piano at one of the casinos . . . one of the bigger ones.

ALEXANDER: Well, I don't know how you heard that, because I was playing guitar on the street. I think perhaps you enhanced the story in your head since that's what you'd like me to be doing.

HELENA: Why do you do such things, Alex?

ALEXANDER: What are you talking about? Do what things?

HELENA: Things so beneath you. Playing guitar on the street. I know your mother has set no example whatsoever.

ALEXANDER: I don't know what you're talking about.

HELENA: Running a worm store for one.

ALEXANDER: It's not just worms or bait. It's tackle and rods too. She makes decent money. And she has time to go hiking and be outdoors. It's much better than half the jobs in the big cities. Sitting in an office at a computer, looking out the window at rusting fire escapes all day.

HELENA: Yes, but she was a lovely actress.

ALEXANDER: She hated doing that. You just made her.

HELENA: I did not. Anyway, I'm just saying that she has never encouraged your—

ALEXANDER: Oh God, no. Are you doing this again? Don't blame, Mom. She doesn't discourage me about anything. She says I should do what I want.

HELENA: See, that's exactly what I mean. You shouldn't be doing what you want. You're special. You have a gift. You're an extremely talented and accomplished pianist.

ALEXANDER: No, I'm not. I'm just slightly better than the average Joe. I know that now. I've been out of Vermont.

HELENA: This is simply false. I was just telling the new artistic director of the Grande Ole Theater about you. I gave some guidance to him recently over in Burlington so they can re-open. They have an incredible season planned. We'll go to every opening night.

ALEXANDER: I know. Mom told me about that.

HELENA: She told you about the season?

ALEXANDER: No, that you gave them $25,000 dollars.

HELENA: I don't know the exact amount. What is money anyhow?

ALEXANDER: A lot. I think money is a lot now. Now that I've been out in the world. It's power.

HELENA: Well, being in Las Vegas *would* make you think that. The point is that I didn't want the theater to close. It's a fabulous theater. My father invested in that building.

ALEXANDER: I know. You've been giving them money for years. The theater's not even that big. It's not like they have that much overhead. And yet they never seem to break even.

HELENA: It's not the money that's important. They needed more guidance, which I was more than happy to give to them. They agreed to do one Shakespeare, one O'Neill, one Miller, and one grand musical—probably Rodgers and Hammerstein. Doesn't that sound fabulous? Doesn't it?

ALEXANDER: Yes. How much money do you have left?

HELENA: That's a rude question. I believe I'll ignore it. Now, what I was going to say is that I told the artistic director of the theater that my grandson, Alexander, an enormously talented musician, is coming home for a visit this summer. It's a rare treat. We'll convince him to stay. And he'll play for your musical. He agreed.

ALEXANDER: You shouldn't have told him that. I don't want to play.

HELENA: What? You don't want to play?

ALEXANDER: No. I don't want to play. I don't like to. I actually hate it sometimes.

HELENA: I don't believe you. I've never seen a child who sat down and produced such an amazing sound as you do. You're a natural. You learned Chopin in less than a week. Now, the problem is that we never had a teacher who could keep up to speed with your immense talent.

ALEXANDER: That's not true. Mr. Hall was a great teacher. He played professionally in Boston. He wasn't a virtuoso, no, but he made money playing professionally. I was lucky to have him every summer.

HELENA: He was an idiot who didn't know how to foster your talent.

ALEXANDER: I don't want to be a musician, Helena! I don't know why you always push me to do that!

HELENA: Because you're gifted. You could have gotten into Juilliard instead of—

ALEXANDER: No, I couldn't!

HELENA: Well how would you know? Despite the many times I encouraged you to audition—

ALEXANDER: I know.

HELENA: How?!

ALEXANDER: *(Pause.)* I tried.

HELEN: You did? *(Beat.)* When?

ALEXANDER: Two times. The first audition was three years ago. Right after I graduated from high school. I looked like an idiot. I was so cocky at that first audition because you always told me how good I was. How talented. You pumped me up and exaggerated my true talents.

HELENA: You are good.

ALEXANDER: Maybe. Good. But not good enough. The second audition I did last year. They told me I needed more work, or maybe I should consider something else.

HELENA: That's ridiculous. You just need a better teacher.

ALEXANDER: No. I don't want to keep trying to live out some fantasy that I'm not even sure is mine.

HELENA: Many great talents are not recognized immediately. Van Gogh's genius wasn't recognized until he was dead.

ALEXANDER: Well, I don't want to wait until I'm dead. Besides, he's a painter in case you didn't notice. Mozart, Beethoven, and Chopin were all child prodigies. Their talent wasn't just recognized by their grandmother. They were playing salons and for large audiences at a very young age. There was no question.

HELENA: You played for the Summer Festival.

ALEXANDER: I know.

HELENA: *Moonlight Sonata* was perfect for the affair. It was wonderful. Everyone was so impressed.

ALEXANDER: Of course they told you that. I was your grandson.

HELENA: I don't think they just told me that.

ALEXANDER: Look, I came back here because I heard about your tests.

HELENA: I don't think one would audition twice if one didn't enjoy it. I remember how you'd play for me for hours. And then remember when you and I did that interpretive reading of *The Raven*? You were thrilled.

ALEXANDER: Did you hear what I said?

HELENA: Yes, I heard you. You're just like your mother.

ALEXANDER: She says I'm just like you.

HELENA: How's that?

ALEXANDER: Stubborn.

HELENA: I am not stubborn! *(Beat.)* I'm not! Absolutely not! She is!

ALEXANDER: I've come to take care of you.

HELENA: As if I need taking care of. I have a whole summer at the theater planned. I'll take care of you.

ALEXANDER: Mom's afraid that you're giving away all your money to that theater. When Grandpa was alive, he'd put a stop to it. She doesn't trust that artistic director there now.

HELENA: Your mother is very stingy. And so was Grandpa. And there's no reason for it. I come from money. I shared it freely with them. I don't know why they gave it a moment's worry. They had no need. *(Beat.)* I wonder if we could get in and watch a rehearsal.

ALEXANDER: Why do you ignore reality, Helena? Why do you have to embellish everything?

HELENA: Why not? Do you think anything great was ever accomplished by being realistic, Alex?

ALEXANDER: I don't think anything great was accomplished by lying.

HELENA: I never lied. Maybe stretched a little. Maybe. You are brilliant.

ALEXANDER: Lies, lies. Would you stop? God, I wanted to do anything to get away from music once I realized I wasn't good enough. I was a delivery man, a receptionist, a dog walker. But sometimes it would overcome me, and I'd end up in some high school music room somewhere practicing. I wound up playing guitar on the street because I needed to play to fill the void. But it's all stupid because I'm not good enough. It's all idiotic because I'll never get anywhere. It's all because of your lies, your insistent lies. You puffed me up so much, and now I've fallen so low. I feel like nothing.

HELENA: You want to blame me for natural disappointment? That's life. If you're never disappointed, you've never lived.

ALEXANDER: I don't want to live like that.

HELENA: I never intended to hurt you, Alex. Never. Whether you believe me or not, I meant what I said. I was proud of you. I still am. And you know, there's nothing wrong with having passion for music. It's the sound of God on earth. At least that's what I think.

ALEXANDER: It may be the sound of God on earth, but if you're not a virtuoso, and you know you're not, there's no point in doing anything with it. You even said so yourself. Being a street player is beneath me. Only Juilliard is grand enough.

HELENA: You're right. I have said those things, but it's because I worry about you. I wouldn't want you to live on the streets. It's dangerous. It's not that I don't find street performers wonderful. I was enchanted beyond belief by a violin in a subway once. I guess I just wanted to know you'd be safe. I wanted the best for you. And I never doubted you could do it. I'm sorry if I put so much pressure on you. I got carried away I guess.

ALEXANDER: I was so ashamed when I didn't get in. I thought I failed you. I thought that's why you always loved me so much . . . because of my playing.

HELENA: Oh Alex. It was the other way around. I loved your playing because I love you so much and I saw how happy it made you. That's what I really wanted for you—that joy. *(She hugs him close.)*

ALEXANDER: I was happy, wasn't I?
(She nods.)

HELENA: Mr. Hall noticed that all the time. He used to comment on that along with praising your abilities

ALEXANDER: He did? Really?

HELENA: *(Nods.)* I heard he's coming back this summer.

ALEXANDER: Oh yeah. Maybe we could take a second look at "the idiot." Give him a second chance. See if he's improved. See if he can really "foster my talent."

HELENA: Alexander darling, if you're going to quote my words back to me. Choose the smarter things I've said. *(He smiles. Beat.)* Well, maybe something can be arranged. I think my piano has been getting a little dusty. But there are two conditions. Firstly, they'll be no moping or moaning about my physical state. And secondly, no lecturing me on how I spend my own money. My spirit is a very happy one, and it remains so when I am giving to those who create. Those who give me wondrous music, fabulous performances, and booming voices quoting the words of William Shakespeare.

ALEXANDER: Okay, okay. You can give to the theater, but not—

HELENA: *(Putting her hand up to stop him.)* Mmm.

ALEXANDER: Sorry. But you'll at least tell me what the doctor said?

HELENA: It's all very boring. The cancer has returned. We'll do a lot of wiggling our fingers, and crossing our toes and eating fresh fruit and vegetables, and getting under the evil giant iron again. It would be nice though to have someone to hold my hand.

ALEXANDER: I have a hand.

HELENA: I know. And it's a good hand. I think it will do. And you'll play when I'm feeling a little sick and low?

ALEXANDER: Of course. I don't think I could find a better audience.

HELENA: If I do die, Alex, and I don't plan on it, but if I do, I want you to remember that I always loved you. And I too, like your mother, want you to do whatever you want with your life. But never forget how music makes you feel. That I insist upon. Do you understand?

ALEXANDER: Yes. I understand.

HELENA: Right. All right then. Let's go over and watch a rehearsal of *MacBeth*. I love the witches. And Lady MacBeth. Always reminds me a bit of myself. Very inspirational. Very dramatic.

(Holding a hand out to her. She takes it.)

ALEXANDER: And very stubborn.

HELENA: Hush. I'll get my coat.

AND ALL I LOVED

Gary, a 26-year-old social worker, met Julieanne, a 24-year-old art school graduate, a few months ago at an "arty" bar in Boston on "lesbian night." As it turns out, Julieanne was there to make sure her artwork was properly hung. Gary had gone with a woman friend to keep her company. Gary and Julieanne began talking and immediately hit it off. Julieanne warned the flirtatious Gary that she wasn't good with relationships, but Gary turned on the charm. Julieanne ended the night by asking Gary to come home for a one-night stand. Gary was startled and reluctant but agreed after she told him there was no chance she would consider dating him. In the months since, they have become friends but have never gotten romantic again. Julieanne introduced him to her very warm and religious roommate, Mary, hoping he would fall for her instead. As it turns out, Gary has fallen in love with Julieanne despite himself, and Mary has fallen for him. Today, Gary has decided that he can't bury the truth anymore. Gary has been driving around for hours this evening when he sees the light on in Julieanne's apartment. He unexpectedly comes to her door.

GARY: Hey you, want to dance? I know I'm not a woman.
JULIEANNE: How many shrinks did it take to figure that out? *(He smiles.)* I was a little feisty that night, huh? Actually I should consider myself lucky. I mean, how often does a girl get hit on by a guy on lesbian night, sleeps with him, and later becomes friends with him? I think it's a rarity. You're lucky I wasn't a lesbian.
GARY: Yeah, lucky. You probably would have smacked me.
JULIEANNE: No, I probably would have taught you a lot

about women. Would have told you to stay away from my type. Anyway, what's up?

GARY: Is this too late?

JULIEANNE: No. But what's going on?

GARY: Well . . . I've wanted to talk to you for a couple weeks. I was driving around thinking and . . .

JULIEANNE: Funny. I was going to call you tonight too. I have some . . . some news.

GARY: Really? What?

JULIEANNE: Um. No. You go first. There's no rush.

GARY: Well, I guess I wanted to catch you without Mary for once.

JULIEANNE: Oh. Well, no such luck. Mary's home. But she crashed about an hour ago.

GARY: What about the rally? I thought it was supposed to go all night?

JULIEANNE: You don't understand Mary-speak. "All-night" generally means nine-thirty. Those self-righteous Christians never have the energy of us sinners. They have a way of falling asleep at the most crucial moments. *(Putting her finger to her lips.)* Don't tell Jesus.

GARY: I'm surprised she ended up going. She knew how you felt about it. Are you angry?

JULIEANNE: Not at all. I absolutely, positively disagree with her. I think that kind of thinking will send women right back to alley abortions, but at least she's committed to her cause. How do you feel about it? I've never heard you take a stand.

GARY: I don't know. I think it's for the woman to decide.

JULIEANNE: Yeah, why should you bear any responsibility for the choice if you don't have to?

GARY: Okay, fine. The truth is that I don't believe in abortion. If it were me having a baby, I wouldn't do it. But I won't ever be the one carrying the baby. It's the woman's body, so it's up to them to decide.

JULIEANNE: And when or if the woman decides to abort the

baby, you tell everyone it wasn't your choice, but you stood by your girlfriend.

GARY: I guess.

JULIEANNE: You end up smelling like roses. No responsibility and you're not the one to blame.

GARY: Who says they'll be any blame? And I *would be* responsible. I'd be part of the decision process.

JULIEANNE: If it were your child, would you take care of it—raise it on your own?

GARY: On my own? I don't know. It would depend entirely on the circumstance. I suppose I don't feel like I could afford it or would know anything. I would find nice parents to adopt it I guess.

JULIEANNE: Strangers?

GARY: I don't know. Why are we talking about this? This is not what I came here to talk about.

JULIEANNE: Sorry. I didn't mean to get into any heavy-duty debate on it. I was just curious. So I heard from your agent friend today. He likes some of my stuff.

GARY: That's great! Is that your news?

JULIEANNE: (*Shakes her head no.*) No. But I am happy about it. Thank you.

GARY: Welcome. I brought a bunch of photographs of your work, even the new self-portrait.

JULIEANNE: He probably had a good laugh at it.

GARY: I think he used the words "frightening and provocative" actually.

JULIEANNE: It was hilarious.

GARY: Hollowed-out eyes. Funny as Hiroshima. (*Beat.*) Why?

JULIEANNE: It seemed accurate. Besides, what do you care?

GARY: I care a lot. I wonder what's going on with you sometimes. I think you hold a lot inside.

JULIEANNE: Oh, that's deep, Gar. That's why you and Mary make such a great couple.

GARY: Couple? Julieanne, Mary's great. She's fun and sweet . . . the kids at the home love when she volunteers but—

JULIEANNE: She's a great woman. She's been my best friend since forever.

GARY: I know, but that's not what I'm getting at.

JULIEANNE: She really likes you, you know?

GARY: *(Surprised.)* What? No, she doesn't. Not like that.

JULIEANNE: Yes, she does. She told me tonight. She's a good person, Gar. I know she's kinda thick on the religion thing these days, but I think it's just this weird phase. She had a hard childhood.

GARY: Don't you get it? I'm not interested in Mary.

JULIEANNE: Oh, you doin' someone on the side?

GARY: No! I mean . . . no, nothing like that. I mean . . . I'm interested in you.

JULIEANNE: Oh God.

GARY: Gee, you know how to put a guy at ease.

JULIEANNE: We all have our talents. It's just, it would really complicate things.

GARY: Like what?

JULIEANNE: Look, I told you from the start I didn't want anything that would pin me down here.

GARY: Can't you even consider us for one second? You were attracted to me from the first moment we met. I could tell. Why can't we go back to that moment?

JULIEANNE: Yes, I was attracted to you. And I wanted a fling. I wanted some physical attention that night, but that's all. I was honest with you about not wanting to be involved in anything ongoing. And I don't feel any differently now that I know . . . Look, my best friend has feelings for you now.

GARY: No, she doesn't. Not really. She's just lonely. Besides, this is not about Mary. It's about how I feel about you. Why do you keep pushing me and Mary together? You know I've always wanted you.

JULIEANNE: Very unhealthy of you by the way. Look, basically I'm telling you, Gary, there's no possibility for us.

GARY: I don't believe you.

JULIEANNE: Well, that's not my problem. It's yours. This is

so weird. This whole day. Of course, you don't know the half of it. You do know, though, that none of this was supposed to happen?

GARY: Well, what was supposed to happen? Do you know that?

JULIEANNE: Sure. I was supposed to go away and paint like mad. Be some sort of recluse in California for twenty years. Pop out for art openings. Never get tied to anything or anybody. Just free. I don't do connection right. It hurts too bad when it runs amuck. And it always runs amuck.

GARY: How would you know? You never let it go that far.

JULIEANNE: I watched my mother. She had one disposable relationship after another. Each time the man professed his love and devotion. Each time—gone. Maybe when I'm forty-something, I'll settle down. When I don't need anybody, but I'll enjoy the companionship. Some recluse type. A lousy poet slash burnt-out social worker type like yourself. But until then, I fly solo. That's the plan.

GARY: And if the plan is circumvented by passion or love?

JULIEANNE: Love? I don't know if I believe in that. Once the challenge is gone, that's when things change.

GARY: No, when the challenge is gone that's when you can allow yourself to be at ease. You can express your love even more without worrying that you'll be rejected.

JULIEANNE: *(Pause.)* You'll change your mind like Dennis and all my mother's men.

GARY: Who's Dennis? I've never heard his name before.

JULIEANNE: He was my high school boyfriend. First one.

GARY: High school? Well, I hope you're not holding him accountable for changing his mind. He was a teenager. That can be chalked up to youthful naïveté.

JULIEANNE: Yes, but all love is naïveté. *(Beat.)* I was crazy about Dennis. He wore saddle shoes and he didn't think it was cool to get drunk and throw up.

GARY: Very mature—this Dennis.

JULIEANNE: In the right ways. He was thrilled when I asked

him to Sophomore Semi because most girls thought he was a complete nerd.

GARY: Sounds familiar.

JULIEANNE: Until I took him to the dance. Everyone realized that he had this great sense of humor, and he could draw these cartoons. He drew them all over the napkins that night. Girls started to notice his beautiful eyes and his incredible talents. He called me every day for a week afterwards. He adored me, and we had the best talks. Real equals. We even made out a bit. Only, this girl, Cynthia, began to call him too. She would laugh hysterically at his jokes. She never told her own. I could tell he liked her. Once Dennis and I were having this great conversation about Donald Duck at this party and Cynthia got jealous and went out on the steps to cry. He saw her crying there and was overwhelmed at her emotion for him. She told him she was jealous, and falling in love with him.

GARY: She just sounds high-maintenance to me.

JULIEANNE: All my witty replies and interesting quips could never add up to how she cried. I tried to cry for him too, but I couldn't. I still can't cry even though if anyone had a right to cry it would be me. Sometimes I just can't feel things. A stone face is nice for poker but of little use in a relationship.

GARY: (Quoting Poe.) "From childhood's hour I have not been as others were. I have not seen as others saw. I could not bring my passions from a common spring. From the same source I have not taken my sorrow. I could not awaken my heart to joy at the same tone; And all I loved. I loved alone."

JULIEANNE: Umm, deep. Yours?

GARY: Poe's actually.

JULIEANNE: He's cheery. You're lucky I'm not a slit-my-wrists type.

GARY: You don't have to feel what you don't. I like a stone face. When you finally crack a smile, I'll know I really earned it.

JULIEANNE: You'll resent having to earn it eventually. Trust me.

GARY: Maybe if you trust me, it'll all come easier than you think.

JULIEANNE: Nothing's going to be easy between us, Gar. It's all very complicated now.

GARY: It doesn't have to be.

JULIEANNE: I'm afraid it does. You don't know about our problem yet.

GARY: Problem?

JULIEANNE: Yes. I went to the doctor today. I was worried for the last three months. I thought it was just stress, but . . .

GARY: *(Realizing.)* Um . . . Are you saying you're . . . ?

JULIEANNE: Yeah. I'm pregnant.

GARY: Are they sure?

JULIEANNE: Oh yeah.

GARY: What are you going to do?

JULIEANNE: What are *you* going to do? It's yours as much as mine. I guess we had quite a one-night stand, huh? *(Pause.)* Don't feel like serving up any more poetry?

GARY: That's not fair. I'm shocked. This is all coming at me all of a sudden.

JULIEANNE: Yeah, well, this all comes naturally to me of course.

GARY: And it's definitely mine?

JULIEANNE: What?! How can you ask me that? You've seen my social life.

GARY: I'm sorry. I didn't mean that. I'm glad it's mine. I'm just confused since I seem to remember using a—

JULIEANNE: I know. Ninety-eight percent reliable. We must be special.

GARY: Really special.

JULIEANNE: *(Beat.)* Is your infatuation wearing thin like our protection?

GARY: No. I just . . . am surprised. Shocked. I don't know what to say.

JULIEANNE: Look, you can walk away from this. In fact, it's

what I want you to do. I know with all your professing tonight, you think it'll make you look bad, but it may be for the best. I just felt I had to tell you.

GARY: I don't have any desire to walk away, Julieanne. And I don't want to be just your friend. Okay, I'm not sure what to do about this situation. But I still meant every word I said to you. *(Beat.)* What do you want to do?

JULIEANNE: Well . . . if you're not going to walk away . . . What I'd really want is . . . How would you feel about raising the baby?

GARY: *(Beat.)* Wow. I don't know. But I think we should consider it.

JULIEANNE: No. I didn't mean *we*, Gary. I meant you. I can't do it. I have too many dreams that I can't let go of. Even if I'm not a total recluse, I want to travel and paint and be free. I'd resent you keeping me from that. I'd resent our child.

GARY: I don't know what to say. I'd have to think about it. I don't know how I'd even afford it. And a baby, *your* baby would be a constant reminder of you . . . of all I want with you.

JULIEANNE: That's how you feel right now, but your feelings for me will fade. You're the kind of guy that falls in love hard. You deserve a woman who'll love you as fully as you think you love me right now. Look, you said you can't stand the idea of abortion. Well, the truth is I can't either. But forgive me if I won't give up nine months of my life to give my baby to a complete stranger. A stranger who may or may not do right by my child. But for you, for you I'd have it. And I'd have no regrets. Because I know you'd be a great father. I've seen you with the kids down at the home. *(Beat.)* And I know you can't possibly make up your mind right now. But think about it. Will you?

GARY: *(Nods.)* Absolutely. If you will think about us one last time?

JULIEANNE: I don't think that's a—

GARY: Please. Just ask yourself . . . When your artwork is being rejected by some snooty gallery in L.A. and the traffic drove you crazy on the way home and your manager at your day job made a pass at you again, who will you turn to? Who will be your shoulder? And when things are going well, your first big show is a hit with the critics, who will you share it with? Who will you celebrate and laugh with about the pretentiousness of it all? And who will you go home to? Who do you want that to be?

(She looks as though she's going to speak, but can't.)

FAMILY PORTRAIT

Georgie, 20s, was born and raised in a small town in Maine. Neither of her parents were happy when she went away to New York to study art and photography at N.Y.U. Her father, mid 50s, a former alcoholic, took it as a direct assault on his lifestyle. He always enjoyed small-town living. As a family portrait photographer, Edison made a decent living taking pictures of the nice folks in the surrounding communities. He would have made an even better living if he hadn't had a habit of hitting the bottle. In the last few years, listening to the demands of his wife, Maggie, and daughter, he has managed to clean up his act. His wife's condition was a great influence on his sobering up. Two years ago, she started to have headaches. Soon after, Maggie began to forget things—strange things. She was too young for senility, but her confusion only worsened. After a series of tests, the doctors concluded that it was a brain tumor. The family was devastated, but Dr. Wu said it would probably disappear if they used both medication and radiation. In the last week, Georgie has received several calls from her parents' neighbor, Frieda, who is concerned about her mother's welfare. Apparently, her mother and father are acting strangely. Georgie has just driven in from New York to find out what's really happening.

EDISON: Snapshot? What are you doing here? Why didn't you call?

GEORGIE: I did. I tried, Dad. Last night. And no one answered this morning either.

EDISON: I didn't hear it.

GEORGIE: *(She gives him a look.)* So how ya doin', Dad? *(She goes to hug him.)* How's Pops?

EDISON: *(Suspicious.)* Fine. Did you bring the tapes you stole from me?

GEORGIE: I brought home Nat King Cole and your favorites. So where's Mom?

EDISON: She's lying down.

GEORGIE: Is she okay?

EDISON: Why wouldn't she be?

GEORGIE: Well, she's got this little thing called a brain tumor, Dad.

EDISON: And I have a bum knee. Life goes on.

GEORGIE: Well, there is a subtle difference. *(Reaching up.)* Don't I get a hug?

EDISON: Sure. *(He hugs her.)* It's nice to see you, kid.

GEORGIE: Is it really? You seem to be acting kinda weird about me coming home.

EDISON: Not weird. I'm suspicious. You run outta money or what?

GEORGIE: Money? *(Looking around.)* From the looks of the photo studio, I should be asking *you* that.

EDISON: I know it's a little ragged. We've been real beat. No time to clean up. I had a big family come for a sitting a few days ago. Real nice family, but I haven't cleaned yet. I have a baby—this fat baby for her first birthday coming tomorrow. So I'm stayin' real busy. *(Beat.)* So what's up? Why are you here, Snapshot?

GEORGIE: *(Unzipping her bag, pulling out a few tapes.)* Well . . . Frieda called me, Dad. She said things seemed a little off here.

EDISON: Off?

GEORGIE: She said Mom went out in the middle of the night with no shoes on. She was lost.

EDISON: Oh, for cryin' out—is that all? She wasn't lost, and she had her slippers on. She was just real tired.

GEORGIE: Frieda was afraid things were getting to be too much for you. I think she was afraid that you—

EDISON: I know. Hit the bottle again. Well, I didn't. You know what Frieda's problem is? She watches too many soaps—a little too much "As the World Screws with Your Head." There're no problems here. You can leave Sunday and get back to your precious New "Yuck." *(Looking down at the tapes.)* So where's Judy?

GEORGIE: What?

EDISON: Lose your hearing in that screamin' town? Where's Judy? You tell me you brought back my favorites but I don't see her. It's the least you could do since you decide to pop by unexpectedly. Pop by whenever you please. Pop, pop, pop. Hi Pop. How's Pops? What am I supposed to do? Drop everything?

GEORGIE: I'm sorry, Dad. I was just honestly concerned. *(Hands him a tape.)* Here's Judy.

EDISON: Oh. Thanks.

GEORGIE: You look tired.

EDISON: I'm old. It would be a real stunt if I didn't.

GEORGIE: You aren't old. You know what else Frieda said?

EDISON: I don't care what ole slippery lips said. She's an old bag. An old screwball and a nag on top of it.

GEORGIE: She said Mom wasn't recognizing people.

EDISON: She recognizes me just fine. I don't think she wanted to recognize ole slippery lips the other day. And I admit, she was real tired last Saturday . . . she had a bit of trouble getting David's name out, but she knew who he was fine.

GEORGIE: David? She loves David. Jesus, she adores him. So have you brought her to Dr. Wu?

EDISON: Why bother? He's an idiot. They're all idiots. Nothing's helped.

GEORGIE: That's not true. This is what I was afraid of. This is exactly what Frieda said. You're not taking her, are you?

EDISON: I am. I take her.

GEORGIE: It's probably getting bigger, Dad, doing more damage.

EDISON: The treatment isn't helping.

GEORGIE: Well, how do you know?

EDISON: She told me!

GEORGIE: *(Beat.)* She did?

EDISON: Yes.

GEORGIE: She didn't tell me that. But I knew something was wrong when I talked to her on the phone. That's really why I decided to come.

EDISON: You talked to Mom? *(Beat.)* When?

GEORGIE: Last night. She said you were in the shower or something. It was weird, Dad. Hard to understand her. And for a moment I wasn't sure if she knew who I was.

EDISON: So, I don't always recognize your voice right off. Sometimes it's a bad connection.

GEORGIE: It wasn't a bad connection. She could hear me fine.

EDISON: I hate phones. You lose perspective.

GEORGIE: She really sounded low. I wanted to come and see for myself.

EDISON: Okay, she's having a kind of rough time right now. She just needs a little more TLC.

GEORGIE: I understand, but maybe you need some help with that. Maybe you can't do it alone. Maybe you could use a nurse or something.

EDISON: I take care of her fine. Besides, how are we gonna afford a nurse? I guess you're losing track of where you came from, Ms. New York high society.

GEORGIE: Or maybe just a helping set of hands. You don't necessarily have to pay that much. Maybe an older, retired lady.

EDISON: I don't know.

GEORGIE: And you have to get her to the doctor, Dad. I know she may resist it. But do you want things to get worse?

EDISON: Of course not! Do you? I don't see you helping out.

GEORGIE: Well, I should be. That's why I came home. I've been thinking about it. How I should be home. I'm going to take her to the doctor Monday.

EDISON: Monday? Don't you have to be back for school?

GEORGIE: I'll take a few days off. I don't care. I want her to go in.

EDISON: What about what she wants? She can't take the radiation. She's sick of it.

GEORGIE: The radiation keeps the tumor from growing. If it grows, things will just get worse. I know it's hard for you to take her. You've got a business to keep going. I don't think about those things sometimes, but I'm starting to.

EDISON: Who cares about the business? The business is going fine. It's going. I'll take her to the doctor soon. If there were problems, I would have called, Georgie.

GEORGIE: So why did David tell me that your studio has been closed for days at a time?

EDISON: David? When did you talk to David?

GEORGIE: I stopped by his place on the way here.

EDISON: *(With meaning.)* Oh?

GEORGIE: Get it out of your head, Pops. David and I will never be a thing again. He's content to stay here and teach and live in his mother's house, and I'm . . . well, I'm just not content by nature. But we'll always be friends.

EDISON: Whatever. You'd think he'd try harder. You're a tough one.

GEORGIE: Maybe he's tired of tough. Maybe he'd like it a little more easy.

EDISON: You were a great couple.

GEORGIE: Well, God knows I tried.

EDISON: Don't tell me that thing again.

GEORGIE: I begged him on my knees. I asked him a million times to move with me to New York.

EDISON: That was your mistake. You appeared slightly desperate.

GEORGIE: Slightly? Anyway, the point is, he told me he's seen the lights off here during the day a lot. I just don't want to hear that you've gone back to drinking.

EDISON: One day last week when I had to run errands for Mother's medicine. I'm dry, Georgie. That's not what's going on.

GEORGIE: I don't think David would lie to me.

EDISON: And I would?

GEORGIE: It wouldn't be the first time.

EDISON: I'm not lying. You can see her right away if you don't think I'm caring for her right.

GEORGIE: It's not that. I think you're doing great. But why aren't you taking her to Dr. Wu?

EDISON: By the way, I saw some of those photos you plan to exhibit for your showing thing in New York. Frieda showed me that flyer you sent her.

GEORGIE: Why are you avoiding the question?

EDISON: I was going to call you this week about those photos. I've been sick about it ever since you discussed it with Mom this summer. Do you actually plan to use those photographs you took of her when she was just back from the hospital?

GEORGIE: Mom said it would be fine to use them. She didn't think they were bad—

EDISON: Of course she said that. Because she could see how much you wanted to use them. That doesn't mean she liked them and you know it.

GEORGIE: What's wrong with them? She looks vulnerable and sweet. My professors love them.

EDISON: Your professors don't know her. And she doesn't look vulnerable. She looks funny, weird—lost and confused. She looks sick.

GEORGIE: I don't agree at all. She told me they were fine.

EDISON: That's not what she told me. She told me she was embarrassed. You know your mother likes to look nice in pictures. She likes the house to look nice. You chose the ugliest part of the house—the most run-down area of the library. Caught her at the worst moment, Georgiana.

GEORGIE: Somehow we went from the affectionate Snapshot to the uncomfortable Georgiana. I must have took a wrong turn in Albuquerque.

EDISON: You did. Even David, good-looking David, looks half-dead. You try to make us look like white trash for your own selfish reasons. Pass these photos off in New York as art. Your personal trauma with rural America and the family you can't make sense of. Your personal trauma with your alcoholic father. Your mother's tragic tumor . . . It's all up for grabs. It doesn't matter if you offend one of us. It's art. It's reality. Well, it's not reality. It's your manipulation of reality. The one that makes you look so angst-ridden and downtrodden.

GEORGIE: Are you finished? *(Beat.)* It's funny that you call me manipulative. You're the master. Only you could turn a conversation around like this. I wasn't talking about my art.

EDISON: You call it art. I call half of it pornography. The rest are photos taken at unappealing perspectives, making your subjects look troubled or demented. And the subjects are us. Do you know how insulting it is? I don't understand.

GEORGIE: I don't expect you to. I know we don't agree on art, but right now, I'm talking about my mother's life—her health. Not what *you* want with my work.

EDISON: Do you think she wants to be remembered like that? Does anyone?

GEORGIE: They're the truth. It doesn't have to be pretty to be beautiful.

EDISON: Your mother is full of pride. I won't let you. She had a life—a life to be damn proud of.

GEORGIE: Of course she did—does! You act as if she's dead. Her dignity is clear in the pictures. You can see it on her face. Her mathematics books are in the background—the teachers' editions. I tried to capture her vulnerability caused by this illness. I love that part of her too. Look, photographs are supposed to make you feel something, Dad. Capture an emotion, a mood. If they made you angry, they were effective!

EDISON: Is it more important to be effective or kind to those you love? Art should make beauty where there isn't beauty. You need imagination to see people at their best, Georgie. I thought I gave you that.

GEORGIE: Yeah, you gave me imagination all right. I had to imagine my way out of my room, out of this studio, out of this house, this stupid town . . . I had to because I was so afraid I'd end up a violent drunk like you.

EDISON: Well, I knew I gave you something. *(Beat.)* But don't take out your anger with me on her. She told you you can use them, yes, but she's humiliated. Trust me.

GEORGIE: You made your point. What if I said I wouldn't use the damn photos if you don't want? Will you then tell me why you won't take her to the doctor?

EDISON: You promise you won't put them up for display?

GEORGIE: *(Pause.)* I promise. Now, what's really up, Dad? Come clean.

EDISON: I told her I wouldn't tell you, but you've a right. I took her to some idiot specialists in Augusta in September. Two specialists. They said there's nothing we can do. The tumor's inoperable. Surgery would damage the brain stem.

GEORGIE: I thought Dr. Wu was hopeful? You told me he was optimistic. You made it sound like nothing. That it would be fine.

EDISON: He was optimistic this summer, but now, well . . . he says the only change is that's it's gotten bigger. She doesn't want to live like this, Georgie. She was in pain every day with the radiation. She just asked for a few weeks off. That's all. We're going to go back this week and start up again.

GEORGIE: I know she's in pain, but she has to go every day. It'll cure her.

EDISON: I love her, Georgie. It's been twenty-eight years we've been together. The only thing your mother's ever asked of me in all that time is to stop drinking, make peace with you, and help her through this. This is the help *she* wanted. You don't let someone you love stay in pain even if it means you might risk losing them.

GEORGIE: I don't understand. We can take her to other specialists. Those doctors don't know everything. I don't understand. How could you both keep me in the dark? I never knew . . . I mean, you both let me think she was getting better.

EDISON: She wanted you to stay at school. She knows how you love it.

GEORGIE: I don't care about school! Screw school! She's my mother. I won't go back now. If I had known . . . I would have come home immediately. Are you saying she's going to . . .

EDISON: I don't know. *(He moves in.)* All I know is that she's in a lot of pain.

GEORGIE: You can't give up, Dad, or she'll see it in your eyes! It's this house, this studio—it is full of death. It always was. With all that drinking and depression. I won't let you feel hopeless. I want to see her. *(Shaking her father violently.)* I won't give up! I won't let her die. I refuse to let her! I want to see her, Dad! You'll kill her!

EDISON: *(Grabs her tightly and hugs her hard.)* It's all right, baby. It's all going to be all right.
(She cries in his arms.)

SACRIFICES

Jay, 18, was put into prison at age 15. He was a drug dealer. He was also charged for his involvement in a murder. Jay was a bright kid who had been doing well in school before this occurred, but family chaos drove him to search out companions. Unfortunately, they were the wrong companions. All of his friends belonged to a gang. Jay found their deep commitment to each other inviting. His loyalty to them overrode his loyalty to his abusive, drugged-out father and his passive mother. Though his sister and mother begged Jay to sever ties with the gang, he got more deeply involved with them, selling drugs and skipping school. His mother even threw out her no-good husband to calm Jay's home atmosphere, hoping to convince him to get out of the gang. But he didn't get out. Currently, his mother and sister visit the prison infrequently because it breaks their hearts when they do. Today, Stacey, 17, is visiting her brother, Jay, in prison to ask him an important question.

JAY: It's been a long time. Haven't heard from you all in a long while.

STACEY: Mom was here a month ago, right?

JAY: Try three months ago. For a *whole* hour.

STACEY: Well, it's been a hard time, Jay. Real crazy busy too.

JAY: Oh yeah. Me too. Life's real crazy busy here too.

STACEY: Look, I know it's hard to understand, but Mom and I can't stand—

JAY: *(Getting angry.)* I'm busy *all* the time! I'm living in a giant roach motel, see? It's a real motel kinda place. The accommodations suck. Anyway, I got a lot of exterminations to handle. So real busy. Real, real busy here! You can stomp all you want, but they don't die. Nothing vile ever dies here.

Ever. The more vile, the more it won't die. The cockroaches are like little Arnold Schwarzeneggers—they're huge and foreign. Like eight inches long or somethin'. I'm a fan of the rats actually cause they eat 'em.

STACEY: That's gross. That's disgusting.

JAY: If you think *that's* bad, you can imagine what it's like to watch the guys eat the rats then.

STACEY: *(Disgusted.)* Uuh.

JAY: I'll bring you one of my cell mates next time you visit. Not one of the guys, the giant roaches. *If* you visit. Big *if* there.

STACEY: Look, are we gonna start this again, Jay?

JAY: *(Shakes his head.)* Nah, I'm not startin', Stace. *(Sharp, teasing.)* I was just saying that you can take a creature back to your biology class—a little souvenir of your visit with your loser brother, the inmate. You can do a whole show-and-tell on it. Maybe you can even dissect it for Ms. Hampton to get some extra credit. The anatomy of the prison creature—not pretty—no, but oh so interesting.

STACEY: Look, I'm sorry, Jay.

JAY: I'd volunteer my body to your science class if I thought it would get Mom's attention. But I doubt she'd even notice. But, hey, don't be sorry. None of you. I know, you all got a life. And I, I got the talk shows—Oprah, Rosie, and the psychobabble flavor of the month.

STACEY: Okay. So this is the guilt trip part of the visit.

JAY: *(Seriously.)* It's not just a guilt trip. I'm trying to tell you something. I'm trying to tell you that it's hard as hell being here. Every day I wish I were dead. But what's harder than that is thinking no one cares whether I die or not. No one ever visits. Visits give me some spirit to go on another month or two. Because then I actually think maybe you do care.

STACEY: Oh, Jay. I want to come more often. I just can't stand to see you here. I'm frustrated, ya know? I know what you're capable of. I know what you can do.

JAY: Me capable? Still? In what way? Think about it. I'm an

eighteen-year-old with no education, no friends, a mother
and sister who don't seem to give a good . . . whatever. And
I'm facing ten more years in this hellhole. I don't think I'm
capable of anything anymore. But, hey, maybe you could
fill me in.

STACEY: *(Beat.)* Hope. You're still capable of hope. But every
time I come I see how you've given up, given in. Just like
you did with the gang. And school. I hate that! It's not like
you!

JAY: No, it's not like *you*!

STACEY: You could be out in less than five years. You'd be
under twenty-three. That's a beginning.

JAY: Can you really blame me for losing hope in a place like
this?

STACEY: Who else can I blame? For being here in the first
place. I mean, I'm pissed at you! You had brains! You were
smart, and you just threw it all away!

JAY: Yeah, I also had a father who liked to shoot up and throw
me down stairs daily. And a mother who just let it happen.

STACEY: Oh, come on. She didn't just let it happen. I lived
there too. She tried to get help. She threw him out way
before you were even arrested the first time.

JAY: Ten years too late.

STACEY: She tried to get you away from those guys. We begged
you over and over.

JAY: Yeah, whatever.

STACEY: How dare you?! Mom did everything she could. She
took on two jobs to keep you at St. Joseph's. She knew you
needed a good school. She did everything she could—

JAY: *(Yells.)* I know!! *(Beat.)* But where was *he*? Doped up
maybe? Hangin' with some woman maybe? Where was he?
Selling some stuff? Beatin' on her face? But did she dump
him? Did she ever notice that I had to protect her over and
over again? That I had to fend for my own life with him?!
Did she?!

STACEY: Yeah, she noticed. She just didn't know what to do.

JAY: *(Laughing.)* Oh yeah, that's an easy answer. I stayed with them to escape from Dad. Because I had to.

STACEY: Yeah? You had to? I told you those "friends" would get you arrested or dead within a year. I told you what would happen, Jay. You knew the drug dealing was gonna get you. But you made your own decision. So stop blaming Mom! And everyone else!

JAY: Why did she stay with him for thirteen years? Do you ever wonder that?

STACEY: *(Shrugs.)* She loved him.

JAY: Why?

STACEY: For what he was when she first met him I guess. Not what he was to us. I don't think we ever knew him—the real him. Until maybe now. I do. And good or bad, he is our father, Jay. Not a beast.

JAY: Well, he may be *your* father, but he's not mine. I don't have one.

STACEY: He'd like to visit you.

JAY: *(Beat.)* Since when?

STACEY: He's been begging Mom for the last few months. She didn't say anything because she knows how you feel about him.

JAY: Let him beg. I'm not going to see him. I'd kill him if I saw him.

STACEY: He just wants to meet once. He's changed. Trust me.

JAY: Great. Great news for him. Get a little rehab, did he?

STACEY: Yes, actually. He's been drug-free for the last couple of years. He's different. Nicer. More quiet than anything. He's even a good listener I've found.

JAY: *(Sarcastically.)* Oh great. He oughta counsel. And I'm sure he's suddenly taken God as his Lord and Savior too.

STACEY: Well, as a matter of fact . . .

JAY: I knew it! Of course he turned to God so he can be forgiven for his sins. *(Beat.)* Wait a minute. You don't expect me to forgive him? *(Stacey doesn't speak.)* Oh man! You've got to be kidding me? Forgive and forget, is that it? Well,

I won't forgive. Because I can't forget. Every night I dream—the screams, the torture, the thrown furniture, the broken bones and bruises. I dream about it. I try to stay awake so I won't dream, but I can't. I scream in my sleep. I've scared the other inmates. I dream about your bruised face on Halloween. And watching Mom's glasses shatter one night and hiding under my bed with the wires digging straight into my back because I was so terrified of him. You know! How do you forget these things?! How?! How do you forget them all?!

STACEY: I didn't forget. I can't either. But I put them away.

JAY: Where? Where do you put them? I've tried that. But they don't stay put away. *(Beat.)* Why do you think I joined those guys? To help me forget everything. To just hang out and shoot pool. And when we got to beat the crap out of somebody, I was ready.

STACEY: Mom and Dad made a lot of mistakes. We all did. But at least we're all still alive. We have a chance to set things right.

JAY: Oh really? This is alive? Ya know, if this is alive, I'll tell ya, I'd like to be dead. Dead sounds nice. Maybe that's what you could do. Bring me some dead pills. I wish sometimes *I* was the dead kid lying on the floor that night.

STACEY: Don't say that.

JAY: Why not?

STACEY: I thought you said it was horrifying—his death.

JAY: No, watching AJ shoot the kid was horrifying. Real unexpected, ya know? I thought we were going to rough him up a bit for snitching, but I didn't think . . . Yeah, that shot was . . . There was so much blood. The sound was so loud—the shot was so loud. And I couldn't get my head around what had just happened. *(Beat.)* But actually, looking at his face, the kid's face, afterwards, lying there so quiet, he seemed real peaceful. And happy.

STACEY: So kill yourself. Be happy just like him. Throw away your brains. Your chance to reverse this life. Your chance to tell stories. And write. You still write?

JAY: *(Shrugs. Beat.)* Some.

STACEY: There must be lots of material to draw from in here.

JAY: I already had plenty.

STACEY: You could get a GED.

JAY: I already did.

STACEY: You did? That's great news!

JAY: Yeah, whoopee. I'm working on college credit now. All ready for the future. For the big prosperity of my brilliant life. For the hope to come back.

STACEY: Well, you must have some hope already or you wouldn't be doing all that. And I think it might help everyone if you—

JAY: I know what you're gonna say. I'm not lettin' him. I don't give a hell how he's changed.

STACEY: He begged me to convince you. He's here. Outside.

JAY: What?! How dare you?! Tell him to go home!

STACEY: He just wanted five minutes to say hello. To, to apologize.

JAY: To apologize? And I'm just supposed to accept it? *(She's silent.)* Don't you get it? He's why I'm here! This is his fault! I don't care what you say. He ruined our lives. He continues to ruin mine! Every few minutes I think about how much I hate him! How I'd like to slam his head into those prison bars just like he slammed me day in and day out for ten years. Slam, slam, slam, slam, slam, slam, slam—

STACEY: He's dying.

JAY: *(Beat.)* What?

STACEY: You don't have to kill him. He's dying.

JAY: *(Beat.)* Oh. That explains the God thing then. And the rehab. Everybody always gets all religious and repentant when they're dying. They suddenly see the light. Get all Mother Theresa–like. They suddenly get real scared about going to hell. Well, he can apologize to his God almighty. He doesn't need to apologize to me. Because I don't accept.

STACEY: And that's it? That's final? You don't even want to see him for five minutes?

JAY: What's wrong with him?

STACEY: Cancer. Lung at first. But now it's spread.

JAY: *(Beat.)* Why now? I mean, why didn't he come to my trial if he was so sorry?

STACEY: He did. *(Jay's eyes widen.)* He sat outside the courtroom. Left before you'd see him. He didn't want to upset you.

JAY: *(Beat.)* I don't understand. I don't understand how I'm supposed to forgive him. Or why I should give him the satisfaction.

STACEY: Maybe he's not the only one who'd benefit from it.

JAY: What do you mean?

STACEY: I mean, maybe it would free you—free all that anger you've been holding onto. Of all that anger that you don't know where to put.

JAY: Maybe it would just make me more angry. That he does this now. So he's dead and off the hook. Where were his apologies when I was seven, hiding under the bed with the metal springs digging into my back? Where was he then with all his "sorries"? *(She shakes her head.)* He's really here?

STACEY: Yeah. He was silent the whole way. I think he was praying you'd say yes.

JAY: I'm sorry, Stace. I know you mean well, but I can't talk to him. I can't let him off the hook. He can die like I've lived—thinking I'm a horrible person!

STACEY: Come on, can't you reconsider this a little bit?

JAY: No! I'm not going to reconsider! I can still make choices here! That's all I have. This is my decision, so keep out of it.

STACEY: Jay, don't be stubborn! Listen to me this time! This will eat at you for the rest of your life. This is a chance to put it to rest. You don't have to see him after today. Just hear him out. You don't even have to accept his apology.

But he'll validate everything you've said and more. He did with me. And his words will put things to rest!

JAY: How could I trust that he would validate anything? How could I trust him at all?

STACEY: You trust me, don't you? I've never steered you wrong.

JAY: But I hate him, Stace. I hate him like no one else I've ever known. Why should I give him the satisfaction?

STACEY: Because it may stop the dreams. I don't know for sure, but it's worth a shot. Right? There's no point in hating and wanting to kill him anymore, Jay, he's dying. He's gone.

JAY: Yeah. Well, tell him to come back some other time. I'll think about it maybe.

STACEY: He only has a month or two. So I don't know if there'll be another time. I beg you, Jay, be stubborn with anything else, but this once, listen to me! Do this for you. Do this so you can hear how right you've been all along. So you can hear him say, yes—that's the truth of what happened. He wants to admit it was his fault, so you'll know you're not a horrible person. Then maybe you wouldn't hate yourself so much. And you'd find some hope again. You don't have to forgive him. You can just listen if you want. *(Beat.)* What do you say? *(Long pause.)*

JAY: *(Firmly.)* Five minutes.

NEIL

Kara, 32, and Robert, 35, a very happily married couple, had a baby four weeks ago. Sadly, they never had the chance to bring their baby home. Kara received glowing reports of her baby's health during the course of the pregnancy, but for some reason, the baby had been terribly overdue. After her doctor induced it, Kara spent thirty agonizing hours in labor. Finally, her obstetrician decided to give her a cesarean section. When baby Neil was born, he could not breathe or function on his own. He survived less than a week in the hospital connected to a ventilator and other medical devices. The doctors told them that there was no hope. The baby would not survive unless he remained on the medical equipment, and eventually the baby would die anyway. Kara and Robert had no choice but to take their Neil off life support. It is a little more than a month after the baby's death.

KARA: You got home early, huh?

ROBERT: My appointment with the Schmidts was over like that. They just wanted to look at this short-term investment plan. They whip through paperwork like no other customers I have. Most geriatric types pore over every *and, or,* and *but.*

KARA: Did you pull a fast one on the old folks?

ROBERT: No, I think they tried to pull a fast one on me. They tried to sell me some shares of Schevoka, this start-up their nephew's doing.

KARA: Schevoka?

ROBERT: Exactly. That's what I said. Actually, I couldn't pull a fast one on them. Mrs. Schmidt is either damn lucky or the sharpest investor I know. *(Beat.)* Besides, they were sweet.

KARA: So you told them?

ROBERT: No. They must have heard. Mr. Schmidt and my father both belong to the Kiwanis together.

KARA: Oh.

ROBERT: So you hungry for some spaghetti? I thought it might finally stir your appetite.

KARA: I know you're worried, Robert. I just haven't been hungry. It's not like I'm going to waste away. I think it's even natural. You want some wine?

ROBERT: No. Thanks. I best slow down on that. Don't you want to slow down too?

KARA: No. No reason to slow down. You smell good.

ROBERT: It's the cologne you gave me this summer. *(Starting to rub her shoulders.)* You like it?

KARA: It's nice. Really nice, hon. *(Pause.)* I just . . . so you know . . . I'm not in the mood for anything romantic . . .

ROBERT: I didn't mean to suggest that we'd do anything romantic. I didn't mean to suggest . . . I'm—not in the mood either.

KARA: I know. I just wanted that out there. Ya know?

ROBERT: Sure.

KARA: You're very nice to cook for me every night.

ROBERT: Hey, you eat bon-bons on the couch well. I cook well. We all have to use our strengths in our partnerships.

KARA: Very true. *(Pause.)* Robert, I have something that I should—Hell, why don't I just call it good news. I have good news, Robert.

ROBERT: Yeah? What's that?

KARA: Well . . . well, I quit my job.

ROBERT: *(Pause, perplexed.)* That's good news?

KARA: To me it is.

ROBERT: I don't get it. Why? You never complained about your job.

KARA: That's because I didn't care about my job when I was pregnant. I only cared about Neil. I just wanted something that would allow me flexibility. But now, I just, I don't know. I realize how mediocre it is. And I don't want to do mediocre most of my day. Besides, I need more time. I just feel depressed about going back. I feel like everything got skipped over. I haven't absorbed it yet. It all feels like this terrible nightmare. Like it never really happened.

ROBERT: What? His death?

KARA: No. His birth. My pregnancy. Us. Everything. Like we never even conceived him. Of course, I know that's not true, but I think it sometimes. I never got to absorb, Robert. Having him. It all happened so fast. God, there were glowing reports on everything and suddenly he's stuck on a million machines. I got to give him one bath and change him, and then suddenly, I'm telling my parents that he won't make it—we have to pull the plug. I'm watching him take his last breath. He kept breathing so much longer than we expected, didn't he? I didn't even cry. I didn't feel anything.

ROBERT: It may take years to deal with it, Kara. That's what they said in the group. In the meantime, you have to stay active.

KARA: I know. And in the meantime, my job seems stupid, and frivolous. Who cares in the larger scheme of things, Robert?

ROBERT: Well, I thought we were working toward buying a house next year? I thought that was important to both of us?

KARA: That was when we thought we needed more space to raise a family. I didn't say I wouldn't get another job. I will. Just give me more time.

ROBERT: Going to work has been great for me. It gets my mind off it. It gives me a sense of routine. I need that for my mental health. That's why I think it will help you.

KARA: Fine! Great! I'm not you! I don't always just "do." *(Beat.)* I don't know. Just so you know, I have been tossing around other possibilities for jobs. I've always had this idea that I might want to go into teaching . . . so I thought I might try substituting.

ROBERT: Do you know how little that pays?

KARA: Yeah. So what? It's not like we can't get by on your salary.

ROBERT: This isn't fair. You don't quit your job without at least discussing it with your husband. It's common decency. I really think I would be a lot more receptive to this if I would have had warning. But just out of the blue? Just give two weeks and quit . . . out of the blue?

KARA: I didn't give them two weeks. I told them this was my last day.

ROBERT: Wonderful.

KARA: I didn't want to work there anymore.

ROBERT: Well, it's not like I want to sit around talking financial management 101 with every customer I have. It's really boring to me too.

KARA: So quit. I swear I won't give you a hard time.

ROBERT: Yeah, right. I know things feel stupid or even miniscule in importance to what's happened to us, but I mean, at some point, Kara, you've got to pick up and . . .

KARA: And what? Move on? Is that what you were going to say? That I need to move on?

ROBERT: No, I wasn't going to say that.

KARA: Good. Cause that sounds like "get over it." Which in case you didn't realize, is pretty hard to do since every bit of my waking life for the last nine months has been in anticipation, in preparation, for my child, our child.

ROBERT: I know. I know.

KARA: I prepared every day for what we'd do . . . how we'd celebrate Halloween, Thanksgiving, Christmas. I'd think about how I'd wake him or he'd wake me every morning. We'd be all sleepy-eyed and cranky. Don't you ever think about those things?

ROBERT: *(Looking down.)* I try not to actually.

KARA: Every day I go into his bedroom to look at everything. I want to see that it was real. That he was real. You never go anywhere near his bedroom.

ROBERT: I can't.

KARA: Well, I can't help but go in there. I need to feel everything, Robert, not just go back to work and pretend it never happened. Priorities feel different. Other things have taken on more importance.

ROBERT: Like what? Being online?

KARA: Why does that irritate you so much?

ROBERT: Because I don't understand why you want to keep torturing yourself with all those women—listening to all that crap about their newborns . . . what they're doing, how they smile or coo or whatever. Doesn't that drive you crazy?

KARA: Yes, but at the same time, we all were so excited for our babies—we bonded . . . I don't know. They're good to talk to. Maybe I need them to give me hope. To say I could have a—okay, maybe it's a little like torture.

ROBERT: You don't even know those people, Kara. Why would you have to talk to them? You never even met them. You have real friends in life.

KARA: Yes, I have friends in life, but most of them don't even call and ask me how I'm doing. I know they're afraid they are going to upset me by bringing it up, but it's not like I'm thinking about anything else. So just talk to me. But they don't. So I talk to these women online. At least, they give me support and hope. Hell, at least they talk about it. They're willing to talk about it, which is more than you do.

ROBERT: I talk about it. We've talked about it so much. There is nothing more I can say right now.

KARA: You cook for me, and you hold my hand, and you take care of me, but you don't talk about him. I need to talk about him.

ROBERT: Sometimes I don't know what to say. No words come.

KARA: I feel like there's this stuff underneath that you don't say. Like you're thinking something about . . . things but you don't say it. This whole week you just shut the door and watched TV.

ROBERT: It had nothing to do with you. I just need to shut down sometimes.

KARA: It's bad enough that we lost our son, but now I feel like I'm losing you. We can't even communicate anymore. I just don't understand how you don't need to talk about him all the time because I do. So then when I bring him up, I feel like I'm bringing you down.

ROBERT: I don't feel that. I don't.

KARA: I don't want to forget him! Ever!

ROBERT: I don't either!

KARA: I was proud of him.

ROBERT: So was I!

KARA: So why didn't you tell me that?

ROBERT: I thought it would make you feel worse.

KARA: How could I feel worse? We had him, and we lost him. But we *had* him. We should be doing as other parents do— bragging about our child shamelessly. Instead we're in silence. You always with your head down like we should be ashamed. *(She folds over.)* Uhhh. *(Sighs.)* It's just my stomach again.

ROBERT: Maybe this whole talk is making you sick.

KARA: No. It's not making me sick. I want to talk about it. I want to say I'm in pain. I don't feel like eating, and maybe I am drinking too much, but what do you expect?

ROBERT: I just don't feel comfortable with the whole drinking thing.

KARA: And the TV isn't your drug of choice? We all have our drugs. Look, Robert, I don't always do things neat and easy like you. I'm messy. Occasionally, completely unreasonable. But you knew I was like that when you married me. I didn't pull any surprises on you. I want to scream at the top of my lungs at some of our friends who never came to see him. I screamed at Lucy today. And you know what? It scared her to death. I didn't care. She's supposed to be one of my closest friends and she wasn't there.

ROBERT: I think she didn't know what was proper. The same with George. They felt awkward.

KARA: Well, screw awkward! Life's awkward. Ignoring us or not calling us for weeks is awkward. It makes it all the worse. You know it too. Why do you have to be so damn diplomatic and forgiving of people? Doesn't anything ever piss you off?

ROBERT: *(Thinking.)* His dying pissed me off.

KARA: At me?

ROBERT: *(Taken aback.)* What?! Of course not!

KARA: Cause I kept thinking you might blame me for not insisting about the C-section earlier.

ROBERT: And that's your fault?!

KARA: I don't know. I guess I thought that—maybe thought that—

ROBERT: No. If anything, I was angry at *me* for not demanding more from the doctor. I'm supposed to protect you . . . so is he. Here you were exhausted and obviously suffering and I should have said something. I should have demanded more from Dr. Barton.

KARA: Let's just say "Dr. Barton SUCKS" real loud.

ROBERT: Why?

KARA: Don't think. Just do for once. Will you? We can count to five and scream like crazy.

ROBERT: I don't think I can.

KARA: He's not here. We won't hurt his feelings. Let's scream it continuously. As loud as we can. One, two, three. *(Counting off with her fingers. Kara encourages him.)*

ROBERT/KARA: Dr. Barton Sucks! Dr. Barton Sucks! Dr. Barton Sucks! Dr. Barrrrrrrrtoooonnnn Suuuuuuuuucks!

KARA: *(Starts singing.)* Dr. Barton Suuuuuuccckkkkkks! Dr. Barton Succkkkkkssss

ROBERT: *(Yelling now.)* Succckkkkkkkkkkkkks. *(It grows in pitch to a real scream. He collapses.)*
(Kara stares for a moment—shocked by his outpouring.)

KARA: *(Long pause.)* Robert . . . ?

ROBERT: I'm fine. *(He stands.)* I'm sorry.

KARA: No. Don't be. It sounds stupid, but I think I heard you in that. *(Beat.)* Are you okay? Are you crying?

ROBERT: *(Turns.)* No. I only cry on the trains to and from work.

KARA: What?

ROBERT: I cry on the train. Behind my paper. I've done it for the past two weeks. I didn't tell you.

KARA: Why not?

ROBERT: I was supposed to stay strong. I wanted to stay strong.

KARA: Oh Robert. You don't have to be strong. You are strong.

ROBERT: It's safe with nobody I know there. I pass the places I would have taken him—the ballpark. I think about the places I've been in my life, and everything I've ever wanted passes by in the window and he, my beautiful son . . . passes . . . in the window . . . Then I just start . . . I never intend on it.

KARA: It's okay. *(She hugs him.)* I understand.

ROBERT: Do you think we will ever be happy again?

KARA: Yeah. We will. *(Pause.)* I love you, Robert.

IN MY DREAMS . . . IN
MY IMAGINATION

Lauren, 24, the oldest child in a large Catholic family, has never felt particularly close to her father, Bruce, 55. It's not as if Bruce would wish this. He loves his daughter. He even greatly admires her intelligence, warmth, and efficiency. In fact, when she was a teenager, he fostered her talents by having her work at his own engineering firm. "She was the best employee ever!" She always looked fondly on those days. The problem for Bruce is that he never knew how to really talk to his girls, in particular, to Lauren. She was always a bit too "literary"—her friends too arty. As the years passed, Lauren moved away from Indiana to Chicago to pursue her interest in theater. Bruce threw up his hands. How could she waste her mind and take such risks? But nothing would prepare him for the announcement she made eight months ago. Lauren told both her parents that she was a lesbian and had fallen in love with a woman. Bruce reacted quickly and strongly. He scolded her behavior, calling her selfish and ungodly. In the end, he left her apartment in a fit of discomfort. In the months since, when she visits, things remain strained. This weekend, when Lauren returns home, she feels she must broach this subject. She finds him staring down at the pool.

BRUCE: You kids enjoy the pool, you love the pool, but none of you have a clue how to take care of it. I have to practically knock John's block off to get him to clean the damn thing. All you kids know how to do is have conversations. All these deep conversations where do they get you?

LAUREN: Are you referring to the conversation I was having with Mom?

BRUCE: No. That I would not call a conversation. I tell you, my father would slam my head into the wall if I talked back the way John does to me these days.

LAUREN: Why wouldn't you call that a conversation?

BRUCE: Because I wouldn't. The volume for one thing.

LAUREN: I wasn't yelling and neither was Mom.

BRUCE: Anyway, it doesn't matter.

LAUREN: Yes it does. Do you know what we were talking about?

BRUCE: I don't *want* to know what you were talking about.

LAUREN: You know exactly what we were talking about. You're just pretending not to.

BRUCE: Right. That makes sense.

LAUREN: Which is why you came out here in the first place. Looking at the pool, checking the pH. You already did all that last night.

BRUCE: That's because it's off again. Look, if you want to talk about something specific, Lauren—let's talk. Otherwise I don't know what you want from me.

LAUREN: She wanted me to come home for her Fourth of July picnic. I refused.

BRUCE: She doesn't realize that the drive from Chicago is a pain in the butt in bad traffic.

LAUREN: The drive's not the reason. I would make the drive in a second if . . .

BRUCE: So you've got plans. I don't blame you. You're young. I'd get out of it too. Lord knows I can't take that potato salad she makes every year. I love your mother, but God help us, that is the worst crap I've ever tasted.

LAUREN: I agree, but that still has nothing to do with it.

BRUCE: She'll get over it. It's no big deal. I thought you were going to bring your car over to Buddy's today so he could check your transmission while you're home?

LAUREN: I haven't had any problems with it since I brought it into the shop.

BRUCE: Well you might want to double-check their work. Those folks could be ripping you off. They fix it so it'll break again. I know.

LAUREN: I had a recommendation for the place I took it to.

BRUCE: Recommendation or not, you really ought to take advantage of Buddy while you're home. He's happy to do it. He does a great job. I think he's got a little thing for you.

LAUREN: I know he has a little thing for me, which is exactly why I don't want to go there.

BRUCE: You don't have to marry the guy. He's just lonely. Just talk to him.

LAUREN: I don't want to talk about my car. My car is fine, Dad!

BRUCE: Fine! I was just trying to get ya a deal. I know you've been having trouble with money.

LAUREN: I'm not having trouble with money.

BRUCE: Oh yeah? They finally give you that raise?

LAUREN: Well, sort of—

BRUCE: Aw, Lauren, I thought they were giving you a raise right away?

LAUREN: They are! The paperwork hasn't gone through yet.

BRUCE: Didn't you tell me that on Mother's Day? Get paid what you're worth, honey. My admin makes forty-two thousand and we're talking Indiana. And you're doin' much more than her!

LAUREN: Are we done with the laundry list?

BRUCE: Laundry list? You want to do my laundry?

LAUREN: You know, the things you use to distract us from really talking. The car, the job, my health. Are we almost done? Because everything is fine. The car's fine, the job's fine, and my health's absolutely perfect. And thanks for asking.

BRUCE: You've got to tell them you're willing to go elsewhere if you really want a raise, Lauren.

LAUREN: Urgh. I'm not talking about the raise! Screw the

raise! I don't want to come home because she won't let me bring Sarah.

BRUCE: *(Pause.)* I'm going to go get Brian to help me finish the yard.

LAUREN: Did you hear me? You do remember Sarah?

BRUCE: I heard you, and I'm not discussing this.

LAUREN: We need to discuss it.

BRUCE: No. I don't need to discuss anything. We're at my house, under my roof, and it's my day off. All right?

LAUREN: No. It's not all right.

BRUCE: Well, then go home. Nobody's keeping you here. You can go home to your friends and your crazy lifestyle and talk till your heart's content about everything making your mother sicker than a dog right now.

LAUREN: Oh please. You both do that. You try to make me feel guilty or feel sorry for one or the other of you. How do you think I feel about the way you guys are reacting? I know Mom's unhappy, but she talks to me occasionally when I force the issue. You're afraid.

BRUCE: Afraid? No, sweetheart, I'm not afraid. I just don't want to get angry on my day off. I don't want to get into it with you on my weekend. I don't want to tell you how many ways I think it's wrong.

LAUREN: How can loving someone be so wrong?

BRUCE: Because it's not natural for you to love a woman like that.

LAUREN: Why not? You do!

BRUCE: Don't be stupid, Lauren.

LAUREN: I'm not stupid! I'm really asking you.

BRUCE: It's selfish and unhealthy and completely against God's will, but you know all that. So I don't know why you need me to say it. I don't want to think about it in the first place.

LAUREN: How is it selfish? That confuses me.

BRUCE: You could have been a doctor, a lawyer, a teacher. You had a great mind. Great grades. The best in the family. You would have been a real example to the rest of them.

LAUREN: Oh, I was suppose to set an example instead of doing what I cared about, what I loved?

BRUCE: What difference did it make? You're working in admin just like I told you. What did that degree buy you? You had so much to give to the world.

LAUREN: I think theater does give to the world. Besides, I thought you told me I was talented.

BRUCE: You are talented. But being an actress is not practical, which you've discovered, no matter how talented you are. And it's not a giving profession. In fact, it's the most selfish, self-absorbed, self-involved profession that ever existed. That's the problem. It draws those people. Weird, unhealthy people who obviously influenced you in this.

LAUREN: Nobody influenced me. I was born like this. I just pushed it so far down my whole life. I remember when I was a kid, when I was a teenager. You must remember too.

BRUCE: Remember what? You were a normal kid.

LAUREN: Yes. But I always liked girls. And I'm normal now even despite that.

BRUCE: I'm not going to change my mind about this, Lauren, so why bother talking about it?

LAUREN: Think about it scientifically, logically. A person's genetic makeup is determined by random selection. It's a random occurrence. You get a blonde in a family of brunettes.

BRUCE: There're no recognizable genes for that as far as I know.

LAUREN: Well it's not as if it's been studied for that long.

BRUCE: If it's so normal, why doesn't the government recognize it? Can you get married? Live legally as a married couple together?

LAUREN: You can live together legally in Vermont. You may not be able to get married, but you certainly can live together legally.

BRUCE: One state and you know that'll be overturned in a year. Why isn't the majority of society applauding it?

LAUREN: Because most of society is closed-minded I guess.

BRUCE: And if you want to get graphic, why can't you reproduce? Why can't you make children together if it's so natural?

LAUREN: I don't know. I can't answer that. It's a biological way to keep population at a reasonable level.

BRUCE: Oh come on! Bull—

LAUREN: We can have children if we want. It's done all the time.

BRUCE: Now don't tell me you're going to have children. That would be completely unforgivable.

LAUREN: So how come you didn't mention that "society thing" about Sandy's marriage? Do you think most of society applauds interracial marriage?

BRUCE: You can't even equate the two. Your sister married a man.

LAUREN: A black man. Forty years ago they wouldn't be allowed to be married in our church. Do you know the uproar it would have caused? Society would not be applauding. Society learns things. Learns about other people, understands differences. It's really not that big of a deal. And since when did you take your cue from society at large?

BRUCE: *(Shaking his head.)* You're grasping for straws now. The situations aren't even similar.

LAUREN: Why can't you just get to know Sarah? Meet her as a person? See what you think? Maybe you'll actually like her.

BRUCE: You're not to bring her here. Ever.

LAUREN: She is the most important thing in my life now. And I can't even talk about her—mention her without you leaving the room or Mom giving me the silent treatment. Do you know how that makes me feel?

BRUCE: We love you, Lauren. Always. Your mother and I are just not going to accept this part of you. Ever. We can't tell you what to do with your life anymore. You're all grown up. We just pray that you rethink this.

LAUREN: It's not a thinking thing. It's how I feel and it wins out. Because that's what's in my gut. And that's what you taught me. To follow my gut.

BRUCE: I taught you that? Well, I don't remember telling you to ignore your mind either.

LAUREN: You taught *all* of us that. Why do you think we're all so incredibly different and gutsy and fearless? None of us have taken an easy road. None of us have followed "societal rules." Even religion—your religion, doesn't tell us to listen to society.

BRUCE: But not about this. There's no question it's wrong.

LAUREN: God, Dad, don't you remember how badly it hurt when Mom's parents rejected you? As I remember from you, they didn't even want to speak to you.

BRUCE: I respected them. I understand their reaction even more now. Your grandparents believed in the Baptist religion wholeheartedly. I don't think I'd be too happy if a man came along and wanted to convert *my* daughter.

LAUREN: It just feels unfair. It's so unfair. Tanya gets pregnant before marriage. You're pissed but she gets a huge wedding and all kinds of lavish attention. Sandy and Derrick get a bigger and more beautiful wedding and everyone's thrilled beyond belief once they get used to the idea of a black man. The boys manage to get themselves constantly in and out of trouble—give you weeks and years of worries. And then there's me. Lauren, who got the good grades and made the strange choices. Who never caused you a moment's worry. At least before I became another screwup. The oldest who was supposed to set the example. Lauren, who is alone at every single family event. Whose relatives look at her with pity and sadness because she never seems to find anyone. I'm not an ugly woman. I'm pretty. I'm smart. I'm fun. Don't they even begin to wonder? And as the months go by, I think someday you'll mention what I told you about myself one November afternoon. Maybe you'll start to wonder and read books and talk to me. In my dreams you give me and Sarah a chance. You invite her to a family dinner. It's not comfortable yet, but you actually like her. You see how well she treats me, how much she loves me. And one day, we get married and you're all there. In my dreams.

BRUCE: I'm sorry this hurts you so much. It does the same to me. In my . . . imagination you decide it's all wrong for you. You meet a good man, and I help you find a wonderful house. You have beautiful, smart children who have a talent for music like you do. We all occasionally take a nice vacation together. You show off Europe to me like you've always wanted to. And I spend way over my budget. That's what I wish for.

LAUREN: So. I'm right. *(He doesn't speak. Beat.)* You don't really want to know about my life. What I care about. Ever know the real person I love.

BRUCE: I am happy to hear about your life, Lauren, but not if it includes that. If you were born like this, like you say, maybe you shouldn't be with anyone.

LAUREN: Are you saying you'd rather me be alone for the rest of my life?

BRUCE: *(Sighs.)* Yes. I guess that is what I'm saying.
(Lauren is left without any words. Long pause.)

BRUCE: I'm just asking you to think about it. Pray about it.

LAUREN: No. I think *you* should. Can you open the garage door please?

BRUCE: Where are you going?

LAUREN: Home.

BRUCE: Come on, Lauren. We can function together. We just won't talk about it. I knew there wouldn't be any point anyway.

LAUREN: Forgive me if I don't just want to function together. That's not what I want from my father. I guess there's no point in ever talking about anything. It'll just be more awkward moments and laundry lists that mean nothing.

BRUCE: I know this has caused problems in our relationship.

LAUREN: Relationship? We've never had a relationship, Dad.

You tell me what to do. I listen. And then you tell me what I've done wrong. This just makes it more clear.

BRUCE: No matter what I've said to you about this, you know I love you. I'll always love you.

LAUREN: I love you too, Dad. But that's . . .

BRUCE: That's that. That'll never change.

LAUREN: It's not enough. I'm not even sure it's true. You can't possibly love someone if you can't accept something so fundamental about them. I have to go.

BRUCE: No, now I can't have you leaving like this. This is crazy.

LAUREN: Get out of my way!

BRUCE: I don't want you driving like this. Come on now.

LAUREN: Don't tell me what to do! I'm leaving!

BRUCE: So, when will we see you again?

LAUREN: When you change your mind.

BRUCE: That'll never happen, Lauren. It just won't happen.

LAUREN: Then maybe I'll never be back. *(She hugs her father quickly.)* Good-bye, Daddy.

BRUCE: Don't worry. You'll be back. You'll be back, hon.

WINDOW OF OPPORTUNITY

Julia, 23, and Duncan, 23, have been best friends since first meeting in their college dorms. After school, they decided to live together. They both have a kooky sense of humor and enjoy a periodic game of spying on people in the apartments across the way. Each time, Julia and Duncan pretend they are the characters they are watching. Today, they have their own dramatic scene. As it turns out, Duncan has been in love with Julia for some time, but he has never told her. Here he courageously decides to admit his true feelings for her. However, she has a surprising announcement of her own. As the scene begins, they are watching a couple across the way.

JULIA: *(Looking through binoculars.)* Oooh. Great dress! Why is she wearing a dress?

DUNCAN: *(Looking through binoculars.)* Um, she's formal. Dresses for him maybe.

JULIA: You think? Screw that. God, Dave is lucky when I comb my hair.

DUNCAN: Yeah, well he's lucky in general.

JULIA: Thanks.

DUNCAN: Scenario?

JULIA: Umm, dinner, I think.

DUNCAN: And the relationship?

JULIA: *(Looking.)* Hummm. I'm thinking friends.

DUNCAN: *(Looking.)* Agreed. But with romantic overtones. He pretends he's Chef Monsieur de la Grande Rotisserie. In reality though, he only cooks every few months. Real cooks never wear aprons like that.

JULIA: Agreed. It's a desperate measure. *(Looks up.)* We're going to get arrested for this some day you know?

DUNCAN: Well, *you* will. It's common for men, but for

women—it's just not done. Ever hear of a peeping Thomasina? No. Right? It's very sick.

JULIA: No, it's not. And it's not sexual either. It's innocent curiosity really.

DUNCAN: Yes, that's true, completely innocent.

JULIA: Exactly! The original reality TV, without the TV.

DUNCAN: Yeah, right. So will they get it on tonight or what?

JULIA: Definitely not.

DUNCAN: Oh really now? She's cozying up to him. *(Points.)* See.

JULIA: She's also sneaking gulps of wine when his head turns. She's downing it for a reason.

DUNCAN: Why?

JULIA: It's the end obviously. She's not in love with him anymore. Maybe she loves somebody else.

DUNCAN: How is that obvious? She gives no indication of that at all?

JULIA: Yes she does!

DUNCAN: How?

JULIA: *(Beat.)* Okay. See her body language? See how she's leaning her chest away from him? That is a clear sign of her true desire to get away. And then there's the fingernails.

DUNCAN: Fingernails?

JULIA: Yes, she's not looking at them afraid they might be chipped. They are her savior right now. She's hiding in them, playing with them, giving her eyes a place to look instead of looking at him. If she were hot for him, she'd be using them to her advantage, showing them off—flashing them everywhere. Chopping veggies with her pinky posed. Plus she hasn't done a hair toss once.

DUNCAN: *(Thinking.)* You flipped your hair when you came in. So what does that mean?

JULIA: No, that was different. That was like a sweep, not a toss.

DUNCAN: Oh, right. Just making sure. So . . . Dialogue?

JULIA: *(Going into dialogue as she watches. Put-on voice.)* I'm so nervous tonight, Frederick.

DUNCAN: Frederick? That's a terrible name. He doesn't look like a Frederick.

JULIA: *(Staying in character.)* Ummmmm, Lawrence, wow, that looks beautiful. I love pineapple chicken.

DUNCAN: *(Putting on nondescript accent.)* Oh, Gloria— *(She rolls her eyes.)* that's my problem. Everything always looks great when I cook up a feast. But it's the taste that's the problem. It's the substance of things I can't get a hold of— I disappoint so many.

JULIA: I don't think you disappoint. Except maybe yourself. It's a lack of confidence, Larry.

DUNCAN: Yes, I lack confidence in love I'm afraid.

JULIA: Why is that? Why do you lack confidence?

DUNCAN: Insecurity, I suppose.

JULIA: That's the problem right there. You live in fear. Fear, fear, fear! Why, I ask?

DUNCAN: I have reason—nothing has ever worked out as I wanted. The women who love me, I don't want, and the women I love are completely uninterested.

JULIA: Well! That happens to the best of us! But you have to get back on your horse, Lawrence. You have to remount many times in life. Just swing your leg up and do it! You can't keep pining away for me forever.

DUNCAN: How can I end something that's never really begun, Gloria? That you've never even given a chance to begin?

JULIA: Oh good God, Larry! *(Stopping the act.)* Ooh. I'm sorry. It seems I just lobbed a carrot at your face, Frederick. *(Points.)* Did you see that?

DUNCAN: Yes. And my name's Lawrence, Gloria. Oh my God! Did you just see *that*?!

JULIA: *(Gasps.)* Did she just put a pineapple chunk where I think she did?

DUNCAN: Yep. And he seems to be diving in for it.

JULIA: Oop. There go the blinds.

DUNCAN: Damn! So much for the lack of hair toss.

JULIA: Shut up. It's usually very accurate. She's clearly abnormal.

DUNCAN: *(Smiling.)* Um-hmm. *(Beat.)* So you want to do another?

JULIA: I'd love to, Dunc, truly, but I can't. I've gotta shower before it gets too late.

DUNCAN: For what? I thought you were hanging here tonight?

JULIA: I'm going out with Dave in an hour.

DUNCAN: Again?

JULIA: Well, yeah.

DUNCAN: Geez, you guys are liked glued to each other.

JULIA: Well, it's been getting kind of serious I guess.

DUNCAN: Oh. Really? You were acting like it was so casual.

JULIA: Well, it was. At first. But, well . . . things changed all of a sudden. It got serious.

DUNCAN: What does that mean? You guys have been dating less than five months. How serious can it get? *(Joking.)* I mean, should I be looking for a new roommate?

JULIA: Maybe.

DUNCAN: *(Shocked.)* Are you serious? *(Beat.)* And you didn't even tell me?

JULIA: I don't know. I was going to tell you—you know you'd be the first person I'd tell, I just . . . I didn't say anything because I wasn't absolutely sure yet.

DUNCAN: Not sure about what?

JULIA: About . . . I don't know. Dave and I possibly moving in together.

DUNCAN: Now? *(She nods.)* But that's crazy! You're so young. And, and you haven't even experienced all the major holidays once through yet. You have to do that first. And what about me? You were going to leave me hanging without a roommate? We have a lease. Besides, he's not right for you at all! I think you have totally lost your mind here. It's been like six months and he's not even your type.

JULIA: You know, I didn't ask for your opinion.

DUNCAN: Excuse me. I thought I was your best friend.

JULIA: We're thinking five months from now anyway. When our lease is up. I would never leave you high and dry. I can't believe you said that.

DUNCAN: When the hell did all this come up anyway?

JULIA: You know, I thought you might be happy for me.

DUNCAN: I am happy. I'm happy. I didn't say I wasn't. It's just . . . I've fallen in love with you.

JULIA: What?

DUNCAN: I'm in love with you, Julia. I have been for a long time.

JULIA: Since when? What is this? Where is this coming from? Are you trying to get me to not move out, Duncan? Is this some kind of screwed up game? Because it's not funny.

DUNCAN: No, it's not a game. I was actually planning on telling you tonight. Unbelievable timing.

JULIA: God. I don't know what to say, Dunc. It's not like . . . I just . . . I don't know what to say.

DUNCAN: I guess I'm just making things awkward between us.

JULIA: No. I'm—I know how you feel—

DUNCAN: Here comes the huge "but." The mammoth "but." I know what follows . . . "you're too much like my brother" or "we're too good of friends" or "it just doesn't feel right."

JULIA: I . . . Look, Duncan, I can't say that I wasn't attracted to you or ever wondered sometimes because I did—I have. But for some reason, it never happened and I have to think there was a reason for it. We're good as friends. It's better that way.

DUNCAN: For you maybe. Do you think it never happened because I'm a freakin' chicken and I never told you how I felt?

JULIA: No. It's not that. I mean, I felt the same way about you about a year ago, and I was going to say something, but I felt foolish. If I knew that you . . . Maybe if I hadn't met Dave, something might be possible now, but—

DUNCAN: Oh God! Don't tell me that! Don't tell me any of that! I'm such a jackass.

JULIA: No you're not. Look, you want me to be honest, don't you?

DUNCAN: Yeah.

JULIA: Well . . . The thing is . . . I think I've fallen in love with him.

DUNCAN: No! You can't have! He's all wrong!

JULIA: No, he's not. He's a really good guy. He loves me, and he's good to his family. He's a good communicator when things don't go right. He fixes stuff up around his mother's house. He's a really good guy.

DUNCAN: But he's boring, Julia. And formal. He introduces himself by his first and last name every single time he calls. Every time! I know who he is. You told me yourself that you couldn't stand how long he takes to read the paper every Sunday.

JULIA: I know I said that. But sometimes it's nice to sit around for hours reading the paper and listening to NPR. It's grown on me. Like people who are different from you do.

DUNCAN: He'd never play the Rear Window game, or stay up all hours talking, or play water bomb day, or build a castle on the beach spontaneously. He'll always play by the rules. Go to bed early, pay all his bills on time, eat all his vegetables, and color inside the lines.

JULIA: I know. He's not you, Duncan. And I don't want him to be. Listen, no one can or will replace you. Ever!

DUNCAN: But I love you, Julia. I know I only fully realized it a few months ago, but I've known in my heart for much longer.

JULIA: You know what? This is bull. You had four years to fall in love with me, Duncan. You had four years to act on it. For whatever reason, you didn't. Now someone else is crazy about me and you're suddenly smitten. That doesn't even give you the slightest pause? *(Beat.)* I know you, Duncan. You're whole life has been about competition. Getting the best grades, sweeping the track team finals, competing with other freelancers for the best story. You know what I think? I found someone who loved me, and you got scared that you'd be alone. So suddenly, you're in love, right?

DUNCAN: No, I didn't tell you a couple of years ago because I was too self-involved to notice. Or maybe I was just too afraid you'd reject me.

JULIA: Well, you're stupid for that. Because I wouldn't have rejected you. But now, what I have with David is right, Dunc. I can feel it. And I won't jeopardize that for something I'm not sure of. Sometimes things happen for a reason. *(Beat.)* Come on now, pick yourself up, sir, and get back on the horse. You're a braver man now than you've ever been.

DUNCAN: I'm the dumbest man alive.

JULIA: Brave and dumb. Not a bad combination really. Now, I'll go catch that shower. I'm not leaving tomorrow or anything.

DUNCAN: Maybe I should go to Roger's place for a few days.

JULIA: If you feel you need to, go. I understand. We all get hurt, Duncan. I know you haven't before, but it opens a door in a way—opens up the possibility to something real. Which requires that you be vulnerable sometimes. I'll never throw this in your face or use it to hurt you. Honestly, I'm flattered. Really.

DUNCAN: That's why you suck. I can't even hate you when you're flat out rejecting me. Anyway, get outta here. *(She doesn't move.)* Don't sit there staring at me. Get out, get out!

(She does.)

DUNCAN: *(Beat.)* Get out.

IF ONLY

Shannon, 33, has been in a coma since she and her ten-year-old son were in a head-on collision with an SUV the evening before last. Rob, 35, her husband, has been at their hospital bedsides ever since they arrived. He has had to deal with the questions and needs of doctors, police, friends, and reporters. There is a bit of controversy about the accident, even though it occurred on a foggy night, because Shannon had been drinking at a party. Earlier today, Shannon began to come out of the coma. And now Rob, who has just come to her bedside, has the painful task of explaining to her the extent of her own injuries and those of her son.

ROB: Oh God! *(He hugs her.)* Thank you God! *(Looks at her.)* I love you so much!

SHANNON: I love you too.

ROB: Oh my God. You're awake. God. Don't do that to me. You scared me to death.

SHANNON: Now you're scaring me to death.

ROB: No, no, I'm just so happy.

SHANNON: *(He hugs her hard.)* Oh God. Do I look that bad?

ROB: *(He shakes his head no.)* No. No. You look beautiful.

SHANNON: You're hugging me so hard like I died or something. *(Pause. Looking at him.)* What? What is it?

ROB: *(Beat.)* You were in a coma.

SHANNON: Come on. Are you kidding me? *(Beat.)* A coma? For real?

ROB: Yes. You don't know—I'm just so happy to hold you. *(Beat.)* You okay?

SHANNON: I don't know. I feel pretty rotten. But I don't know how people who wake up from comas are supposed to feel. And anyway that nurse has drugged me up pretty good, so

I don't know how I feel really. She put me on some sort of sedative.

ROB: I know. She wants you to sleep—to get some rest.

SHANNON: Geez, how much rest do I need? I was just in a coma since God knows when.

ROB: Sleep is different I guess.

SHANNON: I guess. She thought I was getting too upset, you know? I want to know how he is.

ROB: I know. I called the nurse's station on my way here. I just went home quickly to shower this morning. Otherwise I've been here the whole time.

SHANNON: I didn't know where I was. I woke up with these two strange women sticking a needle in me. I started my nice steady stream of obscenities and got a little hysterical I guess. I was freaked out, Rob!

ROB: I know. I'm sorry. I can't believe you woke up the one hour I wasn't here.

SHANNON: I can't believe this. This is my worst nightmare. It's like the last thing we need, huh? Life was already givin' us a hell of a time. And how will we ever afford all this—

ROB: We'll be fine. We have insurance. That's the least of our worries.

SHANNON: And what's the worst?

ROB: (Covering.) Nothing. There's nothing to worry about except getting better.

SHANNON: I'm not worried about me. It's Michael I'm concerned about.

ROB: (He nods.) Well he's here. And he's okay.

SHANNON: It was so stupid! I feel so damn stupid! Like all this . . . "if you only did this or you only did that" keeps going through my brain.

ROB: Well stop that.

SHANNON: That's easy to say. You'd feel the same way. I've driven a million times in rainstorms, Rob. I didn't know it was . . . that the visibility would be—How is he? Honestly?

ROB: He's okay.

SHANNON: That means not good. I know you.

ROB: They haven't told me much either.

SHANNON: They had to practically push me back into my bed. I wanted to go see him. So please, please tell me what I've done exactly?

ROB: I am. He's under several doctors' care right now. His main doctor is Dr. Blanch. He seems on top of things. They're running several tests.

SHANNON: God, you make it sound like we've been here for a long time.

ROB: Two days.

SHANNON: Two? Wow. But that's not as bad as I was starting to think.

ROB: *(He nods.)* Well, it's been the longest two days of my life.

SHANNON: I'm sorry. *(He nods.)* So why don't you start with what he does know?

ROB: I don't want to upset you.

SHANNON: Okay, well, now I'm really getting upset so . . .

ROB: He's got a few broken ribs and a broken arm. His face is a little bruised up but that'll heal. *(She nods and gestures for him to proceed.)* They had to do what they call a trac. He couldn't breathe through his nose or mouth. They had to make a little incision through the throat so that he could—

SHANNON: Oh God! He's only a ten-year-old. Do they know that? *(Beat.)* How is he? Is he in pain?

ROB: I don't think so. But uh . . .

SHANNON: What, what?

ROB: He's suffered a head injury.

SHANNON: But he was belted in.

ROB: The seat belt worked enough so he wasn't thrown out of the car—but he hit the windshield.

SHANNON: Jesus! *(Beat.)* So what does this mean exactly?

ROB: There's some brain damage.

SHANNON: *(Beat.)* How bad? *(Beat.)* How bad, Rob? Does this mean he won't stand a chance of being a genius some day or something much worse—something I don't want to think about? What are we talking about here?

ROB: We don't know yet.

SHANNON: Well, why don't they know that?! How many doctors does it take to figure this out? He's been here for two days!

ROB: Relax. You're supposed to relax, Shannon.

SHANNON: How can I relax with what you're telling me? My son is . . . and it was my fault. I'm so stupid!

ROB: It was an accident.

SHANNON: That SUV—that son of a—that SUV was coming so fast. He came right over the center line. The last thing I remember—a couple of headlights coming straight for me. Michael was screaming like crazy.

ROB: It's okay. It's okay.

SHANNON: I want to see him.

ROB: Well you can't right now. Not in your condition.

SHANNON: Screw my condition! He's my son. I want to see him!

ROB: He's in critical care right now, Shannon. They won't let you. Besides, they don't want you to move right now either.

SHANNON: Why not? I can get in a wheelchair. *(Rob shakes his head.)* I can do it. Why not? *(Beat.)* What's really going on here? I have a right to know. It's my body.

ROB: I don't know enough to tell you anything.

SHANNON: Great. Anyway, it would serve me right if I couldn't walk, wouldn't it? For what I've done to Michael.

ROB: They don't know anything for sure. And you don't deserve to be punished for anything.

SHANNON: *(Pause.)* What happened to the other driver? And please, God, don't make it bad news.

ROB: He's okay. A couple of broken bones.

SHANNON: That's all? Honestly? *(He nods.)* Thank God, even though it was his fault. Is his insurance company going to pay? I mean, we need to get Michael to a specialist immediately.

ROB: Why are we talking about all this? The important thing is that you're awake and safe.

SHANNON: Yeah, well what about Michael? Is he awake and safe? We can't wait on these things, Rob. He needs to be seen by the best doctors.

ROB: Can we *not* go into panic mode? Can we *not* go into I'm going to fix-this-right-now-in-an-organized-fashion-and-demand-everything-from-everybody?! I just want to talk to you. I want to be here with you and take you in.

SHANNON: I know, but I feel helpless here. I feel like I have to take charge because I'm responsible. I mean I have to do something. I have to help somehow.

ROB: This time the best way you can help is to rest. Talk to me for awhile. I've been here around the clock since it happened. Your mother and father want to see you right away too.

SHANNON: I can't see them now.

ROB: Why?!

SHANNON: Because I feel like Mom will blame me.

ROB: Are you kidding?

SHANNON: She always manages to do that somehow even when she doesn't mean to.

ROB: Don't you realize that they thought you were dead?! They've been here all night!

SHANNON: Okay, okay, I want to see them, I do, but I need to know what happened first. *(Beat.)* Did you call Fred?

ROB: Your mother did.

SHANNON: Of course.

ROB: He'll take the case. But I'm afraid it's not so . . .

SHANNON: What?

ROB: Not so clear-cut. There's a witness who said it may have been your fault.

SHANNON: What? Well, she's wrong! You don't believe that?

ROB: *(Beat.)* You had a couple of beers at Sarah's party, Shannon.

SHANNON: That was in the afternoon. I ate afterwards. I

didn't leave until five. What are you implying? That I was drunk?

ROB: No.

SHANNON: You think I was drunk? That I put our son in danger? Is that what you're telling me? You're blaming me for this?

ROB: I'm not blaming anyone. I'm just telling you the truth—like you wanted.

SHANNON: This witness said I was drunk?

ROB: *(Shakes his head no.)* No. She said you came over the center line. Sarah and a couple people at the party said you had a few drinks.

SHANNON: *(Exhales.)* I see.

ROB: The police questioned them. *(Beat.)* They ran a blood test here to look at your alcohol levels.

SHANNON: And you just signed the okay with no problem I guess?

ROB: Did I have a choice?

SHANNON: But you *assume* I was drunk?

ROB: I didn't say that. The police didn't tell me the level. But then again it's not as if you've always had the best judgment.

SHANNON: That was a long time ago and you know it.

ROB: I don't know anything right now. All kinds of crazy things have been going through my mind. You don't realize. I've been going through hell the last few days.

SHANNON: Oh yeah, and this is a real picnic for me, Rob!

ROB: I know this is hard for you. I know that! But will you just think of *my* side of things for once?! I've been pacing the halls in this godforsaken place for the last two days, praying you'd be alive. I haven't eaten. I haven't slept. I just wander from room to room asking for more reports about you and Michael. More reports from doctors who just don't know anything. *I've* been furious too. I totally lost it yesterday with some doctor for not doing things fast enough. Furious with all the people asking questions—the police, the insurance company, friends. A million forms to fill out and a million people that I don't know how to deal with. I'm holding your hand for hours while people come in and out acting as if I've already lost you. I want to throw furniture out the window. My whole life has changed in an instant. I don't know if I'm alone in the world. Do you know how that feels? I don't know if my son will ever walk or be able to live with me. I don't know whose fault it is. I should have been with you instead of working on a Saturday. And you shouldn't have driven in that damn weather when you were . . .

SHANNON: *(Beat.)* No . . . I shouldn't have.

ROB: I didn't mean . . . It's just . . . I hear the "if-onlys" in my head too. And all you can do is tell me what I haven't done. What I should have done.

SHANNON: I'm sorry. I guess you're pretty angry with me.

ROB: I don't want to be.

SHANNON: No. *(Beat.)* But you are all the same. I'd be furious at you too, if it were the other way around.

ROB: You would?

SHANNON: *(Nods.)* But the thing is, Rob, I would never put Michael's life in that kind of danger. You can think I'm stupid for driving in that weather. You can think whatever you want about my abilities, but please know that I was not drunk, not even tipsy. Because if I were, I wouldn't have gotten into that car. Not in a million years. *(Beat.)* Do you believe me? I need you to believe me.

(She looks to him for an answer.)

BURNING DOWN THE HOUSE

Tony and Marissa, 30s, have been married for some time. Marissa's quirky hypochondria and obsessive-compulsive behavior has become worse since having their baby a year ago. Lately, her behavior has become less quirky and more harmful to their relationship. In the last few weeks, Tony has received some devastating news about his health. He has Multiple Sclerosis. He cannot bring himself to share the news with Marissa, however, because he believes she will fall apart. Tonight, Tony, who is completely frustrated with Marissa, reveals everything he has been suppressing.

TONY: What are you doing? We're going to be late again.

MARISSA: So we're late. Better to be late than burn down the house. I think I might have left the stove on.

TONY: You didn't. Trust me. Besides, I'm sure Patty will notice. She's a good baby-sitter.

MARISSA: I didn't say she wasn't good. But she's upstairs with Timmy. She won't be anywhere near the kitchen for hours.

TONY: This is the third time we're meeting them late for dinner.

MARISSA: So what? They'll just get a drink. I want to check the stove is all.

TONY: *(He stands in front of the door.)* No.

MARISSA: What? *(Looks at him.)* Okay, I know what you are going to say. What's the big deal? You know I'm like this. I've always been like this.

TONY: Just don't. Okay? Don't. Start by just not doing it once. Stop the thought.

MARISSA: What do you mean, "Stop the thought"? It's no big deal. I just feel like I left the stove on.

TONY: When would you have left the stove on? You didn't cook anything today.

MARISSA: That's not true. I made lunch.

TONY: Yeah, a veggie burger. In the microwave.

MARISSA: But I made tea at some point. I used the kettle.

TONY: Hours ago. We would have noticed if the stove's flame was on.

MARISSA: Maybe I left it on low. That's easy to do without noticing. It's really not that big of a deal. I'll just run in there and make sure it's not on. This conversation is taking longer than if I just checked. Now, you go get the car.

TONY: No. I would let you check it, but you already checked it once. So, no.

MARISSA: No I didn't. When?

TONY: Right before I went to put my jacket on. I saw you in there.

MARISSA: Well, I didn't check it. I maybe looked in that general direction.

TONY: You touched every knob, Marissa. I saw you.

MARISSA: Well, I want to be careful. Besides, you know how I am about things like this. You knew that before you married me. If it bugged you so much . . .

TONY: It's gotten worse.

MARISSA: No, it hasn't. Maybe you've just gotten more sick of it.

TONY: Well, that's true. I have. All this energy wasted on stupid things.

MARISSA: It's not stupid! It could be very serious. The one time I don't check is the one time it'll be on and you know it. So let me just go check it once. Patty's going to hear us and get concerned.

TONY: (Blocking her way.) So what if she hears us?! I hate that. Worrying all the time about tiny details. Little nothing things that don't really matter that you preoccupy yourself with. It makes me concerned about what real things you're blocking out?

MARISSA: Oh my God. What are you talking about? There's nothing I'm blocking out.

TONY: Are you unhappy with me?

MARISSA: No. I'm not unhappy with you. Of course not. This is ridiculous. Besides, this stupid habit of mine didn't materialize from nothing.

TONY: I know it didn't materialize from nothing. But you only left the stove burning once in your whole life. You left one pot of eggs boiling. So the hell what—so what?! It was once—one time.

MARISSA: I could have burned down the whole apartment complex.

TONY: But you didn't. And there is nothing you can do about that event now, so you can stop beating yourself up for it. The point is that you're so careful now that you could never do that again.

MARISSA: Oh, no. Don't say never. I'm pretty absentminded.

TONY: What if I told you that I would take full responsibility if the stove were left on tonight?

MARISSA: It doesn't matter who's responsible. We have a son upstairs, remember? The point is that I don't want anyone to get hurt.

TONY: That's not the point anymore. The point now is that you *have* to check it. And it's not for anyone's welfare exactly. And you don't have to just check the stove. You check the sink in the bathroom to make sure the faucet isn't on. And that light switch. I know you do. I've seen you when you think I'm not watching. Then you check the shower. And then you walk over to the candles, that haven't been lit for days, to make sure they're put out.

MARISSA: Well, remember Mrs. Hershel with the potpourri? She had no idea. She lost everything.

TONY: Ha! There are all kinds of mistakes and accidents out there, Marissa. There're undetected gas leaks and carbon dioxide poisons and knives left in wrong places. There are dangerous chemicals left near open flames. Faulty wiring that you would have discovered had you had the electrician come in that one more time. The whole house is a horror if you let it be.

MARISSA: Oh, you're exaggerating about me.

TONY: Am I? And it's not just about the house anymore. Last week do you know how many tests you asked to have run on Timmy?

MARISSA: *(Beat.)* Well, it's better to be safe. I've been reading.

TONY: Don't read, please!

MARISSA: You don't think it's important to be up on health issues? Look, I know you think I'm nuts on the lead poisoning thing but this house could be full of it.

TONY: No, I think health issues are very important. But sometimes, it doesn't matter how careful you are. Things just happen. Do you know Dr. Harrison pulled me aside and asked me if you were obsessive-compulsive?

MARISSA: What? He did not!

TONY: Yes, he did. He didn't blurt it out like that. He said he was concerned with the number of tests you wanted run. Timmy is a perfectly healthy baby . . . and he felt you seemed to be overly concerned about everything. Very casually he asked if you'd ever been tested for obsessive-compulsive behavior. He said it was more common than people think and often caused by anxiety. His mother-in-law has that same problem. I didn't know what to say. He's not the first to bring it up though.

MARISSA: Oh great. Great! Who else?

TONY: My mother. Your sister.

MARISSA: What? She was joking. We just like to joke about it. I'm just picky.

TONY: She wasn't joking. She told me it started when your father lost his job years ago. Right around when he started drinking.

MARISSA: Well, I'm not going to say I wasn't stressed out then. God, everybody's diagnosing me. This is really something. All over a stove.

TONY: I've noticed that ever since you went back to work, things have gotten worse. I've heard there are medications for that kind of thing.

MARISSA: No, no, no. I won't do medication. And it's not like I want to go back to work. I don't want to miss any part of anything Timmy does right now. These years you can't have back. You understand that.

TONY: Yeah, of course. I wish you didn't have to. But we need your insurance right now. I wish I were making enough so you didn't have to go back.

MARISSA: Well, maybe someday soon we'll win the lottery and neither of us will have to go to work ever again. *(Pause.)* What's the matter?

TONY: I think I need you to get help, Marissa.

MARISSA: *(Beat.)* Help? Where is this coming from all of sudden? Help because I check the stove too often? And because I'm a worrisome first mother?

TONY: Yes.

MARISSA: *(Pause.)* You know what would help me? If my husband were home a little more often in the evening instead of out with his buddies all the time. Or that he didn't seem preoccupied with his painting business or whatever has him staring at walls for the last few weeks. Or that he'd make love to me without me having to ask. I don't know! Maybe I am crazy. Maybe I'm a psycho like you all think, but I won't go on medication. And I'm sorry I'm not a deadpan person like you about everything—that I get emotional and worried. Frankly, that may be why you can't get the business going, Tony. Ever think of that? There is a bit of passion needed to make things happen. Even me saying that isn't pissing you off, is it? You just—you just take it. Maybe it's you who needs help instead of me. Now, if you want to go to dinner right now, you go right ahead, but I'm not. You can just tell them I'm sick. It isn't even an excuse, according to everyone's diagnosis apparently. I can see by your face that you think I'm acting irrational. But don't I always? So screw you!

TONY: I have M.S.

MARISSA: *(Beat.)* What did you say?

TONY: I have Multiple Sclerosis.

MARISSA: That isn't the least bit funny.

TONY: I wouldn't joke about this. That's where I've been in the evenings. I wasn't out with the guys. I was at the hospital having all kinds of tests run. It's also why I'm so concerned about you lately. About you getting help. I need you to be strong, not worried. And I don't want Timmy panicking about everything as he grows up.

MARISSA: I can't believe this. How come you didn't tell me? How long have you known?

TONY: Two weeks.

MARISSA: Two weeks?!

TONY: Before that, Dr. Shapiro thought it might be some other neurological problem, but then I had numbness in my face and hands. The M.R.I. showed M.S.

MARISSA: So why didn't you tell me all of this?

TONY: At first, I thought it was nothing. No need to tell you. I mean, you get crazy when I go for a routine blood test. I didn't want you to get nervous over nothing. And then, I wanted to make sure first.

MARISSA: So it's for sure?

TONY: *(Nods.)* I didn't even plan on telling you tonight. It just slipped out. I'm sorry, I was afraid to tell you.

MARISSA: Why?

TONY: Because . . . I don't know . . . maybe there wouldn't be room for me to feel my feelings I guess. That all the room would be taken up by you. With your fears and your worries about me. That I couldn't feel my own loss because I'd be spending all my time comforting you.

MARISSA: *(Pause.)* Wow. I sound pretty selfish.

TONY: I don't mean on purpose. But right now I need you to have complete and utter faith, Marissa, no doubts, no worries. To believe I can get better. I started medication this week. There hasn't been much change yet. I've been staring at walls for days because I'm trying to figure out how to run a business when I have M.S. John said he'd help me out. He's the only one who knows about this.

MARISSA: You didn't tell anyone in your family either? *(He shakes his head no.)* Why were you doing this alone? *(Hugs him hard.)* I love you, Tony. And I'm so sorry you thought you needed to do this alone.

TONY: I don't think you're selfish. I don't think you choose to worry.

MARISSA: *(She hugs him harder.)* You are the man I waited for my whole life. I won't lose you. I'm strong when I need to be.

TONY: I know.

MARISSA: You are meant to have a long, long life, Tony. And you will. I know it. I believe it.

TONY: I'm so scared. I've never been so scared in my whole life. *(Marissa holds him and nods.)* And the worst is I don't want Timmy to grow up without me.

MARISSA: He won't! We'll just follow exactly what the doctor prescribes. And I think we should find someone who specializes in this.

TONY: No reading up on this.

MARISSA: No, I will read everything. Not to worry me, but because we need all the information we can. *(He looks unsure.)* If I were sick, would you expect me to go it alone? *(Beat.)* Would you? *(Tony looks to her.)* I know your fears now . . . about me. And I understand. I'll make an appointment Monday to see someone. I won't promise I'll go on medication, but I will consider it. I just never knew how much . . . I didn't realize it affected you too. Now I do.

TONY: You are the love of my life, Marissa J. Proust.

MARISSA: Now, let's go to dinner. There's no need to stay home and mope. We'll call them from the road. We can say we were having baby-sitter delays. And then tomorrow, we'll spend the day talking about all the things we haven't talked about. I'll make you brunch.

TONY: *(Smiles.)* I just might attack you.

MARISSA: Let's hope. Now, let's go. Let's go and put it away for now.

TONY: What about the stove?

MARISSA: Well, if it were on, I'm pretty sure the house would be burned to the ground by now.

TONY: *(Looking up at it.)* Doesn't seem to be the case. *(She nods. He takes her hands gently.)* Try not to think about it. *(She nods.)*

MARISSA: You too.

THE HOOD'S A BETTER PLACE

Kyra, late 20s, and Eddie, 30s, are former lovers from a rough neighborhood on the North Side of Chicago. Eddie, a lifetime car thief, is sort of a Robin-of-the-Hood. He steals cars and commits petty crimes but is considered a hero in the neighborhood for keeping away the dealers. When Kyra was in high school, he saved her from a terribly abusive family situation. He also taught her the ways of a life of crime. By the time she was twenty-two, she had tired of this lifestyle. Though they were engaged, she decided to leave Eddie and his line of business. Strangely enough, she chose to become a cop. Today, the two lovers meet up under different circumstances. A murder has taken place—a notorious drug dealer from the "hood" is dead. One of Eddie's neighborhood kids is being charged. Eddie has been called in for questioning as well. Kyra, who has just been promoted and moved to a precinct in her old stomping ground, has been asked to informally get as much out of her former fiancé as possible.

KYRA: *(Feigning surprise.)* Oh my God. What are *you* doin' here? *(Throws up her hands a little.)* What am I saying?

EDDIE: No, good question. I always ask myself that when I end up in this smelly precinct.

KYRA: Well, you might not end up here if you kept your hands off other people's things.

EDDIE: Hey, I never touch their things. Their cars—yes, but not their *things*. It's a victimless crime as far as I'm concerned. They get their insurance money. I take away their parking nightmare. It's sort of like a service. I should be paid, not charged.

KYRA: Yes, I remember your thinking on it. So . . . Is that why you're here?

EDDIE: *(Shrugs.)* So this is quite a surprise. I thought you worked downtown writing traffic tickets, Lady Cop.

KYRA: You thought wrong.

EDDIE: So when did they assign you to this place?

KYRA: They moved me here a few days ago. I got a promotion.

EDDIE: Congratulations. So how long have you been at this thing anyway? I lost count.

KYRA: Four years.

EDDIE: Four years?! You worked your way up to detective quick, huh? Not bad for a former shoplift-oholic. Oh. You probably didn't tell them about that?

KYRA: No, I told them. And about my past bout with crime.

EDDIE: Oh, well, that's sweet. To be remembered.

KYRA: They assigned me to the twenty-fourth because they knew I was familiar with the neighborhood.

EDDIE: Yep. You might be able to provide all kinds of interesting information for them. *(Beat.)* So is that why you're talking to me now?

KYRA: What are you talking about? *(He shrugs.)* Oh, you mean because I know you? I can get the inside scoop?

EDDIE: Knew me, slept with me on a regular basis, dumped me for this glorious line of work—what have you. Now they think I'll give you a kinda off-the-record account.

KYRA: Of what? I don't even know what you're in here for, Eddie. I'm too new. I don't even know where the john is.

EDDIE: *(Points.)* Over there.

KYRA: Thanks. So what the hell did you do that has you so paranoid? Did you do another mass car racket? *(He shakes his head.)* Well, look, if you don't feel comfortable talking . . . *(She starts to go.)* I have a mountain of orientation papers to weed through.

EDDIE: It's changed—the hood. I'm a grade school nun next to most of these guys here today.

KYRA: Yeah, that's what I've heard too. *(She looks around.)*

EDDIE: Whatcha looking for?

KYRA: Nothing, I . . . I should be doing that paperwork.

EDDIE: Oh. Is this going to make you look bad—*(Gestures to himself and then her.)* us talking?

KYRA: No, no.

EDDIE: Cause I don't like to do that—make anybody look bad. That's *your* style.

KYRA: Oh come on. Get off it. That's not true. It's never been true. I just didn't want to live that lifestyle. I told you that a million times. You don't have to either, ya know?

EDDIE: You're right. I could move up to what you have. Dealin' with the same folks, but worse because they *pretend* to be good. Looks like the only difference is you got a lot more paperwork. You don't look happy, Skinny.

KYRA: Yeah, well, I am. Besides, who is—really happy? At least I'm a lot happier than I was.

EDDIE: Yeah? So did you sleep your way to the top or did you do it the hard way? Course sleepin' with a bunch of cops *is* the hard way.

KYRA: Oh God. I thought you had to be over this by now.

EDDIE: Over it? You don't get over your fiancée leaving you. Are you over it?

KYRA: *(Sighs.)* You want some coffee, Eddie?

EDDIE: Nah. I don't like to be jittery, period, but especially when I'm getting interrogated.

KYRA: Interrogated? For what exactly?

EDDIE: Are you honestly telling me you don't know? *(She shakes her head no.)* Kees is dead.

KYRA: No way. Really? *(Eddie nods slowly.)* You must be thrilled beyond belief. Hell. I'm thrilled beyond belief.

EDDIE: I'd be lying if I said anything different. I've wanted to kill that guy for at least ten years. If I could have gotten a hold of him, I would have strangled him with my bare hands. He got so many kids hooked on that shit.

KYRA: Oh God. Do they think you had something . . .

EDDIE: Nah. It's worse than that.

KYRA: What could be worse than that?

EDDIE: They're holdin' Tot for it.

KYRA: Tot? No way. *(He nods.)* Tot? Our Tot?! *(He nods.)* Why?

EDDIE: Geez, I can't believe you don't know this crap. It's the biggest thing goin' on around here. You're some new detective who knows the hood. They don't tell you nothin'?

KYRA: You have to earn respect when you go to new places. Sometimes that means you have to do things you don't like for awhile to earn it.

EDDIE: Sounds and feels just like a gang to me.

KYRA: Sometimes it just takes time.

EDDIE: Whatever. *(Beat.)* Hey, you think you could do somethin' for him?

KYRA: What do you want me to do?

EDDIE: I don't know. You know the kid. He's a good kid. He's had a rough couple of years. He's been hooked on coke and was just startin' to get off when this thing hit.

KYRA: I'm sure they're holdin' Tot for a reason. And it's not like I'm big enough here to pull strings. Besides, I haven't seen Tot in years. I don't know what he's capable of.

EDDIE: Well, he's not capable of murder.

KYRA: Well, how do you know that?

EDDIE: Cause I know.

KYRA: Well, they must have something on him or they wouldn't be holding him.

EDDIE: Yeah, well, he had the weapon in his possession. Some kid saw the gun and reported it.

KYRA: What the hell was he doin' with the weapon? *(Beat.)* Anyway, there's nothing I can do. If he's innocent, the truth will come out.

EDDIE: Yeah? Truth ever come out about your dad hitting your mom so hard he made her blind?

KYRA: That was different. She denied it.

EDDIE: *(Beat.)* No justice is as cut-and-dry as cops like to make it out to be. That's why some people have to handle it on the streets.

KYRA: Is that what happened here? Was someone seeking revenge on Kees?

EDDIE: I'm just sayin' help Tot as a favor—as a huge favor to me or something.

KYRA: A favor to you?! In what way do I owe you a favor?

EDDIE: Well, for one, I helped you get out of that chaos you called a family to live in a nice quiet apartment. You never woulda got through high school if it weren't for me. That's for one.

KYRA: No, I wouldn't have been shot at twice either.

EDDIE: Hey, that was a fluke. That could have happened walkin' down any street.

KYRA: We were stealing his car. He had a reason.

EDDIE: Look, it doesn't matter. You got me back for all that and a lot more when you left.

KYRA: I wasn't trying to get you back, Eddie. I just couldn't do it and live with myself anymore.

EDDIE: Oh, give me a break. Don't give me the self-rightcous bull. I know what cops do. They pretend they're the good guys, meanwhile they lie, take bribes from the drug dealers and give the black kid the work-over when he's just walkin' down the street.

KYRA: Okay, whatever. My point is the life you lead—wrong or right in your eyes—wasn't right for me, okay? I know you helped me out of a bad situation, Eddie, and I'm thankful to you, but I don't think I owe you anymore for any of it.

EDDIE: Fine. No debt due. So take me out of the equation. Think of it like this. Tot grew up in a situation three times as bad as yours. He has no one. And he never hurt anyone or anything in his whole life. 'Member how he helped your mom out that one night with those guys? There's no payback there? *(Beat.)* Do you honestly think Tot is capable of taking down Kees—the biggest drug dealer in the area?

KYRA: Well, neighborhoods change, so do kids. *(He looks at her.)* Honestly? No. *(Beat.)* As far as I know, *you're* the only one who could take him down. *(Beat.)* You want me to get you a smoke?

EDDIE: Now that's a shock. No, I quit.

KYRA: You did? I'm impressed.

EDDIE: Don't sound so surprised. I do have some willpower, Skinny. I see you haven't kicked your habit though. *(She's confused. He looks down at her nails.)*

KYRA: *(She tucks her hands under.)* No. I guess I still get nervous.

EDDIE: Why you nervous? You only used to get that way when you lied. You're a cop now. *(Salutes.)* On the force. No need to lie, right?

KYRA: *(Beat.)* I don't think I can do this.

EDDIE: Do what? *(Beat.)* So you aren't married? I thought someone woulda snatched you up by now.

KYRA: No ones quite as willing to get through the hard exterior as you were.

EDDIE: Oh, it's not that hard as I remember, and most definitely worth the effort.

KYRA: *(Rolling her eyes, smiling.)* Um, I don't know about that.

EDDIE: God you're pretty when you smile. *(Rolling her eyes.)* Don't roll your eyes. It's true. Hey, did I tell you Maggie asks about you from time to time?

KYRA: She does? You still take care of her?

EDDIE: I have her stay with me now cause she can't get around so well anymore. She's one tough old bird. I've been takin' care of the park over there by the beach too. You guys should watch that area. Dealers want it. I took in Tot for awhile too—so as to help him kick the habit, but . . .

KYRA: But what?

EDDIE: It's hard when the dealer keeps shovin' it in your face. What can you do?

KYRA: Nothin'. But kill the dealer.

EDDIE: *(He nods.)* Can I ask you somethin'? *(She nods.)* Do you have any regrets?

KYRA: *(Beat.)* In general or about you?

EDDIE: Both. But about me mostly.

KYRA: Some. *(Beat.)* Anyway I've got work to do. *(She starts to go.)*

EDDIE: *(He gets in front of her.)* No. Don't.

KYRA: What are you doin'?

EDDIE: Being honest for a change. I never fell out of love with you, ya know, and I'm not just sayin' that because of this situation. It's true. I knew you were comin' here. In fact, I've been keepin' an eye on you these past years. I don't know why I'm sayin' this, but I'll tell ya everything. Everything they want to know if you agree to let Tot go.

KYRA: What are you talking about?

EDDIE: Your initiation here in your new district. The thing that wins you respect among fellow detectives. *(Pause.)* I mean, you did a good job pretending that you didn't know why I was here, Kyra. I almost believed you. It was the basic logic that was flawed. Surely, you heard a morning briefing. This is the big story. My name would be tossed around. You'd respond, "I know him." I mean, you'd have to. You're ambitious. They'd tell you to hang around in the front, pretend that you ran into me accidentally and find out all you can. Maybe you'd even get a confession.

KYRA: I know you didn't have anything to do with it, so it doesn't matter what I was put up to.

EDDIE: Oh, now, me having nothing to do with it won't win you any respect, especially since you know it can't be true.

KYRA: Sure it can. You're not a killer. You're not always above-board on everything, but you watch out for your neighbors. You take in the old ladies because they can't get around. You make sure the kids can cross the street to get to school. You're a good guy.

EDDIE: Who steals cars, and carries a gun. I'm a lifetime criminal, Kyra, who doesn't know any other way. I wish I could have changed. So what do you think? Can we get Tot out of it?

KYRA: *(Beat.)* If he didn't do it.

EDDIE: He didn't.

KYRA: Then who did? *(Pause. He looks at her.)* You're covering for him. I know you.

EDDIE: Or the other way around. Don't let your personal feelings get in the way.

KYRA: They'll put you away for life.

EDDIE: He's a lifelong drug dealer. I did them a favor. No tears will be shed. I won't even do three months.

KYRA: You don't know. First of all, it's still murder. Second of all, you're not exactly Mr. Popular around here either.

EDDIE: Hey, if they're mad about anything, it'll be that I got him before they did. They'll get over that. Look, you say you're all about truth and justice. Then Tot shouldn't go down for this. Look at the big picture. The hood's a better place. Tot will have a second chance, and I'll get free dental care for a couple of months. It's the happy ending. You even get to look good. Trust me. It'll be a piece of cake.

CONCERNED CATHOLICS

Gretchen, late 40s, has been working in the rectory and for Father Thomas, 40s, for eight years. During her time there, she has secretly fallen in love with him. Because of recent national news coverage regarding sexual abuse in the churches, Father Thomas' former actions have been called into question. Several years back, he was made aware of an accusation against one of his fellow priests. Some people think he did not react aggressively enough when he heard this. Though Thomas followed all proper procedures, he did not stop Father Patrick from taking on other duties that further exposed him to young boys. Father Thomas fully agrees with his critics. He thinks he left too much up to the church and its leaders, instead of acting upon his own instincts. Gretchen, too, has her theories about who is to blame in this situation. She has decided that all of the recent sexual abuse cases are linked to gays in the priesthood. In fact, several parishioners are considering getting on the warpath to hunt down and expose these gay priests—root them out so as to put an end to this problem.

GRETCHEN: *(Waves her hand shooing him away while speaking into the phone.)* He's eating his dinner now. He has parish duties all day long. I won't disturb him. He's been at the nursing home for the last five hours and before that he presided over a funeral and did a final blessing at the hospital. It's his only time to rest—

FATHER: Who is that?

GRETCHEN: Yes, of course we're well aware of what Father Patrick is being charged with.

FATHER: Okay, now, let me have the phone.

GRETCHEN: Look, Father *Thomas* did nothing wrong!

FATHER: *(Reaching for it.)* Gretchen, give me the phone. *(Firmly.)* Gretchen.

GRETCHEN: *(She covers the receiver.)* No. *(She tries to wave him away again. Into the receiver.)* Leave poor Father Thomas alone. Father Patrick was here less than a year, and he's caused him nothing but—

FATHER: *(Grabbing the phone.)* Hello . . . Yes, this is he . . . Yes, I became aware of that this morning . . . I was in charge of the parish when the accusation was made . . . Uh-huh, well, I discussed it with the bishop and a religious team that included a psychologist . . . I don't know . . . I don't know why they weren't more aggressive . . . No, I wasn't aware of that. But we're rethinking how we should handle this in the . . . No, not now. No. But if you call on me tomorrow morning, I'll talk . . . Yes . . . Yes, fine. Tomorrow morning. *(He hangs up.)*

GRETCHEN: What are you doing? You have a wedding tomorrow.

FATHER: Oh. Do you think we could squeeze in the interview right after the wedding?

GRETCHEN: I don't think you should do it. You're liable to say something that will get you or the bishop in a lot of trouble.

FATHER: So what if I did? If things get complicated, it's God's will. He'll keep me on track.

GRETCHEN: Yes, well, I hope so. This one's very complicated.

FATHER: Well, we've dealt with complicated things before.

GRETCHEN: Yes, and some of them are still unresolved. *(Looks knowingly at him.)* Forgive me for even bringing it up again.

FATHER: Nothing to forgive. *(Holds her hand.)* We're good friends—always.

GRETCHEN: Yeah. *(Breaking it off.)* Anyway, it'll be tight tomorrow. And I don't know why you're giving these people the time. Send them to the bishop. He needs to be accountable too.

FATHER: I'm not going to pass them off. I have my part in it. Besides, the questions they ask are no different than what the people would be asking. People have a right to know.

GRETCHEN: Yes, but the way these people talk to you. Sometimes they act as if you have nothing to do but to be at their disposal. I don't like the accusatory way he was talking either.

FATHER: He wasn't saying anything I don't agree with. I should have been more assertive and reacted faster to everything.

GRETCHEN: It's not your fault at all. You're a trusting, loving man who thought his fellow priest could be trusted as well.

FATHER: You're always defending me, Gretchen.

GRETCHEN: I know you. They don't see you. They don't see what you've done. They don't know the incredible improvements you've made here on the school and the activities you've created for seniors. That's what should have been reported about. How you helped those folks who lost their factory jobs. That's what should have brought you into view, not this sick ordeal with Father Patrick.

FATHER: Yes, but unfortunately, it's not always the good things that we do that get recognized. But I know God recognizes them and that's all that's important.

GRETCHEN: The problem is those journalists act like there is nothing else to report in the world. They're like piranha.

FATHER: It's a big story—a national story. In a place like this, there isn't that much else to report. I just wish I had done things differently.

GRETCHEN: You can't turn back the time. Besides, you followed every procedure.

FATHER: Some of those procedures are not perfect. I should have followed my instincts over procedure. Sometimes the whole "brotherhood alliance" is a problem.

GRETCHEN: What are you talking about?

FATHER: Well, it's like being in a fraternity I guess. You feel this incredible pressure to protect your own. I should have been protecting the boys instead.

GRETCHEN: There should be no need to protect the boys. It shouldn't even be an issue. There shouldn't be priests like that period.

FATHER: I agree, but how are we to know the priest is an abuser ahead of time? It usually crops up later.

GRETCHEN: Well, there should be something that screens them out before they're ordained.

FATHER: And what would that be?

GRETCHEN: Lie detector tests or something.

FATHER: And how would we do that? What would we ask?

GRETCHEN: Well, it's the gays that are the problem. It's the homosexuals.

FATHER: What are you talking about?!

GRETCHEN: Gay men in the priesthood is what I'm talking about, Thomas.

FATHER: Oh no. You haven't gotten all right-winged on me, Gretchen?

GRETCHEN: Are you saying you approve?

FATHER: Of what?

GRETCHEN: Of gay men in the priesthood?

FATHER: I suppose you disapprove even if they aren't practicing gays?

GRETCHEN: You're darn right I disapprove. It's too tempting. It's too powerful a position. I'm not saying we need to shut gay men out entirely. I'm not condoning gay bashing either. Nothing radical. I'm just saying that they shouldn't become priests. It's too tempting.

FATHER: And what about heterosexual men? What about young girls who have been abused through the years? And all those crying wives coming to them. Disturbed about their failed marriages. Wanting advice and support. Isn't that tempting as well? Isn't that a ripe opportunity for seduction?

GRETCHEN: *(Pause.)* That's not . . . You know what I mean.

FATHER: No, I don't know really. How come this has never come up before?

GRETCHEN: Well, it's not as if I haven't thought about it before, but I just had no reason until now to say anything about it. I had no idea the problem of sexual abuse was this widespread. None of us did. I didn't know these gay priests were affecting our children so profoundly.

FATHER: Yes, they are affecting our children profoundly. They're helping save marriages and guiding kids away from drugs and alcohol. Preparing them for first communion and confirmation and bringing God into their lives. Besides, all of these cases aren't due to gay priests, Gretchen. As horrible as it all sounds, many girls were abused as well.

GRETCHEN: Oh no, that's far and few between. I've talked about this with people.

FATHER: No, it's not! That's not what the statistics tell us. Some of these men are just troubled, and sick and willing to abuse their power—they don't discriminate between gender. They're pedophiles.

GRETCHEN: Many of the boys abused are not children. There's the clue. They're adolescents and these priests try to form relationships—homosexual relationships with them. And the young men do it at first because they feel special—privileged until they realize that it's just wrong.

FATHER: Oh my . . . Who's been feeding you this crap?

GRETCHEN: I talked to a woman who leads up a Catholic organization over at St. Alfonzo's parish in Allentown. She called me this afternoon asking if we would be interested in getting involved.

FATHER: Involved in what?

GRETCHEN: In organizing a group here.

FATHER: What kind of group?

GRETCHEN: Of concerned Catholics. Catholics who want to get behind removing these gay priests.

FATHER: *(Sarcastic.)* Well, that's an organization Jesus would have loved. All about patience, kindness, and forgiveness.

GRETCHEN: I'm sorry if we're having trouble forgiving them. You do you realize this has ruined people's faith over and over? It may ruin entire lives too.

FATHER: Of course I realize that! So blame us! Blame the people who put the priests back into positions and exposed the children again. Blame us for being tight-knit and stubborn and stupid as hell, but do not blame gay men in the priesthood. Not all gay men—just like not all heterosexual men—abuse children. I hope you realize that!

GRETCHEN: I can't believe you're defending them!

FATHER: I can't believe you're targeting them! What you're suggesting, Gretchen, is just a huge witch-hunt to me—no different than rooting out communists or even the Jews.

GRETCHEN: Oh come on. That's not an accurate comparison. There's no death at the end of it. And besides, what some of those priests did is much worse.

FATHER: And for the gay priests who have done quiet duty for years at parishes never harming anyone and, in fact, making the lives of the people there much better—you would go after them too? *(She nods.)* What did they do wrong?

GRETCHEN: Nothing, maybe, but temptation may get them sometime. They may break. The parish at least has a right to know. They have a right to know who their children are exposed to.

FATHER: As long as the father is not pursuing any sort of physical or emotional relationships, he is following the word of the Lord, and of this religion as well. Is he gay if he merely feels as if he may have feelings for men, but never acts on them?

GRETCHEN: I'd say so. I don't know. It's hard to say.

FATHER: Well if you don't know exactly, how can you commit yourself to weeding them out? You don't even know what you consider gay.

GRECHEN: Now, you're just trying to confuse me.

FATHER: Gay priests have been speaking to their parish and advising for more than a hundred years. Despite all our denial, they have served the elderly, brought food to the bake sale and given your children first communion. This witch-hunt may not kill the Catholic Church, but it'll do serious damage. If you want to do something, create a support group for the survivors or demand more action if abuse occurs in the future.

GRETCHEN: Why are you so insistent on defending them?

FATHER: Because, because I am them.

GRETCHEN: *(Pause.)* What? No you're not. You can't be. I mean you and I have fee . . .

FATHER: I've always been aware of your feelings for me and I'm hugely flattered.

GRETCHEN: *My* feelings? *(Beat.)* I thought you . . .

FATHER: We're good friends.

GRETCHEN: Of course we are. I had no idea that you . . . I just spend so much time here at the rectory you misunderstood me. I'm a caretaker. *(Beat. Laughs.)* You're just trying to make a point, aren't you? This isn't true about you, is it?

FATHER: I've never acted on it—nor will I. And I would never harm anyone, least of all a child or a young person.

GRETCHEN: I can't believe this, Thomas.

FATHER: It's innocent to love a person. I don't think God believes it's a sin to love. I don't always agree with all the church's doctrine—gay issues, priests not being allowed to marry, but I will abide by it. It's part of my commitment.

GRETCHEN: I think I better go now. It's late.

FATHER: Will you tell this group about me, Gretchen?

GRETCHEN: There're some extra vegetables on the stove if you want.

FATHER: I didn't mean to hurt your feelings. I've wanted to tell you so many times about this, but didn't know quite how—

GRETCHEN: Please, Father. I need to go now. I really need to go.

FATHER: So I'll see you tomorrow at eight o'clock?

(He looks to her, but she doesn't answer.)

YOU BEEN LIED TO

Jack, 18, just found out from a stranger that the woman he thought was his sister his whole life was really his biological mother. He was raised as if his grandmother, Edith, was his mom. Eighteen years ago, Pam, who is now 31, came home pregnant. The details of that youthful pregnancy had long been kept a secret from Jack. Pam, who has spent several years in and out of rehab and living with transient boyfriends, now tries to explain to Jack what really happened and why.

PAM: *(Knocking.)* Come on, come on, let me in, Jack! Let me explain! I'm not going away until you let me in.

JACK: So stay at the door. What do I care?

PAM: I only want to say I'm sorry.

JACK: You and her are so alike. You lie to me for years and then you expect me to accept your apology just like that. It doesn't matter at this point. So please go away.

PAM: There's a lot to explain, Jack. You may understand why we lied if I can just explain. But please don't make me do this out here. All the neighbors will hear.

JACK: *(Opening the door a crack.)* The neighbors? The hell with the neighbors! We're talkin' about losing the basic pieces of who I am. Having everything all mixed up and put together in some twisted new story. You're worried about how the neighbors will look at you? Well, how have they looked at *me* all these years?! Ever think of that? *(Beat.)* You come home pregnant at thirteen. Next thing they know *Grandma's* changing my diaper, and I'm calling *you* sister. They must have been whispering like crazy all that time. Did everyone in this damn neighborhood know besides me?

PAM: No, of course not. And I can't tell you this stuff through a door, Jack. But I will tell you everything. That's why I'm here.

JACK: Oh, how nice. How thoughtful of you to come here and tell me that my entire life has been a lie!

PAM: Look, I know I should have told you about this years ago. I wanted to. I tried to a million times. I even wrote you a letter.

JACK: What are you talking about? I never got any letter.

PAM: I wrote it when I was eighteen. It was right after I moved outta here and in with that guy, Lou. 'Member? *(Beat.)* I wrote you a letter about everything, but she said you wouldn't understand. That it would be bad for you.

JACK: She?

PAM: Mom.

JACK: She's not my mom! Unfortunately, that would be you.

PAM: *(Beat.)* Okay, I know you're mad at me and you have every reason to be but she's heartbroken. She knows it was wrong not to tell you. Do you even know where she is right now?

JACK: Probably crying her eyes out at Uncle Joe's. Doing the martyr routine.

PAM: No, she's not. And I think if you would just talk—

JACK: What's there to talk about? How can I talk to her or you? How am I ever supposed to believe either of you again?

PAM: She's at St. Vincent's.

JACK: Hospital? *(Beat.)* Is she okay?

PAM: Yeah.

JACK: This isn't a load of bull to get me to open the door?

PAM: Come on, Jack, I don't lie about everything.

JACK: Yeah? Well, how am I supposed to know that? *(Pause. Opens door.)* Fine. Come in.

PAM: Thanks. *(Beat.)* She's okay. She just had to go to the emergency room to get some anxiety medication. She got hysterical last night when she went to Uncle Joe's.

JACK: I didn't throw her out of her own house ya know? I just refused to talk to her anymore.

PAM: I know.

JACK: *(Beat.)* When is she planning on coming back?

PAM: Later this afternoon I guess.

JACK: I'll get out of here by noon then.

PAM: What?! You can't leave here, Jack. You don't have any money. You don't even have a job.

JACK: I have a couple of friends I can crash with till I get a job and stuff. I am old enough.

PAM: But what about school?

JACK: Who cares?

PAM: No! That's what I always said. And look at me. I'm workin' two crappy jobs and have nothing to show for it.

JACK: Except a screwed up brother—oh, I mean son.

PAM: *(Pause.)* All I meant is that I think you should stay here with Edith and get an education.

JACK: Are you suddenly trying to be my mother? You're trying to tell me what to do? Like you know anything. You spent three-quarters of your life as a poster child for the white-trash pot smokers of America. I'm not too keen on your love life recommendations either since the two latest boyfriends who were "so nice" were actually felons.

PAM: Okay, that's enough.

JACK: I don't even know what I'm supposed to call you anymore—Sis, Mom, Pam?

PAM: There was a reason for all this, Jack. You don't know everything.

JACK: Well, I'm ready to hear this explanation. Cause this is the most screwed up thing ever. I mean, here I am just hangin' out on my porch one day. Life's as it always is, and some dude starts telling me he went to high school with my mom. I'm thinkin' he means my sister—he's talkin' about you, not Edith—'cause he's your age. So I'm not listening all that well—thinkin' about something else. Then he says, "So how is your mom? Is she as hot as she always was?" I want to pop him in the face, but I'm totally confused at the same time. My mom's about fifty years old, so I don't think she was ever hot to him. And if she was, I want to throw up. I say, "I'm confused," and he starts laughing. I tell him that he must have things backwards because my mom's around fifty, but he tells me I'm wrong. He says he knew my mom, Pam, from high school. She got pregnant like eighteen years ago. She got around with a lot of guys he says.

PAM: That's not true. That's totally not true.

JACK: He says *her* mother, Edith, was not pregnant. He notices that I look about eighteen. He laughs. "Get it?" He says, "Get what I'm sayin'?" I grabbed his shirt—suddenly, like outta nowhere, I just start poppin' him good ones. He didn't even see them coming. He pushes me hard. And I'm laying there. He spits and says real dramatic, "You been lied to, boy." Laughs. *(Beat.)* And I feel like my brain was just put in a blender.

PAM: I'm sorry.

JACK: Yeah, well, that doesn't change anything. And please don't tell me that that moron is my father.

PAM: He's not. He had a crush on me a million years ago. He's a jerk—a complete liar.

JACK: But he wasn't lying about you being my mother was he?

PAM: No.

JACK: Do you even know who my dad is, Pam?

PAM: *(Angrily.)* Yes.

JACK: Well, I'd *like* to doubt that guy about your sleeping around, but it's not exactly like you've been a nun since I can remember. How many boyfriends have you had since . . . oh, last week?

PAM: Fine—think that about me now. But I wasn't at all like that back then. I never slept with anyone!

JACK: Well, you must have slept with someone or—

PAM: Look, I will tell you everything. And I know this is difficult for you, but this isn't exactly easy for me either.

JACK: Oh, I'm so sorry. I might have been less furious about this stuff had you told me sooner. Yourself. But to hear it from a stranger—to hear it like that so randomly.

PAM: I tried to tell you again this past year. I felt more together with keeping the jobs down.

JACK: So why didn't you?!

PAM: I started to a couple of times, but you always seemed like you hated my guts. Besides, Mom thought I should wait till you were out of high school.

JACK: And then I would have been out of high school and she would have said, wait until he's graduated from college. And it would have gone on and on. Why were you listening to her? At some point you have to make your own choices.

PAM: I wasn't that strong, Jack. And if I thought that the idea of it wouldn't disgust you, I might have considered it.

JACK: Might have considered it?! I thought you just said you tried to tell me? That you were gonna?

PAM: I was! That's not what I meant.

JACK: So what did you mean? That it's *my* fault?! It's my fault cause I mighta been disgusted?!

PAM: No! I just think it would have been easier to tell you if you liked me even a little!

JACK: Well, I don't *not* like you! I might've even thought you were cool, but it's hard to like someone who keeps messing themselves up over and over. I mean, why do you go out with losers all the time? Why didn't you go to college? Why don't you now? I'm sure the state would help you out. You're smart.

PAM: It feels too late. Everything feels too late.

JACK: Well, hell, what do you have to lose at this point?! You don't have anything!

PAM: *(Beat.)* I know I'm not who you want me to be, Jack, but I do and I did always love you.

JACK: Yeah, that was real obvious. Going away for ten years to live with loser boyfriends when I was a kid—now that made it real, real obvious.

PAM: I couldn't stay and not want to be the mother.

JACK: So why didn't you? You *were* the mother.

PAM: Because a kid can't have two moms. Edith was the better choice.

JACK: No, the truth would have been the better choice.

PAM: Maybe. Maybe it was a mistake.

JACK: Maybe? There's no maybe about it. *(Beat.)* And Dad?
Who would that be? *(Pause. She looks down.)* What? You're
not going to tell me?

PAM: I didn't say that. I need something to drink.

JACK: No, you don't. I thought you were supposed to knock
that off?

PAM: I have. I just . . . you're right.

JACK: So go ahead. *(She looks at him.)* God, it was bad enough
thinking he was some man we couldn't even bare to mention my whole life. The mysterious bad man in Edith's life
who disappeared into oblivion and everyone hoped had
been lost in some terrible catastrophe. But now the dad
question seems more important somehow. Who is he? A
diamond thief, a powerful mob guy or just some dude who
works at an auto shop and watches TV all night long?

PAM: Maybe it's better not to know.

JACK: No way! Don't you dare do that! You've already kept
so much from me. How dare you keep me from knowing
about him too?

PAM: He's the reason we kept you from knowing so much.

JACK: Okay, so he may have been a jerk in high school, but
that was eighteen years ago. He could have changed by
now. Just because *your* dad wasn't someone you wanted to
know doesn't mean I'll feel the same way! Just because he
was a real rotten bastard doesn't mean my dad is.

PAM: He's the same man.

JACK: What? *(Confused.)*

PAM: He's the same person.

JACK: But . . . *(Long pause.)*

PAM: I'm not the only one in the family with bad taste in men.

JACK: That's disgusting.

PAM: Edith divorced him and threw him out.

JACK: So why'd you even have me?

PAM: Because I wanted you. We both wanted you. Maybe for our own selfish reasons. I wanted someone to love me for me, and I think Mom wanted someone she could protect— since she screwed that up pretty good.

JACK: Is he alive? Did you charge him?

PAM: Yeah, he's alive. And no. It's all over now.

JACK: Is it? Whose words are those? It doesn't seem over for either of us.

PAM: Well you can't dwell in it, Jack. It doesn't do any good.

JACK: Well, what the hell did you do for the last eighteen years but dwell in it with all those stupid guys? Yeah, you can say you shoved it under the carpet and you never talked about it, but you sure as hell dwelled on it.

PAM: Yeah, so what should I have done?

JACK: Set it right. *(He grabs his backpack.)*

PAM: What are you doing? Where are you going?

JACK: I'll be back.

PAM: No, Jack, talk to me. Where are you going? Don't do anything crazy. Come on!

JACK: I gotta go, Mom. I promise I'll be back.
(He exits. Pam is speechless.)

WEAPONS OF MASS DESTRUCTION

Susan and Abe, 30s, have been brought together by their spouses, who are coworkers and extremely ambitious lawyers. Both Susan and Abe have complained to their spouses about the lack of time they have to go out. As a result, their spouses have suggested that they use each other for company. The two have gone out a couple of times in the past few weeks and have enjoyed the restaurants and each other's company immensely; still, something seems odd about their spouses' suggestion. As the scene begins, they are enjoying the view in an upscale bar in Minneapolis in a deliciously intense conversation.

SUSAN: Well, the general population there doesn't know! They don't understand the damage, the kinds of cancer and destruction it will do afterwards, Abe.

ABE: Oh God. It's just a lot of political posturing. Neither wants to look namby-pamby. It's like when a kid says my Willy's bigger than yours. You have to respond or you look bad. And when they say "weapons of mass destruction" that doesn't necessarily mean nuclear.

SUSAN: Well what do you think when you hear that? It's the first thing that comes to mind for me. I think radiation. I think nuclear bomb. There are fanatics over there. Once you cross the line, there's no turning back.

ABE: They won't cross the line.

SUSAN: Sometimes you don't even know when the line is crossed because with crazy people you're not even sure where the line is.

ABE: You act like if there's one wrong word between them, that's the end of the world—boom!

SUSAN: It's not *one* wrong word. It's one wrong word after

years of wrong words and wrong killings and totally con-
flicting values and beliefs. That's a dangerous situation.

ABE: Things aren't that precarious. The leaders want you to
think things are that precarious so they can get money or
support or both from the U.S.! And that's it! It's all about
our money!

SUSAN: Wow. You're feisty about this.

ABE: So are you. I feel compelled to argue with you. It's
very . . . uh . . .

SUSAN: Sexy? I love this kind of conversation when I'm getting a hint of a buzz cause I feel intense and intellectual.

ABE: You have a buzz?

SUSAN: Hey, don't laugh. This is my second drink. I told you
I'm a lightweight. *(Putting her head on his shoulder.)* At
least I'm a cheap date. So how's your martini, sir?

ABE: It's cold and dry. The glass is frosty cold—perfectly
frosty—just like I like it, miss.

SUSAN: Good. I heard this place was good.

ABE: And it is. Very good. And perfect company all around.
How's the daiquiri?

SUSAN: Foo-foo-frozen and sweet—just like I like it.

ABE: So. We're happy. *(Lifts glass.)* To uh . . . to new friends.
(They toast.)

SUSAN: Good friends. *(She smiles.)*
*(They both drink and then put their glasses down.
Awkward pause.)*

ABE/SUSAN: *(Simultaneously.)* Well, this / How's the—

SUSAN: You go ahead.

ABE: I was just going to say this is nice. I mean, us hanging out
again. Haven't been out since . . . well since you and I went
to that really good Italian place last week.

SUSAN: Fiesta. That was good.

SUSAN/ABE: *(Ritual way of saying it.)* Chocolate Mooouuusse.

ABE: I've been looking forward to getting together with you
all week.

SUSAN: Me too. *(They pause.)* I've been meaning to get here with Matt for months, but, well . . . He's at work more than he's home. So you got to come here with me instead—ha, ha, ha. I've heard over and over about the view and the drinks here. Certainly is true.

ABE: Yep. Lydia keeps telling me once this case is over, she'll be home more, but . . .

SUSAN: When I was young if someone would have asked me— would you prefer your husband's money or to see your husband more often? I would have said the money definitely, but now I want someone to talk to, to take a walk around the lake with.

ABE: I'm with ya. Lydia tells me Matt's likely to get partner soon.

SUSAN: Yeah? Maybe. He thinks *she's* going to make partner soon. They're both so ambitious.

ABE: Ambition isn't everything. It doesn't keep you warm at night—that's for sure. *(Holding out his glass.)* To lack of ambition!

SUSAN: *(Picking up her drink.)* Here, here. And slothfulness! *(They clink.)* Is that a word?

ABE: Who cares? I love toasting. Let's just toast periodically for no reason.

SUSAN: Okay. So their method of getting us off their backs seems to have worked.

ABE: You mean— *(Gesturing between him and her.)* this?

SUSAN: I haven't been bugging him as much about going out in the last month. When Matt suggested I go hang out with you sometimes, I was kind of insulted. I know I didn't tell you that before, but now I kind of feel like I can. You aren't offended by me saying that?

ABE: No. Absolutely not! I felt the same way. She kept going on about how you were in the neighborhood. "I'm sorry. Though I'm your wife, I can't spend time with you, but I have a perfect substitute—*and she's in the neighborhood.*" It *is* insulting. As if you're being passed off. If I didn't have a devout passion for Thai food and trying out new places, I probably wouldn't have called back that night.

SUSAN: Yeah, it was a fluke for me too. I just didn't want to stomach another dose of reality TV. What is it with that, huh? It's like bargain-basement entertainment. No creative input, no actor, no writer, no story. Just a bunch of type A personalities having petty fights over how to divide up some lima beans.

ABE: *(Ashamed of himself.)* I know. I love it.

SUSAN: What?! You do? You're kidding? Really? You don't seem the type.

ABE: I'm not. And if you tell my students, I'll deny the whole thing. But I'm a junkie.

SUSAN: I'd rather watch my cat barf up a hairball.

ABE: Yeah, well, now that can be entertaining too. To each his own. *(Toasting.)* To each his own.

SUSAN: *(She toasts with him.)* It is counter to my entire world to have TV be reality. What happened to the mindless sit-com? The melodramatic movie of the week? Now we're forced to watch real people do really stupid things over and over. I don't need that on TV. I have that at work.

ABE: I just like the alliances and the competition factor. The pure evil actually. *(Realizing.)* Course I have that at *my* work.

SUSAN: I really hate that show that supposedly has perfectly happy couples go to an island with the intent of splitting them up. I hate that. How disgusting is that?

ABE: I never watched that one. There's something too humiliating about watching people who profess their love in public suddenly fall apart. Watching people being tempted away by scantily clothed women and men. Or maybe I don't like that one because it hits too close to home. Not the scantily clothed part of course, but losing your partner to another.

SUSAN: *(Pause.)* What are you talking about?

ABE: *(Beat. Pointing to her drink.)* Another? *(She nods.)* Sir? *(He points to the drinks. He nods. Returning to her.)* You've never thought anything was strange between them?

SUSAN: You're saying you suspect something's going on with them?

ABE: Don't you?

SUSAN: Well . . . I told his sister two months ago I knew there was something. She laughed. She thought I was crazy or paranoid.

ABE: I just think it's no coincidence that they paired us up. Not that I mind that they threw us together in a way. I love your company.

SUSAN: But that's beside the point. This is so sick of them. It makes me so angry.

ABE: I was like that a couple of weeks ago.

SUSAN: And now?

ABE: Still pretty angry, but now the thing is, I keep asking myself, is she worth fighting for? Is she right for me anyhow? Do we have anything to salvage?

SUSAN: Are you even certain of all this?

ABE: I did some investigating of bills and . . . I have what I would guess is proof, but . . . I'm sorry. I probably shouldn't have said anything.

SUSAN: No. I'm glad you did. I don't like to be made a fool of. It's not as if I'm shocked really or anything. It's like I did know or I probably wouldn't have gone along with getting together. *(Beat.)* I'm glad we're drinking is all I have to say.

ABE: *(Smiles.)* Me too.

SUSAN: *(Holding up her glass.)* To drinking!

ABE: To us!

SUSAN: And Minneapolis! *(They clink glasses and take a huge swig.)*

ABE: *(Clinking again.)* And this incredible view!

SUSAN: *(Looking out at the view.)* I can't believe this. *(Pause.)* I love this city.

ABE: *(Putting his hand over hers.)* Me too.

SUSAN: *(She smiles.)* That figures. Matt hates it. It's not exciting, it's too cold, and Prince is the only celebrity.

ABE: Lydia never liked it either. If we were here and I said, "Wow, what a view," she would say, "Yeah, but it doesn't hold a candle to the view in Los Angeles, and they have mountains, and forest and beaches." To which I would say, "And traffic, and smog and materialistic egomaniacs." She's from Florida. She likes the warm weather.

SUSAN: Oh.

ABE: We were trying to move somewhere warmer about two years ago, but she'd have to get licensed in another state, which is a pain. And I'd have to look for another tenure track, which for philosophy is a lot like trying to find a trick dog with three legs and a French accent.

SUSAN: I want to go back to school to study education. To teach. PR sucks.

ABE: That's great. I mean, the teaching. It's a great profession. It's an incredibly satisfying job I think. Besides the pay, I highly recommend it.

SUSAN: Yeah? *(Beat.)* Yeah! So screw you Matt, wherever you are. He was trying to discourage me. *(Holding up her glass.)* Scrrrewww youuuuu, Matthew!

ABE: I'd rather not. *(Clinking her glass. Drinks.)* Now his wife . . . is another matter. Not that screw is the right word.

SUSAN: Is that an offer?

ABE: No, just an opinion.

SUSAN: But you like flirting with the idea? *(Pause.)* So why did you marry her?

ABE: At that time I wanted someone to whip me into shape. Someone who had confidence and clarity. Now I realize I was searching for my own clarity. She couldn't give me that. I don't mean that she doesn't have good qualities. She's strong, focused, intense, but she doesn't laugh much. And we fight a lot. She thinks I'm lazy.

SUSAN: Did you ever find your clarity?

ABE: In some ways—yes. I think clarity is overrated. And fun, pure fun is underrated.

SUSAN: *(Clinking his glass.)* I agree! *(She takes a big swig.)*

ABE: Whoa. You downed that pretty fast.

SUSAN: Would you like to get a room with me?

ABE: Um, I . . . I don't—I'm flattered. But I don't think that's a good idea, Susan.

SUSAN: Really? Well you've been flirting with me like crazy. Don't you think I'm attractive?

ABE: Yes. But I don't think . . . Look, you were attractive to me from the get-go, but I—

SUSAN: Me too. So what are we waiting for? We have a husband and wife who obviously want us out of the way so they can move forward. You and I are attracted to one another. Who are we hurting?

ABE: I'm not looking for revenge.

SUSAN: Who's talking about revenge? I'm talking about fun, which is highly underrated. We're both lonely for a good reason. So what's so wrong about some harmless sex tonight?

ABE: Sex is never harmless. It's the most powerful thing I can think of. I mean, talk about your weapons of mass destruction.

SUSAN: *(Angry.)* I don't give a good Goddamn whether it hurts him. I don't care if it destroys his world! In fact, I hope he self-destructs!

ABE: And this is not revenge?

SUSAN: *(Beat. Touching his hand and arm provocatively.)* His being hurt or upset is merely an added bonus of me having a great time with you. And I do think we'd have a great time.

ABE: I do too. But I don't want to just be a way to get back at him. I'm in a vulnerable position here too. If we have sex, make love, I'd like you to remember *me* in the whole of it, not some angry feeling you wanted to get rid of. You know what I mean?

SUSAN: *(Annoyed.)* So you don't want to do it?

ABE: For a good reason.

SUSAN: And what do I do? Go home alone again? Wait in the

dark until he sneaks in? Turn over as if I'm still asleep when he slips into bed? Pretend that everything is as it was?

ABE: I don't know. Maybe you should confront him. I'm going to confront Lydia soon.

SUSAN: And what can he say to amend this? What can he say to bring back a marriage after this?

ABE: You sound as if you've known for quite some time.

SUSAN: Maybe I have. But it's hard to admit failure. All I know is it's lonely. Waiting. My life is lonely. Not as I expected. At all. *(Pause.)* Anyway, we have a cottage. *(Chuckles.)* I have a cottage. We could head there tonight? Just both call in sick tomorrow to hang out on the beach. I'm not talking sex. Actually, I don't want it either. I know I'm all over the place tonight. We'll just go, get on the road, and continue this conversation till whenever. Get up, put our toes in the water. I like you a lot too. And I don't know what that means right now. But I know I don't want to be alone again tonight. Waiting. I don't want him to feel the comfort of me being there again. So I'll call and leave a message, telling him where I went. You could call Lydia and tell her something. *(Beat.)* What do you say?

ABE: It's dramatic. Are you sure it isn't all for revenge or show?

SUSAN: Not sure—no. But it appeals to me. *(Beat.)* I've always thought of the cottage as a healing place.

ABE: *(He looks out at the view.)* Umm. Don't know. But I certainly love the beach.

SUSAN: Me too.

A SWEET PLAN

Katelin and Silvio, 16, have been friends since grade school. They have shared the hard knocks that kids who are a little out of the ordinary face. Both have been bullied by jocks in their high school. Over the last few years, they have joined up with two other boys—outcasts as well—who have formed a "clique." Marky, the leader of the pack, encouraged them to express their anger toward fellow students and their school by reprogramming some computers a few months ago. Now, he suggests that they do a full-fledged attack on the jocks' lockers and a trophy case. Silvio starts to get nervous once he learns that Marky has a gun. In this scene, Katelin is picking up Silvio to go on this "locker rage" they had planned the night before. Silvio is resistant to the idea now. He feels things will get out of hand. He wants to discourage Katelin, who he has a crush on, from going as well. As the scene begins, Katelin comes into his house to find him ill-prepared.

KATELIN: What are you doing? You're supposed to be ready to go.

SILVIO: I know.

KATELIN: The guys are already heading over to the school.

SILVIO: Yeah.

KATELIN: What's goin' on, Silvio? Don't get all chicken on me. Put your shoes on, grab your face mask—let's go.

SILVIO: I'm not sure I want to.

KATELIN: What are you talking about? We promised last night. We all made a pact.

SILVIO: I just didn't feel comfortable saying no to Marky.

KATELIN: He didn't force you. None of us did.

SILVIO: No offense, Katelin, but you're kinda blinded by

things. You don't know how he gets when you piss him off. You haven't seen him when he feels betrayed.

KATELIN: Look how much fun you had when we reprogrammed the school's computers.

SILVIO: No one got hurt then.

KATELIN: Oh, I don't know. You weren't the kid who got suspended for using the computer that went right to the porn site.

SILVIO: That was totally different.

KATELIN: Besides, who's to say anyone's going to get hurt today? We're just gonna shoot up some lockers. Scare a few people. We're not gonna pull a Columbine on them.

SILVIO: I've been thinking all night. Things like this can get out of hand.

KATELIN: It's not going to get out of hand, Silvio. It's going to be fun. And nobody's going to catch us because they wouldn't expect it from us.

SILVIO: I think you're doing this because of Marky.

KATELIN: What?! No I'm not. You know we have a thing for each other, but I'm doing this for me.

SILVIO: He doesn't have a thing for you, Katelin.

KATELIN: That's total bull! I know he does. Don't be stupid. Now, let's get out of here.

SILVIO: Have you thought about what would happen if we did get caught?

KATELIN: It's not going to happen. We have too good a plan. And even if everything went wrong—all we'd get is a slap on the wrist. None of us have a record. None of us have even been sent to detention. You're practically valedictorian. My dad's Mr. Moola. We're a couple of white kids with a higher-than-3.5 grade point average. Sad to say, but we aren't going to do any jail time. They'll say the pressure got to be too much—which it did.

SILVIO: And what if in the whole craziness of things, someone comes after one of us? What makes you so sure no one would get shot?

KATELIN: I know who you think would do that. So you don't have to make it all general sounding.

SILVIO: So what happens then?

KATELIN: We made several promises. I know him. He'll keep his. *(Beat.)* Silvio, I really want you to come with us. I thought we were buds. I thought we were gonna do this thing together. Like when we did the devil's night thing?

SILVIO: This is not toilet papering the trees, Katelin. This is really serious.

KATELIN: Well, I don't get you. Last night we were all shooting off our mouths about all the stuff we wanted to do to that hellhole. I mean, you kept joining in. Like about how all those guys stuffed your head in the sink. You were going on about how all the faculty values is good looks and athletic ability. They treat you like crap. Don't you want to get revenge?! What's happened between now and last night?

SILVIO: Well, I'm not drinking for one. It's easy to get pissed off and complain about teachers and the school when you're hanging out drinking with friends. And secondly, and more importantly, I didn't know he was going to bring a gun till we already promised to do this thing. It's one thing to spray paint the lockers or break chairs, but it's another to shoot a gun at things. That's crazy!

KATELIN: It wasn't crazy to you last night.

SILVIO: Well, he didn't take out the gun till the end. And I didn't feel I could say no by then.

KATELIN: Why? Because Marky was holding the gun to your throat or something?

SILVIO: No. But it did scare the crap out of me when he pulled that thing out. I've never seen one of those before. I didn't even know he had one. Did you?

KATELIN: No. But now we can really scare them. So why do you say Marky doesn't have a thing for me all of a sudden? Did he say something to you?

SILVIO: I met his girlfriend.

KATELIN: What are you talking about?!

SILVIO: She's older. Out of high school.

KATELIN: That's bull. You're totally lying. We just started going out. He doesn't have time for another girlfriend. We're going to hang out tonight after this thing.

SILVIO: I'm not lying. You're just reading way too much into what Marky tells you, Katelin. It's wishful thinking. He even calls you a good friend. Do you not hear that? *(Beat.)* What's it about him that you like so much?

KATELIN: I gotta go. If you don't want to come, fine, but don't sit there making up stories.

SILVIO: I'm not. Why would I lie about that?

KATELIN: You have a lot of reasons. Anyway, if you don't come, it's all right, but don't think that they're gonna hang out with you anymore. I may not even hang with you.

SILVIO: Wait! Don't be like that. I just don't want to get in trouble. I don't want to hurt anyone. Maybe I don't like how things are done at school sometimes, but that doesn't mean that I want to shoot a gun at some lockers. What does that prove? So I don't want to be another stupid statistic about troubled smart kids. Does that mean I'm not cool enough to hang out with?

KATELIN: No, but you don't just agree to do something with your best friends and then back out at the last minute. When it's too late for them.

SILVIO: But it's not too late for you, Katelin. You don't have to go. Neither do they. We can call his cell and say it's off.

KATELIN: But don't you get it, Silvio? I want to go. So do they.

SILVIO: Do you? Or are you just trying to keep Marky's attention? Show him how cool you are?

KATELIN: No, I want to do it for me. For all those years of being made fun of, or for being tortured by those guys. I can't wait till Marky pulls out that gun. I can't wait till I see the looks on their faces. Scare them for a change. Threaten them for a change. I'm gonna grab that flagpole and smash that damn trophy case so fast they won't even know what happened. And I'll love it. I'll love every minute of it. It will be incredible. For once, I'll feel empowered. And we won't be caught. It's too sweet a plan. You have to come with us, Silvio. I know you'll get into it once we're there.

SILVIO: This doesn't even sound like you.

KATELIN: It is me. *(Beat.)* I knew this would happen. I'm taking off. It's late.

SILVIO: Wait! *(She stops.)* You think it's so brave to destroy property? Then go do it without the masks.

KATELIN: That's not brave, that's just stupid!

SILVIO: And if he goes nutty on you—like he did in that video store?

KATELIN: He gave the guy a shiner. He didn't kill him or anything.

SILVIO: He didn't have a gun in his hand, Katelin!

KATELIN: *(Starts to leave.)* I don't have time to chat about this. We've got a schedule.

SILVIO: *(Grabbing her.)* Don't! Please.

KATELIN: *(Pulling away.)* Let go of me!

SILVIO: *(Not letting go.)* No. I only came over last night to hang out with those guys because I wanted to see you.

KATELIN: You're hurting my arm.

SILVIO: I only said I'd do those things because I wanted to impress you.

KATELIN: Well, this isn't impressing me at all. You're turning your back on all of us.

SILVIO: When those kids did that school shooting a few months ago, a couple of them didn't really know what they'd do when they got there.

KATELIN: So that was them. We have a foolproof plan.

SILVIO: Listen to me! They thought they'd scare a bunch of people by firing some shots in the auditorium—not at people, but it didn't turn out that way. I'm sure somebody didn't keep their promise.

KATELIN: I trust Marky and Todd completely. It's you I'm worried about.

SILVIO: Eight kids were injured. One died. They just kept talking about all the blood.

KATELIN: You're hurting me, Silvio!

SILVIO: You're hurting me. Since I was thirteen, all I've tried
to do is protect you. I'm trying to now. Do you want to hate
yourself over the next, oh say, ten years because you made
one lousy choice and it ruined a good life that could have
been? You want to be lumped in with the pasty-faced kids
who play Dungeons and Dragons all day and kill their class-
mates for no good reason?

KATELIN: Ahhh! We're not talking about killing anyone?!
How many times do I have to—

SILVIO: So what would we be doing? What statement is made
by destroying some lockers and a trophy case? Jocks suck?
How deep! How amazing! The problem is the message gets
lost anyway. The message becomes nothing next to the
crime. And I'm not just talking about jail time. I'm talking
about how you feel about yourself afterwards. Have you
thought about that?

KATELIN: How does invigorated sound? Is that the right
word? Maybe exhilarated—maybe alive for once.

SILVIO: Well, if that's what makes you feel alive, maybe I'm
wrong about you. *(He lets go of her.)*

KATELIN: Maybe I was wrong about you. You think you'll feel
bad—like you did something wrong against God or karma
or something? You're just scared. *(Putting on a voice.)* "If
Mommy ever found out, whew, would you be in trouble.
She's hard." You're a coward. Later.

SILVIO: What if I told you I'm going to call the police?

KATELIN: What? No way. You wouldn't do that to us.

SILVIO: I'll tell them who you all are and what you're planning to do before it even starts.

KATELIN: If you do, I'll never speak to you again.

SILVIO: I would do anything to stop you from getting hurt. I
don't care if you hate me.

KATELIN: You're so chicken! Marky was so right about you.

SILVIO: Don't go, Katelin. Please don't go!

KATELIN: I'd hate you, Silvio. I'd hate your guts if you did that. Why can't you just let us have one glorious day where we rule? Is that so much to ask?

SILVIO: And what about the day after? What are you gonna have to do next to get a thrill? Because it's gonna keep having to escalate—to outshine what you've already done—until you *do* wind up killing someone.

KATELIN: Are you coming or what? *(He shakes his head no.)* You can meet up with us later if you change your mind.

SILVIO: I won't.

KATELIN: I know you, Silvio. You may want to narc on all of us, but you won't. You and I are buds from way back, right? Sometimes I wish I could like you the way you want me to, but I just don't feel that, ya know? I'm not trying to hurt you. But you can't force things that aren't.

SILVIO: No. You can't.

KATELIN: So see you later. 'Kay? I know you won't turn on us.

BRING BACK PETER PAUL RUBENS

Marlene and Jerry, 20s, are a happily married couple in Michigan. Marlene, an overweight woman, has entered a magazine modeling contest and has made the second cut. She is looking forward to the finals in New York City. Jerry, also overweight, realizes that Marlene's chances of getting to the final cut are slim. The issues of weight and approval have come up over and over again for this couple. Today, Marlene is trying to convince Jerry to make plans to go with her to New York.

MARLENE: You'll take time off to come to New York with me, won't you?

JERRY: I don't know. It's been really hectic at the shop lately.

MARLENE: Why can't Peter cover?

JERRY: You said it's on a Friday. I have to train a manager. I have reps coming in. I have to order tools that day.

MARLENE: Can't you order them early or the week after? It's not as if the hardware store is going to have a huge run on drill bits or whatcha doohickeys.

JERRY: That does happen. Depending on the doohickey we're talking about.

MARLENE: Okay. The idea is it's not life or death. The city will not be suffering from mass pandemonium if some thingy isn't available that week at the hardware store.

JERRY: What if the thingy is an air conditioner and we get a massive heat wave?

MARLENE: Why don't you just say, "Honey, I don't want to come?"

JERRY: Honey, I don't want to come.

MARLENE: Jerry, why not?!

JERRY: It's a modeling contest, honey. Only a handful of people make it to the end.

MARLENE: Love that vote of confidence.

JERRY: There's no lack of confidence. It's just—there's a lot of competition and it's tough to be sure that you're the one who is going to make the final cut.

MARLENE: You don't understand—not many have gotten passed this second cut. Only twenty-five of us are going to New York.

JERRY: Well, that's still a lot. How many do they pick—one or two?

MARLENE: The magazine editor—Mr. Stewart—he told me that they cut thousands of women on the first cut and seven hundred in the second. I'm in the remaining twenty-five. Considering those numbers, I have a pretty good chance.

JERRY: Well, your portfolio is pretty hot. I'd date ya.

MARLENE: So what are you saying? I look better in the pictures than in person?

JERRY: No.

MARLENE: Well, you think I look fatter in person?

JERRY: No. I never said that. I'm not getting into this discussion with you. I know how it ends. So who judges this thing?

MARLENE: Modeling agents.

JERRY: Hmm.

MARLENE: Hmm? What does that mean? What did you expect? You obviously don't think they'll ever pick me.

JERRY: I didn't say that.

MARLENE: You didn't have to. I can tell. It's not just for the skinny girls. I'm going for the plus size model category. You do get that, right?

JERRY: Even those women look skinny to me.

MARLENE: True. They don't accurately represent the plus size population like me. But I do have a chance, you know. It would be exciting even if I could make it to the final fifteen. If I can, cool, I may be able to do some modeling, which would be great money for us.

JERRY: I just don't want you to be disappointed.

MARLENE: Why am I necessarily going to be disappointed?

JERRY: I just said you might be. I don't want you to be.

MARLENE: Well stop being all negative. I'm nervous enough myself. I don't need you to be doubting me.

JERRY: I'm not. It's just you've been talkin' it up with everyone and I don't want you to, to . . .

MARLENE: Feel foolish when I lose? Is that what you were going to say?

JERRY: No.

MARLENE: Are you embarrassed of me or something?

JERRY: No! No, of course not. But I'm confused about why this is so important to you.

MARLENE: Why wouldn't it be important to me? Women are subjected to unrealistic expectations of what they are supposed to look like. There are so few accurate and realistic portrayals of women's bodies as they should be. I have a chance to be a healthy role model for women. Maybe being overweight isn't the best thing in the world, but it's not nearly as harmful as being an anorexic, size two, twelve-year-old who is forced to sell herself as a sex fiend. And who's over-the-hill—trashed—by the time she's twenty-five.

JERRY: Okay, okay, I understand that, but you have a perfectly good job.

MARLENE: I'm not going to quit my job. I love planning events. And I'm good at it. That's what you were thinking the whole time I was talking? That I was going to quit?

JERRY: No. I don't know. I don't why it bothers me.

MARLENE: I do. It bothers you because you think I'm never going to be a finalist, or worse, I will be, and you'll have to watch your wife parading around in a bathing suit. Walking around in public with all of her fat hanging out.

JERRY: That is absolutely not true.

MARLENE: Isn't it? Remember Brad's Fourth of July cookout?

JERRY: Oh God.

MARLENE: "Oh God" what? You kept wanting me to change out of my shorts.

JERRY: I did not. I didn't care. I just thought you were going to be cold near the lake.

MARLENE: So it had nothing to do with the fact that I was meeting your college buddies? That you'd be embarrassed by your fat wife?

JERRY: No. It didn't. I told you that I thought you were going to be cold. That's all. *(She gives him a look.)* I did.

MARLENE: So why did you keep trying to cover me up then?

JERRY: I didn't. *(Beat.)* They were just a little too short. I thought you might turn the other guys on.

MARLENE: Oh please. You were emanating embarrassment. And it's not like you're not fat.

JERRY: Thanks. Thanks a lot. I don't want to talk about this anymore.

MARLENE: Why not? I mean, all I'm saying is that it's not fair. You were wearing shorts, and I didn't tell you to cover up your big belly.

JERRY: I never call you that.

MARLENE: What?

JERRY: Fat.

MARLENE: But you think it. And I am. I'm fat. And so are you. So here we are.

JERRY: I don't feel like having this discussion anymore.

MARLENE: That's great. Just shut down. All that tells me is that I'm right. You are embarrassed of me showing off my body in a modeling contest. And you know what? Even though it hurts my feelings, that's your issue. Not mine. You're just as bad as everyone else. Worrying that people will think less of you because there's "more of me" on your arm.

JERRY: If that were true, I wouldn't have married you.

MARLENE: I was wearing a gown then. My body was covered.

JERRY: The point is that I'm obviously not ashamed of the way you look.

MARLENE: No, it's not obvious or we wouldn't be having this discussion.

JERRY: You know how turned on you get me. And you know I'm not faking that.

MARLENE: I know. And you turn me on too. But that's not the point. We're talking about being in public. About being embarrassed by what *others* think—which means that not only are you buying into the "skinny stereotype" as the ideal, but you're more concerned with other people's opinions than what *you* believe.

JERRY: That's not true.

MARLENE: Then let me ask you a question. What if we didn't have to wear bathing suits? Only evening gowns? Would you feel more comfortable?

JERRY: *(Unsure about how to answer.)* Well, I . . . probably. Yeah.

MARLENE: *(Irritated.)* So what does that tell you?! And don't tell me you're old-fashioned because you aren't.

JERRY: I don't know. I'm just telling you how I'd feel. You wanted me to be honest.

MARLENE: Yeah, I do. But now you're agreeing with me. You're embarrassed of my weight and how people perceive you because of it.

JERRY: No, I'm not. It's just . . . Okay . . . when my father died, I started gaining weight. I mean, right when he died. Everybody and their brother kept bringing all this food to us. It's what people do. I don't know why. It's not like food would make up for my dad being gone. My dad was dead, but we had pies and cakes falling off our counters. I was always real confident before that too. My mother didn't want to talk about my father's death. Every time I brought it up, she'd invite me to sit down and eat. It was like it was supposed to make me feel better or something. And it did in the moment—until afterwards. It was kind of an obsession. Like keeping me connected to my dad. Before I knew it, I had put on fifty pounds. I couldn't believe it. I'd suddenly become . . . fat. I was dating this girl, Samantha, at the time.

MARLENE: You mentioned her once I think.

JERRY: We were in gym class one day. We had one of those stupid rope things. I couldn't get up at all. I just kept slipping. My hands were all raw and burnt. And I was sweating like crazy. That never happened before. I was always pretty good in gym. And then these guys started laughing at me. Then they started cracking jokes about how fat I was. One of them turned to Samantha and oinked. He just kept oinking over and over. "It must be fun doing it with a pig! I'm amazed he hasn't squashed you yet." And then they all burst out laughing. Samantha broke up with me that very same day. She couldn't even look me in the face.

MARLENE: Oh honey, I'm so sorry. How come you never told me that before?

JERRY: I don't know. It never came up before. It's not like it's the happiest memory.

MARLENE: I'm your wife. You can tell me the bad as well as the good.

JERRY: I didn't mean to hurt your feelings about the whole weight thing. I guess I didn't even realize I had so much shame about it. I suppose in this weird way, I didn't want you to put yourself in a position where people could laugh at you. Not because I don't think you're beautiful. I do— body and all. But because I know how narrow-minded and cruel people can be. And modeling, more than anything, is about being judged in superficial ways.

MARLENE: But don't you see that you're making it easy for them?

(He looks at her puzzled.)

MARLENE: I can't change their opinions of what is beautiful— I can't change the images stuck in their narrow, little brains by not showing up. By avoiding potential embarrassment. I have to be there, with confidence. I won't let them laugh at me because I know that I'm something to look at as well as someone to look up to.

(He smiles. Beat.)

MARLENE: What?

JERRY: Nothing. It's just . . . you are. *(He kisses her and starts to leave.)*

MARLENE: Hey, where're you going?

JERRY: Booking our tickets to New York—what do you think?

FLYIN' HIGH

Tommy and Agnes, 29, went to high school together twelve years ago. Today, they run into each other in a cooling center in a bad section of New Jersey on a hot evening. Both have been on different paths and ended up in the same place. Tommy was the star basketball player destined for the big time; Agnes was an overweight overachiever who expected to and did take care of her sickly parents for years. Somehow forces bring these two opposites together to reanalyze what it means to be successful.

TOMMY: Hey, uh, Miss, do you have fifty cents on you? I want to pick up a cup of iced coffee.

AGNES: *(Still reading her newspaper.)* No. Sorry. I don't do that.

TOMMY: What do you mean you don't do that? I'm just talkin' fifty cents.

AGNES: *(Barely looking up.)* Hey, I don't need to get hassled here. I don't do it cause I've seen too many people in this neighborhood, including family members, who use every penny to buy drugs and alcohol. So just forget it!

TOMMY: I wasn't going to do that. *(Beat.)* Fine. *(Sits.)* I understand. *(Sighs.)* Man, it's hot, huh?

AGNES: *(Putting her paper down.)* It's horrible. I had some stupid kid throw a brick at my air conditioner this morning. I coulda killed him. I had to drag the damn thing to the repair shop on a wagon you pull behind you. I hate coming here. It makes me feel poor.

TOMMY: Well, at least it's cool. It beats sittin' in a room that's a hundred degrees. My air is out too.

AGNES: It just stinks in here. Do you know when this place closes? *(He shakes his head no.)* You look familiar. Do you play bingo?

TOMMY: Do I look seventy? *(Beat.)* Ya know, I think this place stays open all night.

AGNES: *(Putting her paper down.)* They can't. It's not a shelter. They need permits for that.

TOMMY: It's an official cooling center. It's run by the city.

AGNES: So. That doesn't mean it stays open all night.

TOMMY: So what do they think? People don't need to get cool at night? It's been ninety-eight degrees for the last four nights for God's sake.

AGNES: Hey don't get snippy in my direction. I was just asking a question. If you don't know when it closes, fine. The weather gets a little warm and everybody has an attitude. Are you sure I don't know you?

TOMMY: I said I don't know. Do ya?

AGNES: *(Seeing him.)* Oh my God. You're . . . Are you . . . ? You look exactly like . . . You're not Tommy Ramsey, are you?

TOMMY: *(Beat.)* Yeah, yeah maybe. Why?

AGNES: Maybe?

TOMMY: Yeah, yeah, I'm him. So?

AGNES: *(Laugh.)* Tommy Ramsey is asking for some change?

TOMMY: No. No, I wasn't. *(Chuckles.)* Oh. I was kiddin' with ya about that. I knew I knew you from somewhere. And I knew that right from the start. So I was teasin' you with that askin' for the change bit. I just left my house in a rush—left my wallet there.

AGNES: Wow. This is amazing.

TOMMY: Nah, it's not that amazing.

AGNES: I didn't know you lived in this neighborhood.

TOMMY: I don't. Well, I moved back.

AGNES: Get out! Nobody moves *into* this neighborhood. They only move out of it.

TOMMY: Well, it's not that bad.

AGNES: What? Every other building is burnt out. I'm the only one on my block with a legit job. That's why I don't have any money of course. Not that I'd ever resort to selling drugs like them. So what's happenin' with you? Do you still play basketball?

TOMMY: Some.

AGNES: Oh God. *(Hits her head.)* I'm so stupid. You probably don't remember my name. I'm Agnes Hawthorne. I was a junior when you were a senior? I headed up the Spanish club. I carried the flag for big class assemblies too? *(He nods.)* They used to call me fat Agnes.

TOMMY: Oh. Yeah. I remember. I mean, not cause of that. The flag thing. So you still live here?

AGNES: Yeah. Yeah. I never moved out of my mother's house.

TOMMY: Yep.

AGNES: I never saw you around before tonight. Not that I go out much.

TOMMY: I'm not big on goin' out either.

AGNES: You move into one of those ritzy houses on Park Street?

TOMMY: Yeah, yeah. Got a place on Park. *(Chuckles.)* How'd you know? You must be psychic.

AGNES: Where else would you move? So. Um, I don't know much about basketball, so I don't know what to ask. Did you ever get in with a team?

TOMMY: Yeah.

AGNES: Oh. Which one?

TOMMY: Well, ya know . . . Not professionally exactly. But I did play for Duke.

AGNES: Oh. Good. You got a scholarship there, right? *(He nods.)* So what did you study?

TOMMY: Umm. I guess you could say "Women Studies" mostly.

AGNES: No kiddin'? Really?! How crazy. That sounds really—

TOMMY: No! I'm jokin'. I meant, I played around a lot—dated a lot of women and . . .

AGNES: Oh. So what did you get your degree in?

TOMMY: Well . . . uh, I—didn't. Hell, I don't know why I'm

not tellin' the whole truth. I mean, what do you care? I didn't even get to stay on the team after the first half of the year.

AGNES: What happened? You were so good. I remember it seemed like you flew when you made baskets.

TOMMY: Ya know, I don't feel like talking about it. People always want to talk about me. Why can't we talk about the weather or them? Let's talk about you.

AGNES: Me? My life's boring.

TOMMY: Why? You look good, Agnes. Pretty—like you settled into your self more.

AGNES: Oh yeah, several things have settled that's for sure.

TOMMY: No, I mean, you look good—happy.

AGNES: *(Flattered.)* You think? *(He nods. She smiles.)* Thank you. I never heard anyone say something like that before . . . especially someone like you. Course you're like a ladies' man so you probably say that all the time.

TOMMY: No. Not anymore. *(She smiles shyly.)* So what have you done with your life?

AGNES: Huh. Taken care of my sick parents for the past twelve years. First my mother then my father—boom, boom. She died six months ago now.

TOMMY: Oh. I'm sorry to hear—

AGNES: *(Waves his sorry away.)* Nah. She wanted to. But I'm sure glad he went first. He woulda been so mean without her. Course he was mean anyway. He was an alcoholic. That tends to make people mean. I can spot an alcoholic like that. *(Snaps her fingers.)*

TOMMY: Yeah?

AGNES: Is that what happened to you, Tommy?

TOMMY: Where the hell did that come from?

AGNES: It was just a question.

TOMMY: It sounded more like an accusation.

AGNES: Well, you gotta admit it's kinda obvious. Here you are—good looking, a natural talent, with this golden opportunity to get out of trashville. And you blow it—real fast.

There's only two possibilities really—drugs, or alcohol? So which was it?

TOMMY: Look, I told you I didn't want to talk about it.

AGNES: So you still do it?

TOMMY: What do you want from me? I've been through three programs, okay?!

AGNES: *(She flashes him a look.)* Easy.

TOMMY: *(Beat.)* I'm tryin' to quit it. I don't need you to harp on it.

AGNES: Well trying doesn't cut it, Tommy. You either do it or you don't.

TOMMY: Look, Agnes, I don't need a lecture. I don't know you. Just cause you cheered for me in high school doesn't mean we know each other or that you can talk to me like that. I know you're probably all lonely living in your mother's house but I don't need—

AGNES: Lonely?! You have a lot of nerve. I certainly don't need the company of a washed up, drunk guy who still thinks he's a big high school hotshot if that's what you mean?

TOMMY: I'm not acting like I'm some big hot anything. I didn't walk up to you to say, "I was this hotshot basketball player from your high school. Remember me?"

AGNES: No, you just came up to steal my hard-earned money.

TOMMY: I told you before I was only kidding about asking you for money.

AGNES: Yeah, like hell. Like you really recognized me from the start. You don't even remember who I am now I bet. Do you?

TOMMY: *(Beat.)* Give me a break, okay? I've had better times, okay? I wish I knew you back then. You seem real. You know how it is with the booze. It ruins things. I just wanted some iced coffee. I left my wallet at home. Coffee can help sometimes.

AGNES: I wouldn't give you one cent especially now that I know who you are. You make me sick. You had a golden opportunity in your hands. There were tons of people in this neighborhood, including me, who would have given their right arm to find a way out of this trap. And you were handed it on a silver platter. You want some change for coffee? Get real—be honest. You don't live on Park Street. I don't even think you have a place.

TOMMY: I have a place.

AGNES: Where? *(Beat. Looks at him.)* Oh, right, I forgot, your air's out, right? Then go home and get some change, Mr. Park Street.

TOMMY: At least I tried to do something with my life. Maybe I didn't make it, Agnes. Maybe I had some problems, but at least I tried to get out. That's more than you and a lot of people did.

AGNES: You don't think I tried to get out? That I still don't try every day? I'm workin' sixty hours at Walgreen's for piss. Nobody ever gave me anything in my life.

TOMMY: You got a house to sell, what's your problem? I'm not the only one with opportunities.

AGNES: What's my problem? My problem is the roof's a mess, there's something wrong with the foundation, there's some question as to whether the dump three miles away has toxic waste left there. These are my problems. That and then there's this gang that gives the place it's little charm. My mother's house—it's just a golden opportunity for me.

TOMMY: Your mother's dead, right?

AGNES: Yeah. I told you that.

TOMMY: So why do you still call it her house?

AGNES: *(Beat.)* Oh, how deep. You want to get deep on me. How do you go through three programs and still say you're *tryin'* to quit? Just quit. Forget the tryin'. Get a clue. Tryin' hasn't worked!

TOMMY: *(Beat.)* You're right.

AGNES: I am? Course. Damn right, I am.

TOMMY: Why does everyone who runs into to me from high school feel angry? Why do they care? Even Martin Hays, the dealer—he almost knifed me when he realized what had happened.

AGNES: Don't you get it? You stood for hope. Whether you chose to or not. If you couldn't do it, hell, nobody can. There is no hope. Definitely no hope for him or any of us.

TOMMY: *(Realizing.)* I didn't know I was carrying everybody's hope then. That's a lot of weight on someone's shoulders. I guess I should have known. I was too young and stupid to be carrying everyone's hope. I was an idiot.

AGNES: *(Sighs.)* Oh well. We never do what we think we will in high school. Otherwise I'd be a translator traveling all over the world instead of working as an assistant manager at Walgreen's.

TOMMY: Do you think there's some happy medium? Some place in the middle between what we dreamed and what we are? Something that would be better than here but possible?

AGNES: Yeah. Maybe. If you're older and smart enough to make a commitment. I think pretty good exists.

TOMMY: I never had anyone talk to me like this. I mean, they adore me or hate me. You're just kinda yourself or something. It's cool. You got me talking. That doesn't happen much.

AGNES: Oh God, is this your little womanizer routine? Cause you aren't stayin' at my house.

TOMMY: No, no! I'm just sayin' I don't really have a good friend. I may have had a "golden opportunity" like you call it, but I never had a real friend. My mother drank herself to death. And she was closest thing I ever had to that. Anyway . . . *(Points.)* it looks like you were right. Things are closing up here. I guess I should get going.

AGNES: Where? Where you headin' to?

TOMMY: Why? You want to know that I don't have a house on Park Street? Well, I'm sorry for lying. I have a room over on St. John's. Going there.

AGNES: No, I was just . . . uh . . . You want to grab a cup of coffee? Iced coffee?

TOMMY: *(Looks around jokingly.)* With me? It'd be on you I'm afraid.

AGNES: I know. Tell you the truth? Things do get a little lonely. Besides, I think I'm gettin' a kick out of the fact that I'm hangin' out with Tommy Ramsey. Even if he ended up a drunk loser.

TOMMY: *(Smiles.)* Ha. Ha. Failure isn't so bad sometimes. It levels you. The people I met since I've fallen are much nicer people by and large than those when I was flying high—like a bird.

AGNES: *(Beat.)* Very deep. You comin'?

TOMMY: Yeah. Yeah, I'm comin'.

THE BEAUTY OF LIFE

Garth, mid 20s, an ambitious reporter for National Public Radio, has come to speak to Ms. Li Huirong in hopes of writing a feature on the recent AIDS crisis in China. His article would bring to the forefront the Chinese government's lax infection control measures in taking the blood of rural Chinese peasants. These conditions have produced thousands of new AIDS infections across the country. More specifically, they have caused the pain and anguish of families like Ms. Li's. However, when Garth comes to the door, he is met by Ellen, an English teacher and good friend of Ms. Li. Ellen, an American, mid 20s, has a very different plan for Garth.

GARTH: I'm here to see Ms. Li Huirong. My name's— *(Starts to reach out his hand.)*

ELLEN: Mr. Diggs. *(Waves him in.)* Come in. We've been expecting you.

GARTH: We?

ELLEN: Yes. Can I get you some tea? Or maybe you want something more leaded—I have coffee.

GARTH : That would be great. My Mandarin is pretty bad, so I'm glad you're here to translate. So are you a friend of Ms. Li's?

ELLEN: That would be me. I understand you're from NPR.

GARTH: Yes.

ELLEN: I love NPR. I'm a junkie.

GARTH: Well, thank you, uh—I think I missed your name.

ELLEN: No. You didn't miss it. I never said. *(Hands him his coffee.)* Ellen Holt. Ms. Li told me all about you the day you visited the hospital. Is your wife still here?

GARTH: *(Surprised by her mentioning his wife.)* Uh . . . yeah.

My wife doesn't always come with me when I work, but she's so fascinated with China. She decided to tag along.

ELLEN: That's great.

GARTH: Yeah. So you're aware of why I'm here? You know about Ms. Li's condition I assume?

ELLEN: Yeah. We've known each other for awhile now—good friends. It's not uncommon in Wenlou. Her husband died of it two years ago. A lot of people around here have AIDS. They're poor. Not well-educated. They all thought giving blood was safe. The money was easy. Like some sort of down-pouring from God. Now, they're outcasts. And the government, and other people, don't give a good—all right. I'm already getting on my soapbox. So how do *you* like China?

GARTH: Well, uh . . . I don't know. I've only been here a week. It seems like a mysterious place.

ELLEN: Yeah, the whole place makes me paranoid.

GARTH: Paranoid?

ELLEN: Well, it's no secret about the recording devices. If the government isn't happy with you, they have a way of letting either you or your family know about it. They don't play fair. People tend to disappear. *(Beat.)* And then, well, the roads always piss me off too.

GARTH: I hired a driver to help me navigate here. He got lost. Who ever came up with the idea of not mapping any of it?

ELLEN: Ahh, but if you map, people can spy.

GARTH: Ahh, but if you don't map, no one will visit. No tourists, no money.

ELLEN: Ahh, but you see, the tourists come for the beautiful buildings, sir. There's tons of new construction while everyone's starving. It's all about saving face and impressing people. All the gorgeous facades full of garbage inside. Impressive swimming pools that are only filled once a year. An amazing new library, but they can't afford the books.

GARTH: That's ridiculous.

ELLEN: Yes. But people here have a lot of pride.

GARTH: So do I, but it doesn't take a genius to know that if you can't use a space for it's purpose, if it's only there to look pretty, it has no life—it crumbles or becomes corrupt just like a politician with no power or responsibility. *(Ellen nods, smiles.)* What?

ELLEN: I like you. We think a lot alike.

GARTH: Thanks. *(Beat.)* So how do you know Ms. Li?

ELLEN: I came to China to help teach English at the University. I was working on my dissertation on Asian studies—still am three years later. Wanted to experience things here. I hated it at first. I planned on leaving, but I made the mistake of volunteering—just being an extra set of hands with an organization that provides medical assistance for people with AIDS. That's when I met Ms. Li and others, but she was special. So smart. She wanted to learn English so badly. I started to teach her. She picked it up fast. We were finally able to communicate, and the rest is history or "herstory" if you want to be annoying.

GARTH: Are you the one who sent the note to my hotel? *(She nods.)* To tell you the truth, I wasn't sure whether to expect to hear from any of them. I got the feeling that they were afraid to speak about how they were infected.

ELLEN: Well, we're not talking about people who feel comfortable speaking freely anyway. So many people disappeared during Mao's Cultural Revolution. Just for practicing religion or reading philosophy or painting a flower for God's sake. These people remember that if you step out of line, even a little, you will be erased. Now, they've contracted AIDS from government blood donations. They know that if they start talking to foreign media, like yourself, government people will be very unhappy.

GARTH: So what if they're unhappy? Besides hasn't it all come out anyway? Dr. Chou told the press a week ago that the government blood facilities weren't sterile.

ELLEN: It goes far beyond not sterile, Mr. Diggs. *(Beat. He looks at her.)* This is not for the record, okay? *(He looks at her as if to agree.)* They were taking the blood of a bunch of people at the same time, putting it into a huge vat, and removing the plasma for medicine and blood products. They then put the mixed blood back into the arms of the donators.

GARTH: Oh my God.

ELLEN: It's even how the government advertised it. We give you the money, and we even give you your blood back. Unfortunately, it wasn't just your blood. If only one person in the whole group had HIV, it's now likely that everyone who gave at the same time did.

GARTH: That's unfathomable. Okay, I'm not going to quote you, but I need to verify what you just said with another source so I can write about it. Do you know anyone who would be willing to talk about this?

ELLEN: I'm afraid I don't know anyone with a death wish— no. Anyway, we didn't call you here for the story. We have a much loftier proposition.

GARTH: What do you mean by "we didn't call you here for the story?" Who's we?

ELLEN: Ms. Li and myself.

GARTH: Where is she? I was wondering when you were going to bring her out. She is here, isn't she?

ELLEN: No.

GARTH: What?! Then how can we do an interview? This is why I came.

ELLEN: Did you know that the health officials in Henan are preventing Dr. Chou from getting a passport? She's been detained ever since she spoke to the foreign press about the non-sterile conditions five days ago.

GARTH: Look, I promise I won't use Ms. Li's name or yours either.

ELLEN: You're in China now, Mr. Diggs. China doesn't like bad news. Especially if the bad news is about their responsibility in infecting hundreds of thousands of people. It's not very impressive. The government of China will do anything to stop a story like that from escaping, even if that means you have to lose a few people in the process. It won't matter. They were poor and sick anyway. Do you understand what I'm saying?

GARTH: Yes. But how will they know?

ELLEN: I told you about the recording devices and the people who disappeared.

GARTH: You also said you were paranoid. Look, the reason I want to tell this story is because of this incredible injustice. If I don't use your name or her name, what does it matter? I'll disguise myself for the interview if need be. Please just talk to her about meeting with me. You can trust me.

ELLEN: Remember the day you came to the hospital trying to get one of them to talk to you? *(He nods, looking puzzled.)* Ms. Li could see that you had a kind face. And then when she saw your wife and how you smiled at her, she knew. She told me that day to find you and meet with you. *(He looks even more puzzled.)* She wants you to take her youngest daughter—to adopt her. She believes you'll do it.

GARTH: What? What is . . . This is . . . I don't even know her. Besides, she's not dead. She didn't even look that sick.

ELLEN: Looks are deceiving. Ms. Li has full-blown AIDS. She's already had pneumonia twice. She has no money for the medication she needs to live. There is no life here for people who have AIDS. There is no cocktail like in the U.S. that keeps her alive for ten years. She has three children. Two are boys, ten and eleven. Friends have agreed to take them. But her youngest, who is only four, is a girl. And well, you know how popular girls are here. If the girl is not adopted, she'll starve.

GARTH: Oh my God. This is exactly why we need to tell this story. People need to hear this. They'll be moved. She'll have no problem having the girl adopted.

ELLEN: But you don't understand. She doesn't want just anyone to adopt her. She wants you.

GARTH: But why?! I'm just some foreign reporter she doesn't know.

ELLEN: She's seen you. She trusts you. I can't answer why. It's just a feeling. Ms. Li wants you to sign the papers and take her daughter as soon as you can. You can write the story when you get back home.

GARTH: But if I wait too long, the story might have already broken.

ELLEN: Screw the story! This is better than any story. We're talking about a beautiful child.

GARTH: So why aren't you taking her? You obviously know the girl.

ELLEN: I tried, but she doesn't think I'm the one. I'm not married. And I'm staying here for a few more years at least. Ms. Li wants her daughter to grow up in the United States.

GARTH: So what? You obviously care for Ms. Li and the girl. You'll take her to the U.S. eventually. You'd be a better choice. She must see that.

ELLEN: She knows I'd struggle to afford it. I'm not even out of school yet.

GARTH: Look, I know you're trying to help this poor lady out. She's had a hard life, but I can't just come here and just immediately adopt this child.

ELLEN: Why not?

GARTH: Well, I have a wife for one!

ELLEN: Who's incredibly fascinated with China. Why don't you ask her at least?

GARTH: I came here on assignment. I had no intention of adopting—

ELLEN: I understand. But what was your intention then?

GARTH: What do you mean? I'm here to write a story like I said.

ELLEN: But why? Philosophically why?

GARTH: To show people what's really going on in this country. From the mouths of the victims. So that this can never be allowed to happen again. To, to force a much needed change.

ELLEN: You don't force change. It just happens. I mean, let's not get overly ambitious about this. Every country has had their AIDS scandal with the government handling things badly. Big yawn. You'll make people on the freeway shake their heads as they drink down their Starbucks. They'll say, "Oh, those poor people—It's shocking. It's terrible." A minute later when the traffic gets ugly—just like all things shocking and terrible in the U.S.—it will be forgotten. I know you might be naïve enough to believe if you tell this story, the government will never pull this again. But terrible atrocities have occurred constantly throughout history, even when a bunch of reporters covered them. You can't change a world, but you most definitely can change a life.

GARTH: If we don't tell the story, nothing will happen. No one will start funds for health. No one will assist in adopting these orphans. No medical centers will send their talent to help. Dr. Chou put herself at risk by stating that illegal blood collection centers still function in these rural areas so that we could at least effect change here. If we don't call the Chinese government on this, they won't stop. We're talking about changing public health policy here and saving lives.

ELLEN: And I'm talking about a little girl. All these things you're saying are uncertainties. It is certain this girl will starve if she's not adopted. You're here and her mother has said you're the one. Is there anything more important than this? Really? *(Beat.)* Is there?

GARTH: Okay, I hear what you're saying, but what about the hundreds of other little girls? Don't you think their mothers feel the same way? That saving their child is more important than the bigger issues? What am I supposed to do? Adopt them all?

ELLEN: Yeah. You and everyone you know. I know it sounds ridiculous. You think I'm crazy—we're crazy. That's the beauty of life—sometimes something that seems wholly ridiculous is the one and only thing that truly makes sense. Actually, it reminds me of the one thing I truly do love about China. The way people sometimes meet you and immediately trust you for no apparent reason. It's not based on anything logical. It's just a connection—a feeling, an intuition. *(She points to a picture on the table.)* There. That's her—Shen.

GARTH: *(Ellen nods at the photo. He looks at it.)* She's adorable, but . . .

ELLEN: But what? Ms. Li's life has been a living hell, Mr. Diggs. She would have loved to study and go to school like us, but she was forced to work in the fields. She would have loved to travel to other places and visit, maybe write stories, but she's a woman. She would have loved to watch her babies grow up, but she donated blood to the government for forty yuan to help pay for shoes. She told me once, "When I look at my daughter, I see hope." She wanted her to go to the U.S. one day. Her hope was fading. That is until she saw you at the hospital. She knew you were the one. *(Beat.)* So are you? What do think?

GARTH: I think—I think, this is crazy, I think this is an incredible story, this is nuts . . . I, I think—I think—I think I better call my wife.

ELLEN: Your wife?

GARTH: She likes when I consult her on these matters. You know, when I buy a car. When I switch jobs. When I decided to adopt a baby from China. She's funny that way.

ELLEN: I knew we could count on you.

GARTH: I'm not promising anything yet.

ELLEN: I know. There's the phone. *(Beat.)* You won't regret it.

GARTH: And the story?

ELLEN: Tell it. Tell it when you get home with Shen.

GRIEVING SPACE

Kim and Andy's four-year-old daughter was kidnapped from her bedroom while they were making love one night. Kim's mom, who lives with them, had taken a trip, their little girl was sound asleep, and they were enjoying their romantic time alone. Kim blames Andy for the incident since it was his idea to make love. Maybe if they weren't preoccupied, she thinks, they would have heard something. It is now seven weeks since this event took place. The couple, both in their late 20s, has organized searches, papered neighborhoods, and nagged authorities in order to find something—anything. Unfortunately, there have been no breaks in the case. Tips have led only to dead-ends. The pressure and frustration has begun to destroy their relationship. Tonight, as usual, Andy has not been able to sleep.

KIM: What are you doing?

ANDY: Just listening. I couldn't sleep. I hope I didn't wake you?

KIM: No. *(Beat.)* I didn't know you liked classical music?

ANDY: Yeah, I used to listen when I was in college more. I thought I was being so sophisticated.

KIM: Really? Did you take that pill?

ANDY: Yeah. Took two. Didn't do anything. Come sit?

KIM: I should go back to sleep actually. Maybe I'll take one.

ANDY: I forgot how moving it is. This music can grab you. Right in the gut. Reach inside. Stir up the entire spectrum of emotions—from deep sadness to rage to incredible passion. Ya know?

KIM: Sure. Did you ever check with your brother-in-law?

ANDY: About the friend? The FBI friend? *(She looks at him.)* I forgot.

KIM: You forgot? I thought you said you were going to call him yesterday so he could get started right away?

ANDY: I said I forgot. I'll call him tomorrow.

KIM: Oh. I just don't know how you could forget something so important.

ANDY: I don't know. Maybe I'm losing my mind. Maybe *you* should take his number down and call him.

KIM: Maybe I should. I know you didn't mean to, but—

ANDY: Fine. His number's next to the phone where I left it. Where I planned to call it. Now, why don't you sit with me for a second? Just for a second, Kim. Please?

KIM: I'm tired. Don't you think we ought to get to bed?

ANDY: What's the point? We don't sleep anyway.

KIM: Yeah, but we can rest at least. We have a bunch of places to search tomorrow. Lots to do.

ANDY: Yep. "Lots to do."

KIM: Why'd you say it like that?

ANDY: Because that's what you always say—every damn day. "Lots to do." What? What can we do now, Kim? What can we search? We've been everywhere.

KIM: We haven't searched the East River region. Margie got a team together.

ANDY: What do you think we did last week?

KIM: That was so quick.

ANDY: Eight hours is quick?

KIM: It wasn't as long as Sheridon Park. Besides Detective Thompson said they received a tip about that area. He said he's optimistic.

ANDY: Just like the three million other tips he received that never panned out.

KIM: Hey. He's trying. It's what we have right now.

ANDY: Let's be honest. We don't have anything. We don't have a God-blessed thing.

KIM: I'm going to bed.

ANDY: Wait! I don't mean to be blunt or discouraging about this, Kim.

KIM: Then don't!

ANDY: I'm just being honest with myself for the first time.

KIM: Sometimes you have to weigh whether it's better to be honest or it's better to have a little faith. That's always been your problem, Andy, that you have no faith in anything.

ANDY: No faith? So it has to do with God then? Having never converted to Catholicism? This is why our child was kidnapped? Is that what you're saying?

KIM: No. And don't put words in my mouth.

ANDY: Look, I'm frustrated as hell with this too. I can't think anymore because all I do is think over and over, all night about what I should have done. What could have happened? Where she could be?

KIM: So do I! I think about what it would be like if my mother didn't go away for the weekend. If we didn't suddenly get the idea to be romantic.

ANDY: That was so bad? That was so terrible and horrible of us?

KIM: No, no. I didn't say that. I just think if we maybe weren't so self-involved in the moment we might have heard her. That we would have checked on her before we did that.

ANDY: You mean if *I* weren't so self-involved, don't you?

KIM: *(Beat.)* All right. All I'm saying is that we might have been able to run after whoever took her. *Might* have. I don't know for sure. We can't do it over anyway, so I don't know why we're talking about it.

ANDY: Maybe we would have been sound asleep. That's a possibility too. Or maybe they never even made a sound, so it doesn't matter. There are all kinds of possibilities.

KIM: I agree with you.

ANDY: Would you prefer that I never made love to you? Maybe that was my mistake. Making love to you. Now, we're being punished. By God. Because I have no faith, and I made love to you when we should have been checking on our sleeping child.

KIM: Stop being ridiculous!

ANDY: I'm ridiculous?! Ever since this happened, you keep making a point of that. How we should have checked on her. How we were so self-involved. What you really mean is *Andy* was self-involved. I was the one all hot on doing it then. I was the one wanting to take advantage of the fact that your mother wasn't staying with us. I was the one being loud and excited so we couldn't hear her. Right?!

KIM: I said it doesn't matter now.

ANDY: Yes, it does. It matters because it's how you treat me now. Like I'm the villain. I'm the evil one. If I didn't exist this never would have happened. Let me tell you something, Kim, if I didn't exist, neither would Isabella. Don't you see? I'm hurting as much as you are.

KIM: There's no point in going over and over this. I just want to make sure I didn't miss anything. I won't give up. That's all. And I need sleep to make that happen.

ANDY: And I don't really care? It doesn't bother me one way or another? She was my four-year-old baby girl and I'm just totally numb to it and ready to give up?

KIM: I never said that!

ANDY: Directly, no. But it's the way you make me feel. *(Reaching out to her.)* Please, Kim, don't push me away. I miss her like you cannot believe. I'd rather give up my life for hers.

KIM: You say that like she's dead.

ANDY: No. I just—you misunderstand me. I just want you to know that this is the worst thing that has ever happened in my life. I'm her father. I was supposed to be protecting her.

KIM: I know that. *(Touching his head.)* And I don't mean to make you feel guilty.

ANDY: Then don't! I'm already doing it to myself.

KIM: I know. It's just . . . sometimes I think you've started to give up. I can't do that. I won't! You may be in that place right now, but I'm not.

ANDY: It's not like I don't want to believe she's out there.

KIM: Yeah, well, I can't even stand talk like that. I'm going to bed.

ANDY: Wait! Please. I think this is good. I think talking this out is good.

KIM: I don't feel like sitting in a dark room screaming over classical music at three in the morning. Call me crazy, but that's not my idea of what I should be doing right now.

ANDY: What should we be doing?

KIM: Everything possible.

ANDY: Haven't we been doing that already for the last six weeks? Where has it gotten us? Besides angry at each other.

KIM: Next thing I know you're going to tell me that you want to go back to work.

ANDY: *(Beat.)* Well . . .

KIM: Have you given up so completely?

ANDY: No! Definitely not! I'm not giving up. I'll paper a bunch of neighborhoods on the south side tomorrow night. I'll stay out till I finish, but I've got to go back to work sometime, Kim. How do you expect us to live?

KIM: We'll borrow from our parents.

ANDY: They don't have that much. I'll wait until next week. That'll give us a chance to make sure we've covered at least twenty square miles.

KIM: Why do you have to go back so soon?

ANDY: It's been seven weeks already. They've been covering for me and paying me this whole time.

KIM: It doesn't matter about the pay.

ANDY: It's a small office. They can't handle the workload anymore. I really need to get back.

KIM: I would think they could understand. It's not like you're taking time off for a long vacation or jetting around some island. Your child is gone.

ANDY: It's different for teachers. This is your summer vacation.

KIM: It doesn't matter if my summer was off or not. I wouldn't be going back to work yet.

ANDY: Well, I don't have seniority there. They aren't going to be understanding forever. They do have a business to run.

KIM: Then quit. You don't need that job. My brother will help us out. We'll take out a loan. It doesn't matter. You can find something else.

ANDY: I don't want to do something else! I want to go back to work!

KIM: *(Beat.)* What?

ANDY: I want to go back to work. I want something to be normal. I want a routine and a schedule.

KIM: Fine. Go then. Get out!

ANDY: I want to get away from your anger too. *(Kim looks at him.)* You'd think that we could be together on this, be sad and supportive together, but you want to do it without me. And worse than that, you act as if I don't feel it. That's what really hurts.

KIM: *(Pause.)* I don't mean to do that.

ANDY: Some nights I just wish we could hold each other and cry together instead of separately. *(Kim listens.)* I keep seeing so many days in my head. When you first told me that we were pregnant. At the hospital when I watched you give birth. Her first crawl and step and the way she held up her spoon in a triumphant, "I'm done!" But there's one night in my head that keeps coming back to me. I think Isabella was about one and a half. It was fall. Some of the neighbors were burning leaves. I like that smell. Poor little Bella cried all night because she had that terrible, miserable cold. She couldn't breathe—all stuffed up. *(Beat.)* She couldn't breathe. And you'd just about had it. You were so tired. Nothing had worked. She was fighting taking her medicine, and she just wouldn't stop crying all day. Not even Boo Boo could make her feel better. But I told you I'd stay up with her. And you fell asleep on the couch almost immediately. God, I'm so grateful for that night. I talked to her and played with her and cooed at her and rocked her. Finally, in the morning, right before dawn, she fell asleep. I was still holding her when you woke up. She looked so peaceful. I felt really good. Like I had done something right. You put your feet on my lap. We didn't say anything at first. You just smiled at me. Your face was so warm. Both of us were looking at Isabella. And you said, you said—

KIM: *(Quietly.)* You're a wonderful father.

ANDY: You remember?

KIM: Of course. I loved that morning. I didn't know it meant so much to you.

ANDY: Yeah. I guess I never told you that.

KIM: I don't mean to blame you, Andy. I know you're hurting, but I don't know where to put this anger of mine. There is no place for it. It's just there in everything. Why did God do this?! And I can't have space for grieving because I refuse to believe that there is anything to grieve about. Can you try to understand?

ANDY: Yes. *(Beat.)* I just don't want us to lose each other.

KIM: I know. Somehow or other I know we won't. I promise you we won't.

ANDY: Can I hold you?

KIM: I don't want to start crying again.

ANDY: Please? *(He looks to her.)* We can cry together.

(Kim slowly starts to open her arms. They hug each other tightly.)

TARGETED

Stuart, late 30s, an owner of a chain of family restaurants in the Midwest was accused of raping and beating Leslie, 20s. He was found not guilty due to insufficient evidence and several technicalities. This is not the first time he has been charged with this sort of crime. The incident, and more recently the verdict, have devastated Leslie, a young mother who was trying to improve her life before the rape occurred. She lost her husband, her job, and her will to finish school. It's been two weeks since the end of the trial, and Stuart is heading into the parking lot of an abandoned warehouse.

STUART: *(Turns around quickly startled.)* Where'd you come from? I didn't see you.

LESLIE: I was back there. *(Points.)*

STUART: In the woods? *(She looks at him.)* Now, look, I don't want any trouble here.

LESLIE: Who said anything about trouble? I just want to ask you a few things.

STUART: The case is over. There's nothing to discuss. It's late. I'm goin' home.

LESLIE: *(Moves in front of his car door.)* I could visit your mother instead?

STUART: Don't even think about it.

LESLIE: Or what?

STUART: *(Looking around.)* The case is over now. It's all over. I didn't do it.

LESLIE: You said that already. I have friends hiding in the woods if that's what you're looking for. No, they aren't going to attack you. Yet. I just have some questions.

STUART: I'll get a restraining order if you start harassing me.

LESLIE: Get one. I have nothing to lose. I've already lost everything important to me. Besides, it's your word against mine. Just like you pulled in court.

STUART: I didn't pull anything in court. Nothing, lady. I told the truth.

LESLIE: You didn't tell the truth about what you did to me.

STUART: I know someone did that to you, okay, but it wasn't me.

LESLIE: Oh, how sweet of you. To agree that something did happen to me after all the specialists agreed and after the bruises and the black eye and the broken wrist and the many, many pictures of every orifice of my body. That's so sweet of you to agree.

STUART: I don't know why you've gotten it in your head that it must be me who did this to you, lady, because it wasn't. I don't know who the crazy person is who did.

LESLIE: Well, let's think about why. There're many reasons. Maybe the prior offense for one?

STUART: I don't have any.

LESLIE: Not proven anyway.

STUART: I don't have to defend myself to you or anyone.

LESLIE: The woman wanted it, right? She wanted the bruised thighs and the Coke bottle up the—

STUART: I don't have to listen to this.

LESLIE: Why is it disgusting you?

STUART: I have nothing more to say to you. *(He starts to go for his door.)*

LESLIE: She lives at 637 Cherry Road, right? Nice place.

STUART: How'd you know that?

LESLIE: Your mother keeps a very neat garden. I love yellow roses.

STUART: You leave her alone. She's a sixty-seven-year-old lady.

LESLIE: Does she know about that woman—how you dumped her in the alley? With two black eyes?

STUART: That was a completely different story.

LESLIE: Oh, I know. She was a party girl who wanted it rough.

It was a date. Not at all like me. I was hurt by some mysterious person—who wanted my eyes all black too.

STUART: *(Points.)* See that window? My accountant is still working there. All I have to do is wave at him. He'll be here in a second. I don't want to do this, Miss Miller, but I will call the police if you keep this up.

LESLIE: Your "accountant" went home an hour ago. Of course, I don't believe for a minute he's your accountant—dealer more likely. How many accountants do you know who work in abandoned warehouses? Huh?

STUART: You got a problem?

LESLIE: No, you got a problem. Are you getting angry?

STUART: *(Shaking his head.)* No. You seem to be shaking yourself.

LESLIE: Not really. Of course it's easy to get shaky when you face someone who disgusts you so completely. *(Beat.)* Did you get coked-up in there? *(He looks at her.)* You seem nervous.

STUART: I'm not nervous. No reason to be. I just don't need this right now. Okay?

LESLIE: Did you think you'd get off again?

STUART: *(Yelling into the woods.)* Whoever you are out there—I will call the cops. I do know lots of people in the area. There are surveillance cameras out here. So get out!

LESLIE: What are they surveying? Your drug deals?

STUART: What do you want? What do you want from me exactly? Money?

LESLIE: No. To ask a few questions.

STUART: So ask.

LESLIE: Did you rape me?

STUART: Do you really think you could stand here talking to me if I were the one who did that to you?

LESLIE: You didn't answer the question.

STUART: If I were the one, I'd probably be smashing you up against the car right now, and smacking the hell outta you. Those kind of people just lose it.

LESLIE: You seem to know a lot about those kind of people. Are you on your best behavior? Wouldn't want to tarnish your reputation. Couldn't keep the restaurant chain going smoothly if there were more trouble, right?

STUART: I understand you wanting to get even with this person. I sympathize with it even. I'd want to get 'em too, but I'm not going to lead you to believe that I had anything to do with it.

LESLIE: So why did you offer me money a few minutes ago?

STUART: I didn't offer it. I asked you if that's what you wanted.

LESLIE: And what if it was? Were you going to offer it then?

STUART: No.

LESLIE: Good, because it's not your money that I want.

STUART: Is that a threat? Is this an attack on me?

LESLIE: I don't know. Is it? Why don't you answer the question already—directly?

STUART: Look, I'm sorry that you were harmed in that manner, but like I have said over and over—

LESLIE: "Harmed in that manner?" I was raped and beaten and had a Coke bottle shoved up my . . . you're a weasel. You're a disgusting, little, pointy-headed weasel, you know that?

STUART: I wasn't there. I told you that from the beginning. And you can't prove I was. You said it yourself in court. You had a coat over your head the whole time.

LESLIE: I'd recognize your smell anywhere. It makes me sick.

STUART: It's over now! The case is over! There's nothing more to prove because it's over!

LESLIE: Over for you maybe. I've lost everything. My job, my marriage, any scrap of hope I had of pulling things together. I was trying to go back to school for my daughter. I just wanted to get a decent job. It's not over for me because I live in fear every day. I fear walking down the street. I fear parking lots and alleys and men—like you.

STUART: You're not so afraid. *(Nervously rubbing his hands together.)* Not enough to stop you from talking to me right now.

LESLIE: This is sheer willpower. *(Noticing how Stuart rubs his hands.)* Is it the coke that makes you nervous like that? *(He doesn't react. Beat.)* That's how I knew for certain.

STUART: You don't know anything.

LESLIE: I might not have been able to see, but I could hear the sniffing. You sounded just like the coke addicts at the rehab where I worked. The day when they were interviewing you at the station, I noticed. I noticed the bleeding. Your nose was bleeding from coke.

STUART: Nah. It was just dry from the heat.

LESLIE: Why can't you tell the truth now? That's all I want.

STUART: I'm sorry, Miss Miller, but it wasn't me who did this to you. Okay? Not me. *(Starts to walk toward his car.)*

LESLIE: *(Blocks his path.)* You think because the jury found you not guilty that I don't know? Three witnesses put you in that parking lot seconds before it happened.

STUART: And three witnesses put me elsewhere.

LESLIE: People you paid off. How many times you think you can do this and get off, you son of—

STUART: I'm not getting off. It's the truth. I'm getting targeted. I have a little money. Women like yourself see that and try—

LESLIE: Are you saying I'm making this up?

STUART: I'm not saying you're making this up. I'm saying you decided to blame me because it's very convenient—

LESLIE: Convenient?! Why is it only you then? Why does it keep happening to you? What's special about you? You just keep ending up in dark parking lots? Do you think you're the only rich man to be taken advantage of?

STUART: I don't know why it keeps happening.

LESLIE: Well, maybe it keeps happening to you because you keep raping women and beating the crap out of them. And then going to your police buddies and uncle and asking them—maybe paying them—to fix things up. Do you think that might be why? And then you conveniently forget what's occurred.

STUART: Obviously, there is no discussion here. You just want to put all this crap on me. I suggest you don't follow me, or I will call the police. I'll go straight to my mother's so if you plan to make a surprise attack on her, that's where I'll be tonight. Now, I'm out of here, honey.

LESLIE: Okay, good night. *(Pointing to his tires.)* Have a good trip.

STUART: Jesus! What'd the hell did you do? Slice 'em all?

LESLIE: Me? No, that wasn't me. *(Sighs.)* Damn. The kids in this neighborhood.

STUART: I'm pressing charges for this. This is ridiculous. I do not need to be terrorized.

LESLIE: *(Laughs.)* Terrorized? You're terrorized? *(Beat.)* Answer the question now—truthfully.

STUART: I'm not going to answer any Goddamn question.

LESLIE: Just say, "Yes, I raped you."

STUART: You and your friends are going to have to pay for these.

LESLIE: Did. You. Rape. Me?

STUART: You're a nutcase. You know that?

LESLIE: Did you shove the Coke bottle up me?

STUART: I won't put up with this. I do have friends myself.

LESLIE: I said, did you rape me?

STUART: I won't hesitate to call a few people if need be.

LESLIE: *(Screaming, grabbing his shirt to force him to look her in the eyes.)* Goddamn it! Do you hear me? I asked you a question! Did you rape me?!!!

STUART: *(Grabbing her arms.)* What if I did, whore? What are you going to do now? Huh? What are you going to do? *(She backs up and he lets go.)* Huh?

LESLIE: *(Beat.)* Kill you. *(Puts her hands on her hips deliberately—it's a signal.)*

STUART: *(Laughs.)* Yeah? Okay. You're tough. You're sexy too, Leslie. Only problem is—you're a whore. Right, little whore? You're a whore, and your husband knows it. That's why it's over.

LESLIE: *(Pause.)* At least I'm not dead.

STUART: *(Looking around, reacting to the sound of a gun cocking.)* What's that?

LESLIE: Sounded like a gun being cocked.

STUART: Now, come on, I was just kidding. I was just stressed over this whole thing. I can make up for this. I can. I have a lot of money. *(Yelling.)* I have money! I'm gonna help you out! No problem!

LESLIE: I don't want money. I wanted you to admit what you did to me.

STUART: Okay, okay. I did it. I did it. You're right. I did it. Okay? Oh—

(Gun shot. Stuart's shoulder thrusts backwards.)

STUART: *(Grabbing his chest.)* Uh. Jesus. *(Looking at himself.)* What'd you do?

(Gun shot. His body thrusts forward. He grabs his stomach.)

STUART: What'd you do to me?! *(He collapses.)*

LESLIE: Nothing. *(Raises her empty hands.)* Just like you did to me. Right? Just a drug deal gone bad.

WITHOUT YOU

Marilyn, 70s, and Jim, 80s, were very happily married for fifty-two years. They have been blessed with six lovely children and nine wonderful grandchildren. This past year Jim died unexpectedly while in Marilyn's care. It is nearing the end of the Christmas season and Marilyn is having a difficult time. She's talking on the phone with one of her daughters who is checking in with her. Marilyn always insists that her children call when they get back home to let her know they are safe and sound.

MARILYN: *(On phone.)* I'm not being a worrywart!

JIM: Of course she is. But she can't help it. She's talking to one of our daughters.

MARILYN : The snow is falling in big clumps here. The reports say there are lots of accidents!

JIM: *(Beat.)* Isn't she beautiful?

MARILYN: I'm tired. I'm going to bed . . . I'm fine. I just feel the week went way too fast. I can't believe it's already the twenty-seventh. Can you? . . . It went too quick for me. Ahh, it always does.

JIM: Yes. And then the kids and grandkids all go home and there you are again . . .

MARILYN: I might take the pill to help me sleep. Sometimes when I'm so tired it's even harder to . . . What? Yes, of course. I'm fine! . . . I'm not depressed!

JIM: That's what she told me the first Christmas after her grandmother died.

MARILYN: It was nice—too short. And of course, I'm a little bluesy to see Sarah go back, but I know, I know. She has an early train to catch. She's got to get back to work . . . Yes, yes! I'm fine, honey. *(Sighs.)* I just miss him at times like this, when I'm alone here.

JIM: I miss you, too.

MARILYN: Now, you and Sarah go to sleep so you can get up early. Tell Sarah to call me the moment she gets into Chicago, all right? *(Beat.)* Before you go, didn't you turn off the Christmas tree lights before you left tonight? . . . You did. I thought so. Well, that's strange . . . Because I just came out of my bath and they seem to be on again . . . I'm telling you they are! I'm looking at them! . . . All right. *(Calling to Sarah as well.)* Kiss good night! To both my babies! *(She looks around. Pause.)*

JIM: Our babies are in their thirties and forties now. *(Marilyn sighs.)* It's not so bad.

MARILYN: *(Looks around as if she sort of heard something.)* Is someone there?

JIM: It's me. I assume you haven't forgotten. I hope these fifty-one years weren't that forgettable.

MARILYN: Fifty-two.

JIM: Oops. Forgot that one. Fifty-two? *(Beat.)* Yeah, that sounds about right.

MARILYN: Now, why did I say that out loud? Fifty-two. *(Beat.)* Strange.

JIM: It's not that strange. It was very relevant to our conversation.

MARILYN: *(Ignoring him.)* I wonder how those lights got on. *(Calling out. Not seriously thinking anything.)* Is that you again, Jim? Ringing the phone, turning on lights all week?

JIM: Of course. But you never seem to see or hear me. It's futile.

MARILYN: What are you trying to tell me, hon, huh? *(Pause. Sighs.)* Oh. I am old. Only old people and crazy people talk to themselves. But most especially old, crazy people. *(Pained by her last thought.)* Ohh.

JIM: You're not old!

MARILYN: *(Gasps.)* Huuuhh!

JIM: Huh, I think she might have heard me.

MARILYN: *(Panicked. Near speechless.)* Who, who, who—

JIM: She most definitely heard me. *(To Marilyn.)* Now, I don't want you to worry. It's just me—Jim.

MARILYN: *(Still very panicked.)* Well, I, I will worry, whomever you are, because my husband Jim is, is . . . he's, well . . . he's dead.

JIM: Technically speaking—yes.

MARILYN: Technically . . . *(Whining.)* Oh my God! Something is wrong with my head. I'm hearing people now. This is terrible. I have old-timers.

JIM: Oh Marilyn, no. Your head is as sharp as it ever was—as sharp as that young mathematics teacher I married *fifty-two* years back.

MARILYN: Who are you? Why have you come here? You can take whatever you want.

JIM: I don't want anything. I mean, except maybe a Heggie's Chocolate. But I don't think I can taste them anymore. But they sure look good. *(Beat.)* I just wanted to chat with you. I miss you, and I wanted to tell you something. Important.

MARILYN: *(Pointing in his direction.)* I have to warn you, sir, that my children may come over here at any time. My neighbors watch for me constantly. They *all* know me. I'm very, very friendly, so they'll call my son John and his wife and my other children when they see you in here. And then the police will be over here like that.

JIM: Well, they wouldn't be able to reach John, would they?

MARILYN: Sure they would.

JIM: No. John, Cindy, and Marie left for the other grandparents' house in Minnesota. They always spend half the holiday there. In fact, all our kids and grandkids are sleeping or heading to bed in their homes, Marilyn. You know that.

MARILYN: I may know that, I may, but I don't know what I know anymore because this isn't right.

JIM: I suppose our neighbors could call them and wake them if they saw me, but I don't think they can see me. I'm not even sure you can. Can you?

MARILYN: I wonder if I took my sleeping pill. Maybe I'm sound asleep. This is a dream.

JIM: No, no, you're not asleep. You snore when you're asleep. You're not snoring.

MARILYN: Snore?! Like fun I do! You're the one who snores. Fifty-two years of listening to that foghorn nose of yours.

JIM: Well, listen to you. So you do believe me now?

MARILYN: Not in the slightest. I think I left the TV on and you're some sort of character in some movie I left running. I worked you into my dream.

JIM: What movie?

MARILYN: Well, I don't know.

JIM: I just wondered what handsome actor I might sound like.

MARILYN: You don't sound like any *handsome* actor. I just meant that I fell asleep watching *It's a Wonderful Life* or *A Christmas Carol* and the ghosts got all confused in my head.

JIM: Oh, I love those movies. I'll tell you what though, Lionel Barrymore was the best Scrooge ever. He really knew how to make that—

MARILYN: I know. I know. We listened to that tape every single Christmas. I mean, my husband and I did.

JIM: Did you mind that? *(Marilyn shrugs.)* So do you think I'm a good ghost or a bad ghost?

MARILYN: I think you're a big fool. My son John gave me too much brandy in my cider this afternoon—is all. You're just my sour stomach talking.

JIM: So why do you keep talking back to me?

MARILYN: *(Shrugs.)* There's no one else to talk to. So why not my stomach? Better than being alone.

JIM: I'm sorry, Marilyn. I wanted to make it till I was a hundred. I tried.

MARILYN: Yeah. But you wouldn't want to be in a nursing home, would you?

JIM: No. Never.

MARILYN: I figured that. That was my one comfort when . . .
  (*Sighs.*) It's hard to believe, huh?

JIM: What?

MARILYN: That you're gone. That you're really gone.
  Everywhere I look . . . all the ornaments . . . and photographs on the wall . . . the bottles in the medicine cabinet
  and the way I can't sleep but on one side of the bed.
  Reminders. All reminders. I pulled out that small bulb tree
  and started to put it up this year and remembered we
  bought that our first Christmas together.

JIM: Yep. It was kinda pricey if I remember right.

MARILYN: Oh yeah, we paid a pretty penny all right.

JIM: Oh yeah. How much was that now again?

MARILYN: A dollar. (*They laugh.*) My grandmother was horrified by how much we spent.

JIM: Well, a dollar was a lot back then.

MARILYN: My aunt bought that delicate set of elf ornaments
  that Christmas for us too. Only one's made it. I remember
  how each of them broke. I look at that one elf and can't
  help but think of myself . . . dangling . . . at the end of my
  branch. Anyway, I should try to block you out and go to
  sleep.

JIM: No, you can't. I came here to talk to you about something.
  To get you to see something.

MARILYN: No, please. I don't want to talk about these things.

JIM: I think we should.

MARILYN: I was so good, Dad. This whole time. We had
  everyone in for Christmas and we celebrated the next few
  days too, and I held it together. I didn't cry. You know?

JIM: You don't have to hold it together for them, Mother! It's
  okay to cry, to lose control.

MARILYN: No, it's not. Not for me! But you never had any
  trouble with that. You cry at the drop of a hat.

JIM: Is there anything wrong with that?

MARILYN: No. I'm glad I married such a sensitive man.

JIM: Are you? I mean, were you? You didn't have regrets?

MARILYN: None! Don't be ridiculous! You were wonderful. I mean, sometimes you'd go overboard. I'd look over and you were crying at some dumb commercial for long distance phone service.

JIM: It was probably moving.

MARILYN: Yes. It probably was. Still . . . *(Beat.)* Sarah pulled out the old slides and family movies this afternoon and we . . . I thought I was holding it together well . . . but those slides of the kids—when all of them were little and when we were so young I . . . you were handsome and . . .

JIM: Did they make you cry?

MARILYN: No. I just wished to hell I was back there. Even for a moment. I don't remember enjoying it enough, Jim. I don't remember taking it in back then. Taking in and feeling how lucky we were to love each other so much. How lucky to have such wonderful, precious children—all of them so precious . . . All those years of yelling at them to clean up their rooms and "help me with the dishes you crummy kids." I just wanted them back . . . so that I could feel what it was like for one second to have us all be together again. *(Pause.)* But that's a dream.

JIM: So why didn't you let yourself cry? Don't you think our kids would have comforted you?

MARILYN: There's no point in feeling sorry for yourself. You got to get up and move on or you'll fall into a funk. Things change. Kids grow up. We get old. People die. It's just the way it is. That's life.

JIM: You're not an orphan anymore, Mother. I know you always felt like you had to be extra good and extra brave. But none of us expected that Marilyn—not your grandma, or your aunts, or your children, or me.

MARILYN: Once an orphan, always an orphan, Jim. People leave you, wherever you are, without warning.

JIM: I didn't leave you.

MARILYN: Well what else would you call it?! There wasn't any warning!

JIM: I think there was some warning.

MARILYN: *(Angrily.)* Well, you could have given me more warning than you did! Telling everyone all the time, "I'm fine. I'm fine!" You can barely walk across the room or make it to the toilet, but you tell everyone—even the doctor—even the emergency wagon.

JIM: I wasn't lying! I did feel fine.

MARILYN: Like fun you did! I cared for you that night. You were in a lot of pain. From top to bottom. I said, "Do you want to go to the hospital?" "No!" you say, "I'm fine." I'd ask, "How do you feel?"

JIM: With my fingers.

MARILYN: Ahh Jim! Always having to be clever. I knew it was a bad idea to get that test when you were right out of the hospital. But I didn't listen to myself.

JIM: But Dr. Michaels wanted that test, Marilyn.

MARILYN: It was stupid! It was so stupid of me! I shouldn't have let them do it. I should have known!

JIM: It wasn't your fault.

MARILYN: It took so much out of you. You were too weak for that. Back and forth to the bathroom. Nothing left in you. And then that night. What a nightmare! You just kept upchucking over and over. Over and over. I thought the soup had disagreed with you. *(Whining.)* I didn't know what to do, Jim.

JIM: I know. Nobody blames you. I certainly don't. You were the best doctor ever.

MARILYN: *(Getting more worked up.)* NO! Don't call me that! I don't deserve that! I didn't do things right. I called three different nurses. I called the emergency nurse line. I didn't know what to do. I should have called the EMS sooner. I know. And then you keep saying, "I feel fine! I'm fine!!" Well you weren't fine!!!

JIM: I did feel fine. I felt fine because I was with you.

MARILYN: Don't do that.

JIM: This is what I wanted to talk to you about. This is why I came.

MARILYN: I don't want to cry. I only cried once this holiday and it was only for a second and only in front of Lindsey. I hit my head on the kitchen cupboard. Isn't that stupid? I hit my head hard on the cupboard because it was left open. I remembered that I hadn't hit it since you were alive to leave the cupboard doors open. It just snuck up on me.

JIM: Things do sometimes. Even death. I didn't know I was dying. I didn't want to hurt you, or leave you, Marilyn. Never. I love being with you.

MARILYN: You know all those things about a person that irritate you? How you'd take two hours to eat breakfast, or watch the TV too loud or how you'd tap your fingers on the dashboard. All those irritating things? I miss them most of all. I long for them now. You were getting better when we brought you back from the hospital. I know it! I shouldn't have—

JIM: It wasn't your fault!

MARILYN: I was sitting there today looking at those old slides. And I was furious at you. I kept thinking . . . you're the only one who knows my life without me having to retell it all. We could exchange everything in a look. How could you leave me? I was supposed to be taking care of you. *(Crying.)* And you didn't tell me you were going. You just let me be responsible, Jim. And then I had to make the decision at the hospital . . . an awful decision . . . I had to stand strong . . . I had to hold up the fort—

JIM: I know.

MARILYN: You don't know!! You haven't done it like me. My dad died when I was four. I never knew *her.* I had no one but my grandmother and then I had to watch her in the hospital . . . She insisted I put that damn tree up, but I had to go home alone and take it down so we could bring the body back for the viewing. Why did I let you go for that stupid test! Why?!!

JIM: *(Pause.)* My dying wasn't your fault. In fact, it was you who kept me alive for the last seven years. You didn't kill me. You saved me for seven years. And somewhere inside, you know it.

MARILYN: I don't know any such thing.

JIM: You did. And you did the same for your grandmother. You fed me, and nursed me, and showered me, and tucked me in bed, and picked me up off the floor. You cleaned me up when I'm sure it wasn't a fun thing to do. *(Beat.)* You loved me. And you saved me. I want you to know that and believe that. And don't ever forget it.

MARILYN: Well . . .

JIM: I wanted you to know that I trusted you enough to let you take over. And some day, when you really need it, Marilyn, our children will take care of you. And you will trust them. You aren't an orphan anymore. No one who raises six children is ever an orphan again. *(She nods.)* So . . . Do you want to sit here for a moment and just look at the Christmas tree lights? I like to do that. I like to think about all the years. You want to do that? *(She nods.)* Give me your hand, will you?

MARILYN: *(Holding out her hand.)* Oh Jim. It hurts. This . . . without you . . . I just wish . . . I just wish you . . . *(Crying.)* Well, you know. You know.

JIM: *(He nods gently, taking her hand.)* Yes.

THE AUTHORS

Barbara Lhota is an award-winning playwright as well as a screenwriter. The Studio's production of her play, *Third Person*, was selected by the *Boston Herald* as one of the top ten plays of the 1993–94 season. She was awarded the Harold and Mimi Steinberg for *Hanging by a Thread* at the Crawford Theater at Brandeis University. *Green Skin*, her most recent collaboration, was staged at the Producers' Club with Theatre Asylum in New York.

Her plays have been produced at various theaters across the country including the Ritz Theater in New Jersey, the American Stage Festival in New Hampshire, the New England Theater Conference, and the Wang Center in Boston. In addition, her shows have been performed at several off-off Broadway Theaters including Tribeca Lab, Madison Avenue Theater, Love Creek Productions at the Nat Horne Theatre and the Phil Bosakowski Theater.

She received her M.F.A. in Dramatic Writing from Brandeis University, where she was an artist-in-residence and taught playwriting. Barbara now lives in Chicago, where she has had the opportunity to see *Strangers* and *Romance* at the Athenaeum Theatre with Jupiter Theater Company, *Family Portrait* performed at the Bailiwick's Directors' Festival, *Third Person* through Symposium at National Pastime, and *Morbid Curiosity* with Women's Theater Alliance at Chicago Dramatists and with Writers' Block at The Theater Building. At present, Barbara is collaborating with Ira Brodsky on a screenplay called *The Long Shot*. Barbara's plays, *Strangers* and *Romance,* can be found in Smith and Kraus' *Best Women Playwrights of 2001*. If you would like to contact Barbara, you can e-mail her at BLhota@aol.com. Barbara is lucky to have Janet as a collaborator and friend.

Janet B. Milstein is an actor, acting teacher, and private monologue coach. She received her M.F.A. in Acting from Binghamton University in New York, and her B.A. in Theater with Distinction from the University of Delaware. Janet has an extensive background in theater, having performed at numerous theaters with a variety of companies, including the Milwaukee Repertory Theater, the Organic Theater, ImprovOlympic, Writers' Block at the Theatre Building, Tinfish Productions at the Athenaeum Theatre, National Pastime Theater, Stage Left Theatre, Mary-Arrchie Theatre, the Women's Theatre Alliance at Chicago Dramatists, Theatre Q, Cafe Voltaire, and more. Janet has appeared in a number of independent films, as well as working in industrials and voice-overs.

Janet has taught acting to undergraduates at Binghamton University, to apprentices at Fort Harrod Drama Productions, to students at John Robert Powers, Chicago (where she was named Best Instructor), and to children and adults in various acting workshops. In addition, Janet has trained more than 450 talent contestants for competition at the International Modeling and Talent Association conventions in New York and Los Angeles.

Currently, Janet works as a private acting coach in Chicago, training beginning and professional actors in monologues and cold readings. She also teaches various acting classes at ASA Talent Studio.

Janet is thrilled to have had the opportunity to collaborate with the talented Barbara Lhota from whom she learned a great deal about writing and unlearned everything about grammar! Janet is the author of *The Ultimate Audition Book for Teens: 111 One-Minute Monologues* and *Cool Characters for Kids: 71 One-Minute Monologues*.

If you would like to contact Janet, you can e-mail her at Act4You@msn.com.